THE CONSTRUCTIVE REVOLUTIONARY

JOHN

The Constructive Revolutionary

CALVIN

& His Socio-Economic Impact

BY W. FRED GRAHAM

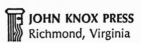 JOHN KNOX PRESS
Richmond, Virginia

Unless otherwise indicated, Scripture quotations are from the *Revised Standard Version of the Bible,* copyrighted 1946 and 1952.

International Standard Book Number: 0-8042-0880-8
Library of Congress Catalog Card Number: 72-107321
© M. E. Bratcher 1971
Printed in the United States of America

PROMPTE   ET SINCERE ·

IOHANNES · CALVINVS ·
ANNO · ÆTATIS · 53 ·
· B ·

Reprinted by permission of Historical Pictures Service—Chicago.

Acknowledgments

I wish to express my thanks to Robert M. Kingdon for his constant encouragement and to the laborers at the Musée Historique de la Reformation, especially Alain Dufour and Alexandre de Henseler.

W. FRED GRAHAM
June 1970

To my own Jean

Contents

Introduction

In the following pages the Reformation leader John Calvin will be presented as the leader of a revolution which disturbed Western society not only in the religious sector, but along the total spectrum of human thought and action. This is not a new interpretation, of course, for the revolutionary nature of Calvinism was as clearly understood in Calvin's own century as it is today by intellectual historians. Nevertheless this interpretation differs from previous ones in several ways.

First, economic, scientific, and political historians are quick to claim the Reformation—and particularly the Calvinist wing of that religious upheaval—as the turning point of modern history. But generally these historians know little about Calvin's own secular ideas. They assume that it was simply the rupture with tradition made by the Calvinists which produced certain changes of life-style which, in turn, affected society in Protestant countries in later centuries. But the heart of this study shows clearly that Calvin himself was aware of the epochal character of his own teaching and of the transforming implications of the Genevan pattern which he had a hand in forming.

In the next place, Calvin's contemporaries believed, and those theologians who understand the Reformation era today share the view, that Calvin's more strictly theological thought was his major contribution to human understanding. This can no longer be maintained. It is true that the great debates within religious bodies have been over such purely theological doctrines as double predestination, the presence (or absence) of Christ at his Table, and correct modes of church polity. But—partly because we live in a period when such doctrines are not of consuming importance, and partly because Calvin expressed his own mundane interests clearly and urgently—I try to balance the better-known theological position of the Reformer with a lucid statement of his social and economic thought and the application of that great mind to the problems of his tiny Alpine city-republic. Indeed, his secular thought is often seen to be critical of his theological thought. This worldly stress is not at all foreign to Calvin's thought. On the contrary, the message of what we might call Christian secularity was preached several times each week from the pulpits of Geneva's three churches—St. Pierre, the Madeleine, and St. Gervais. To insist that Calvin's thought is grasped in the main by a study of Total Depravity, Limited Atonement, Double Predestination, and Irresistible Grace is simply to distort his thought and to study a dead torso rather than a revolutionary thinker.

But there is a third reason for awaking the dead. It is a truism to say that we only understand ourselves today if we know something of our own history, but it is more accurate and exciting to perceive that we go back to the sources (*ad fontes*, as both Reformers and humanists said in Calvin's day) in order to make the future. If history is only a recital of facts for their own sake (or the sake of the reciter, the historian), or in order to bring new generations up to date, then its interest is readily perceived to be antiquarian by anyone interested in getting on with the business of living. But men interested in revolution, in seizing and changing the shape of human history in the future (*sic*), will always be interested in the past as prelude to both present and future. Only the anarchist, always present at times of crisis, as is our *kairos* today, wants to ignore history. And rightly so! For history makes clear that the future of anarchy is inhumanity, the "thingifying" of people, and the final imposition of a tyranny or totalitarian stamp to a nation or people. But true revolutionaries—those who wish to humanize life by freeing captives, healing the ill, opening blinded eyes, and bringing justice to society—know that history discloses how men make their own future. History grants men insight into the misuses of crises and points the ways errors can be recognized and avoided so that man can grapple with the stuff of his own nature to fashion a workable, enjoyable world.

For this reason the historian will note that on occasion I address myself not to him but to the Christian church. I do this in part, I am sure, because I am a Christian. But there is another, more important reason. I have concluded that the church needs not only to be awakened to its past, but to open itself to its future and the possibilities it carries for helping mankind fashion a better world. Because the church has loyalties beyond politics and economics it can resist better than, say, the university the temptations to subsume man's happiness under merely secular, ultimately short-range theories of progress or social well-being. Unfortunately, the church has often surrendered its ultimate loyalty to national, racial, political, social, and economic dogmas and even preached them as part of the gospel. If the church is to recover its prophetic role in human life, its people must see how revolutionary leaders have helped man in the past as well as how their work and message have been perverted. Only thus will the church be alive to the present and be equipped to grapple intelligently and vigorously with the future.

PART I

Setting the Scene

CHAPTER I

The First
Genevan
Revolutionary

ENEVA'S first international revolutionary figure was an immigrant from France. John
Calvin, recognized already as a powerful literary defender of the
revolutionary Protestant religious upheaval, was a welcome refugee in 1536. The city fathers regarded the twenty-seven-year-
old Frenchman as one likely to calm the tumultuous emotions of
the recently reformed city by the application of his cool dispas-
sionate mind to the inflammation of religious anarchy. Quite pos-
sibly Calvin entertained the same hope. But the combination of
Calvin's rational radicalism and the soul-erupting force of Luther's spiritual discoveries was to prove disruptive in Geneva's
internal life and wholly transformative to the character and
thought of Western civilization.

Geneva's second international revolutionary figure was an
emigrant to France. Jean-Jacques Rousseau, descendant of earlier Huguenot refugees, was nursed on the ineffectual struggles
by the small Genevan bourgeoisie in the early eighteenth century to gain power from the then oligarchical city Council. Apprenticed and abandoned by his father, Jean-Jacques fled his city
and was welcomed into Parisian intellectual life because of the
acerbic, visionary quality of his prose. There the famous "citizen of Geneva" (as he styled himself) first amused, then infuri-
ated, the skeptical philosophes Voltaire and Diderot, because of
the ineradicable religious quality of his social sermons. His call
for a society of equals both corrupted and complemented the vision of his Genevan predecessor. It was this vision which in-

formed and inflamed the "second" French Revolution, a revolution which helped give birth to the modern world two hundred years after Calvin's revolution had aborted.

In good puritan fashion modern Geneva refuses to worship her ancestral saints. Rousseau's boyhood home has recently been replaced by a department store. Calvin's gravestone is the size of a building brick, and no one really believes it marks his burial place anyway. The *rue de Jean Calvin*, high in the old city, begins with a "George Eliot Lived Here" sign at one end, includes a heating firm, a German Methodist chapel, and a television repair shop along its one hundred and fifty yards. Number 11 bears a plaque proclaiming that it houses Geneva's Office of Youth, Department of Public Instruction. There are no house tours, no memorabilia—merely a sign acknowledging that Calvin had, indeed, lived at that number from 1543 until his death in 1564, but that the original building had been demolished in 1706. If the visitor negotiates the small alley connecting Calvin's street with the area in front of St. Pierre's Cathedral and enters that schizoid architectural disaster (Rousseau's anti-Gothic generation affixed a classical pillared front to a medieval Gothic church), he will even there find little to remind him of Calvin. But against one interior wall he can see a plaque which recalls the "blessing of God" and "the self-sacrifice of four pious foreigners"—Antoine Froment, who first preached the new religion; Guillaume Farel, who persuaded the city to choose the Reformation; Pierre Viret, peasant and fiery preacher; and Jean Calvin, architect of the Reformed, or Calvinistic, revolutionary wing of the Protestant Reformation.

The modern reader is likely to be unfamiliar with the revolutionary nature of Calvin's message. He lives in a world come of age, secular, with few peepholes into his past. If he thinks of Calvin at all—and even the most active Presbyterian is usually too ignorant of his churchly ancestry to be likely to do so—he remembers a long, pale, ascetic face with a sparse beard, and perhaps connects that face with something called Predestination. And that is all. "Revolutionary" hardly seems to be the adjective to describe such dull dogmatism. The people in St. Pierre's or the

Madeleine Church in the sixteenth century, however, knew they were revolutionary people living in turbulent times. They had watched and cheered as Froment and Farel preached against idolatry, and perhaps they had taken part in the iconoclastic orgies that became so common an outlet for people set afire by the early preaching of the Protestant message. And now they listened to Calvin and Viret and others of the corps of Genevan pastors. These French preachers (for none were native Genevans during Calvin's lifetime there) had escaped the wrath of kings and lesser magistrates to come to Geneva. They were training other preachers who would go back to France and wage war with the sword of the Spirit until the temporal sword harassed them into hasty emigration or burned them to death over a slow fire, a brass ball judiciously stuffed into mouths only too ready to use this last opportunity to testify to the power and justice of God.[1]

We must remember that the so-called "cool" medium of the ear was not a cool medium in the sixteenth century. The evidence is overwhelmingly in the other direction. Wherever the new religion was preached, controversy broke out, families were split, ancient enmities were forgotten that common cause might be made either for or against the new understanding of the gospel. The sermon became the public forum, the city news courier (often complete with gossip column), the molder of public opinion. And the message the populace heard in Geneva was a message of revolution—the end of the old order of antichrist and his priestly myrmidons, the new worth of the individual in the sight of God, the dawning possibilities of justice, the simplification of the court system, the end of the monasteries and the piggish greed of indolent monks. These sermons, many of which have been meticulously preserved for us,[2] do not speak very much of another world and happiness there. They speak of this world— of the necessity of serving God here. They cry scorn against all injustice, whether it be ecclesiastical, bureaucratic, legal, or in the marketplace. They are also stern, dogmatic, and occasionally self-righteous. Indeed, they remind us in many ways of revolutionary preaching in any age, whether by Fifth Monarchy Men or Puritans, Jacobins or American colonists, Marxists or contemporary racists of whatever color. They are visionary and yet practical in an immediate way, harsh when looking out but sternly tender toward the redeemed flock, sharp in denunciation of injustice but perhaps not sufficiently aware of the atrocities which may be committed by the saints of the new order.

This Protestant and Calvinistic revolutionary message was first of all a spiritual one. Sixteenth-century man was burdened by a guilty conscience, the result of listening to too many sermons about sin and regarding too many murals depicting damnation. Medieval preaching did not know much about grace and victory. The Christ of man in the fifteenth century was either an infant, a man dead or dying on a crucifix, or a stern judge filling hell with liquid souls.[3] The sacrament of forgiveness was the only sacrament which did not operate automatically, for the priest's pronouncement of absolution was only effective given certain arguable conditions within the heart and mind of the sinner. The humanists, such as Erasmus and later Rabelais, had both derision and advice for the Christian and for the church, but had no finger on power. It was left for Luther, the tormented Augustinian monk, to wrestle with his sinfulness and teach his university Bible classes until the meaning of St. Paul's words that "the just shall live by faith" came home to him. Not by ritual piety nor by rigorous self-flagellation does the Christian purchase his freedom from guilt, but it is the free gift of God received trustingly by the still-sinful penitent. This message is still wonderful solace to men conscious of their sinfulness, although it may be strange and alien to secular man who feels confused more often than sinful.

Regardless of its value today, the message of justification by faith was revolutionary in the sixteenth century. It spelled hope, and hope realized means freedom. In addition, this message was translated into language men could understand. Erasmus wrote pages about the necessity of translating the Bible into the vernacular. But Luther and others did it.[4] Calvin's message had an impact even stronger than that of his spiritual father Luther. Luther felt God's law primarily as the threat which drives us to God's mercy, and that was the end of its Lutheran usefulness.

For Calvin, the law had a further purpose, that of guiding the believer after he had accepted God's mercy and forgiveness. This meant that the Calvinist was a more "driven" Christian—driven to live a life more in harmony with stern biblical morality, and thus driven also to change society in this direction. This helps explain why Calvin was more concerned than Luther to tell soldiers how they must fight—no rape, pillage, or harassment of noncombatants—and also more concerned to tell the Geneva city Council how it should govern. Luther turned over such legal questions to the political arm, and this in no small measure helped produce in Germany and Scandinavia a more peaceful, less revolutionary movement, when compared with the government-toppling cadres issuing from Geneva.

I have already referred to the unsuccessful "First French Revolution"—the wars of religion which occupied France over a thirty-year period beginning about 1560. It was France, of course, that Calvin wanted most to accept the new religion, as the dedication of his *Institutes* to King Francis I made clear. The theologian wanted no revolutionary war, however. Indeed, all his instincts cried out against social disorder. But the infiltration of pastors into France disguised as booksellers and peddlers and the desire for reform rising in the hearts of town-dwellers and small nobility all over France made repressive measures certain in a century of intolerance. Repression led to resistance and resistance to vicious anti-Huguenot massacres and consequent reprisals, and the nation burst into flame again and again. The conflagration did not cease until the ancient ruling house of Anjou-Valois had been completely extinguished, and the Protestant Prince Henry of Navarre changed his religion for the sake of national unity, granted significant concessions to the Protestant minority, and took the throne as the first of the Bourbon monarchs.

Contrary to the thesis of Marshall McLuhan, it was the *content* of the books and sermons which reached France that produced the revolutionary outburst, not simply the fact of printing as a medium. Spain, a united monarchy, and Italy, a divided hodgepodge of city, feudal, and papal states, also experienced an outburst of printing, but judicious uses of the Index of Forbidden Books and quick execution of suspected heretics effectively eliminated books of revolutionary content and stopped religious ferment before it became serious.[5] Indeed and ironically, McLuhan believes that the advent of the printing industry was largely responsible for the rising tide of nationalism in western Europe, and yet it was precisely the effect that printing had upon men in France which nearly cost the country its national unity in the Geneva-fed Huguenot rebellions.

Calvin desperately wanted his own nation to accept the gospel message which had transformed his own life. It is true that his interests were not limited to France. He corresponded with religious and secular leaders in all the countries of western Europe and with men in Poland, Hungary, and among the Czechs. His severe, rational religious spirit was to transform church life in parts of Germany, the Low Countries, England, Scotland, and Hungary. National rebellions would be carried through successfully by his followers in the Low Countries and Scotland, and later with temporary success in the English Civil War and Parliament's short-lived Puritan Commonwealth. But it was upon France that he squandered his prayers and his life's energy. There his reformation emerged at first vigorous and strong, but soon was crippled by open warfare and covert persecution, until the Huguenots became a static infra-state instead of a dynamic movement. Because this state-within-a-state existed so precariously, it is not surprising that later monarchs found it simple to legislate cruelly against it and finally to abolish it as an unseemly wart on the fair face of France.

The failure of this French Revolution may have been largely due to the fact that its leadership was not taken up by aggressive burghers like those who welcomed Calvin into Geneva. A new world was aborning and—as we shall see in Part III—it was to be a rational world, one associated with the rising bourgeoisie in all of those Western countries which were about to seize planetary leadership. But in France the Reformation leadership came into the hands of the lesser nobility, who carried a strong attachment to the old regional feudal society which a strong national monarchy threatened to emasculate as divisive and unproductive. Because of their amphibiousness, half in the new Protestant-secular world of freedom and self-determination and half in the old world of static feudal segregation, these lesser nobles were easily seduced by the Bourbon monarchs, who turned them into courtiers, sycophants to the depravity of the "golden age" of the antediluvian French monarchy. Unlike the Calvinist Dutch and English, and later the Yankees, these Huguenot leaders were not forgers of the future but representatives of an old way of life which merged with minimal complaint into the new nationalism whose deities resided in Paris and Fontainebleau.[6] The contemporary Scots and Dutch, and a century later the English Puritans, pushed through religious revolutions by uniting them with hatred of foreign control, always Catholic or regarded as crypto-Catholic. But the French Protestant nobility had no outside enemy to unite against, no real commitment to a new world view, no strong secular-national goals, and hence no staying power when the fighting ceased.

Thus France must wait two centuries before revolution will raise its head again, this time to succeed. It will be from our viewpoint in the future the same revolution, but different even as the world at the end of the eighteenth century was different from that of the sixteenth. It will be a revolution avowedly bourgeois, rational, egalitarian, and secular, while the earlier one kept these qualities latent under a deep commitment to religious change. But one thing the second revolution will hold in common with the first: its Genevan parentage.

Just as Geneva's leading citizens often feared what meddling in foreign affairs could mean during Calvin's time, so they both hated and feared what Jean-Jacques Rousseau represented. Born in 1712 on Grand Rue, several blocks from Calvin's old home, Rousseau left the city when he and other teen-aged apprentices were locked outside the city gates when they arrived back at the city too late one Sunday evening after a ramble in the countryside. He was converted for a time to Catholicism and then later to debauchery and shame—or so he tells us in good Calvinist fashion in his *Confessions*. As one reads his social and political

views in the *Discourse Concerning Inequality, Social Contract,*
and *Émile,* one is struck by the parallel between the thought of
Calvin and Geneva's latter-day *citoyen.* Both had a theory of the
Fall of man, a fall from original grace, which renders man's
earthly lot miserable; both were impressed by the need to press
on to change society, not to retreat from it; both expressed aris-
tocratic or republican preferences for civil government, and yet
both believed in the basic equality of men; both—and this to the
sorrow of Calvinists and Romanticists alike—saw religion as a
societal glue which the individual could deny only on pain of
death or exile. "Calvinism," says Michael Walzer, "brought conscience and coercion together—in much the same way as they
were later brought together in Rousseau's General Will." [7]

That in 1762 Rousseau's books were burned in Geneva's old
city at the Hôtel de Ville is less a reflection on the radical nature
of his thought—after all, several Genevan pastors were by now
his good friends—than to the increasingly conservative nature
of Genevan politics. For what he presented, in more secular dress
and yet with the religious element not wholly absent, was a continuation of the attempt first undertaken by Calvin—to transform
French society. Calvin had succeeded to a great extent in imposing his print upon the religious and social life of much of western Europe, excepting only his beloved France. And with Jean-
Jacques a new Genevan revolutionary was preparing the minds
of men for the second installment of that revolt. It should have
come as no surprise to the Christian West to see native Genevans
flocking to the side of Count Mirabeau when he raised the
standard of revolt. The revolution of Calvin had finally found
its French leaders, even if they were partially ignorant of their
own original inspiration.

An underlying persuasion of this writer is that social, political, and economic change—secular change, to sum up in one
catchword all that we persist in seeing as nonreligious—needs
religious meaning and zeal to provide the dynamic to bring it
about. Probably no historian would disagree with this persuasion.
The Puritan revolt needed its Calvin, Milton, John Owen, and
Stephen Marshall; the French its Rousseau; ours in the seaboard

colonies drew on both. The Russian Revolution of 1917 drew on the anti-theistic but nevertheless eschatological religious visions of Marx, and then canonized that thinker and idolized the apostolic Lenin; the black revolt hesitates between Malcolm X and Martin Luther King, both of them martyrs to the cause.

But my more pointed proposition is that Calvin's thought is still capable of direct reformative power in contemporary society. A young Catholic historian affirms that Calvin's thought has continuing religious meaning:

> We are persuaded that the reforming vocation of Calvin possesses a positive significance for the [future] history of the church. To begin with, in the exact measure where it represents a . . . lived witness to the transcendence of God, to the absolute sovereignty of the Word, to the mediation of the unique priesthood of Christ, to the "diaconal" essence of the ministry, to its Christocentric collegiality, and to the ecclesial role of the laity in the heart of a people entirely the priests of God . . . this vocation introduced and still maintains in Christianity a ferment nourished by the whole gospel. Nothing in principle keeps the Catholic Church from recognizing and taking this ferment upon itself in order to profit by its present perpetual interior reform.[8]

Does this perpetually reforming power of his witness to the transcendent God still have power to transform the secular as well? This is an urgent question, not one merely academic. We live in a "revolting" world—this can be seen almost anywhere except the Western white ghetto, where Calvin's followers abound and pray that these revolts (unlike the ones in their own history) will go away. The underdeveloped countries (or, if one likes to employ euphemisms to hide reality, the "developing" countries) are trying to shake off the lethargy of the past and step into the technological world created by the rational West. The black revolution in the United States bids fair to make whites either respond as Christians or react and transform society into a police state. The student Movement—it rates the capital letter—is still searching for goals more specific than dropping out and a rhetoric more convincing than Lenin's prior to 1917.

I think Calvin would have understood many of these revolutionary people. Like him, they have little sentiment for the past or for people who stand in the way of the future. Like him, they speak longingly of justice and mercy, if not (as he did) about walking humbly with God. Like him, they are apt to become impatient with followers who turn reformation disorder into personal profit. The difference between Calvin and many of these revolutionaries is that they want these goals reached at any price. The horrors of the French Directory, the senselessly bloody aftermath of the Russian Revolution, and Cromwell's massacre of the Irish—these are lost on people who know no history but the personal history of their own maltreatment and the misery of the oppressed. Calvin was here conservative. Like the Founding Fathers, Lincoln, and Martin Luther King, Calvin wanted to uproot evil and usher in a new age based on the old, without destroying society. Whether that can be accomplished today is perhaps the contemporary world's greatest problem.

Most of the people who read this book will be likely to talk with representatives of only one of these revolutionary movements afoot today, because only revolting students (and nonstudents) share the reader's social and economic background. If he does talk long enough to hear the goals of the Movement, he will be exhilarated, dismayed, and saddened. Exhilarated because the struggle for freedom which American mythology proclaims to be one of our chief dogmas is here openly avowed by young people who know that neither they nor their parents really have it. Dismayed because so often the enemy—characterized as the System or the Establishment—is understood in such a complete and total way that opposition to it is in fact understood as hopeless before it is even begun.[9] The rhetoric of revolution is very often only rhetoric. And the perceptive reader will be saddened if he has a sense of history, because the articulated long-range goals of this revolution are usually either dull or impractical.

While this is not the place to examine these goals in detail, there is something to be gained by looking at a modern movement just long enough to see a contemporary context to which we might add a revolutionary vision such as Calvin's. One of these expressed goals is socialism, the assumption of control of our industrial system of production by the state. This is not particularly visionary or impractical, but a close look at socialism as now practiced in Europe makes clear that far from being a guaranty of freedom and humanness, it is instead a dull system breeding bureaucrats to do the work of our industrial technocrats, with nothing actually changed. Socialism of the means of production will probably grow in the underdeveloped countries,[10] but this should hold almost no interest for prosperous young Americans searching for meaning. Student radicals who visit the socialist countries of eastern Europe usually find that the students there are, in turn, hopefully eyeing the West, especially the United States, and complaining of the monotonous meaninglessness and unfreedom of their own lives. The suppression of the Czech experiment in free socialism will doubtless increase this discontent.

The other articulated goals—hippie "monasteries," attempts to reduce social and political over-structures by leading a return to medieval guild systems or village economic units—are nicely romantic enough to be attractive and show sufficient ignorance of such movements in the past to have an initial plausibility. But in this instance, ignorance of the past does not mean that we are likely to relive it. It means only that persons engaged in such contemporary Fourierism may safely be ignored by almost everyone but budding Ph.D. candidates in psychology and education who are seeking interesting theses topics. Paul Goodman, Timothy Leary, and even the late and venerable Erich Fromm have not given adequate tools to their young followers.

In contrast, the revolutionary vision and power of the Reformers, especially Calvin, led to pointed action. Like all revolutionary movements, it had its grave shortcomings: dogma sometimes triumphed over people, and economics almost always did; successful religio-political struggles for independence ceased when national freedom was guaranteed but before individual freedoms could be established; the growing Western rationalism of life interbred with rationalistic religious dogmatism and quenched the thirst for beauty, so that Western-Protestant-industrial society—which has done so much in the cause of freedom—has also been suspicious of the aesthetic springs in the human soul. So we have been free only to uglify the world we have learned to dominate. This is but the beginning of the catalogue of charges which could be laid against the new world which supplanted, in northern and western Europe and in our northern American hemisphere, the old world of landed traditionalism.

But, nevertheless, the vision did produce. Critics may point to the misuse of scientific and technological advance. This is undeniable. But the vision has not died—freedom, justice, plenty, beneficial domination over nature. Even the horrible retreat into primordial tribalism—signifying the abandonment of the Western vision by Nazism and Fascism—made it terribly clear that we cannot go back prior to this vision to reconstruct our world. We are, happily I believe, stuck with this goal of planetary domination with its humane consequences. This is not an unworthy goal.

Throughout the first two parts of this study the reader will learn of Calvin's contribution in Geneva to this revolutionary understanding. He should be told, however, that Calvin's own city in effect refused to move beyond Calvin in the experiment to build a new world. Otherwise, Jean-Jacques, its second revolutionary, would not have been forced to maintain his ambivalent stance of styling himself *citoyen de Genève* but refusing to live there. Indeed, Geneva retrogressed in several ways after Calvin's death. Its hardworking, self-sacrificing Small Council became a petty oligarchy. For two centuries the city's financial resources were absorbed in strengthening its walls and defenses, so that maps and plans in the eighteenth century show a Geneva little larger than Calvin knew, ringed by elaborate many-tiered fortifications which gave it the appearance of an overdeveloped starfish. Yet Napoleon took it in 1798 without firing a shot! [11]

And so revolutionary people cease revolting. They petrify and protect their hard-won advances and refuse to proceed farther. In similar modes the psychic energy of plants and animals hardened within physical structures of wood, shell, and bone, thus halting evolutionary advancement, while other weaker but less specialized organisms created the future. Is this an analogy for the Christian world? Has it participated in the advancement of the human dream heretofore, only to be imprisoned within the industrial-military shell now calcifying about Western society? Jesus insisted that the wine of the gospel is ever-new requiring fresh containers. Western men drank it in the sixteenth century and changed their world. If their children eschew both petrifaction and putrifaction and again desire to quaff this heady yet constructive liquor, it may be helpful to understand how it once produced giddy change in an Alpine town and from thence poured forth to intoxicate Western society.

CHAPTER II

Geneva–
Calvin's City

AT THE extreme southern and western neck of Lake Leman, or Lake Geneva, the Rhone River begins its western trek into France before it turns south and heads for the Mediterranean. There Geneva lies on the shoreline of the lake, split in two by the river. In Calvin's time the larger part of the city lay south of the Rhone (today's "old city") and was connected by a bridge to the north city, known as St. Gervais.

A stranger entering the city would have found himself in a crowded, bustling commercial town, bursting at its walls, which were its only defense against the enemy, plagued and blessed by an influx of nearly 5,000 recent immigrants (by 1560), many with families, and with no room to stretch. The streets, he would note, were piled with the ordure of the night and the past weeks, and were ornamented by public latrines and lavatories. The sewers from private dwellings ran into the streets, and cleaning was a constant concern to the city Council. Near the city gates and at the bridges were piled the goods of merchants and fishermen, comprising most of the foodstuffs needed to sustain a city that was not blessed with adequate arable landholdings. Firewood was piled in the public way and was sometimes knocked over, sometimes stolen, and sometimes confiscated and sent to the public hospital when left unattended overlong. Casks of wine, awaiting the seal of the *Seigneurie* (title of respect given to members of the city Council), sat along the streets, and occasionally ruffians would make an opening large enough to insert a straw and suck the heady liquid. Such temptation made for constant legislation.

But the city was not inhabited by humans only. There were ducks, which were not to be shot within the city's walls. There were horses and cows, goats and pigs, chickens and sheep, dogs and, no doubt, rats, though the city's edicts mention all but these hardy alley-dwellers. Smoke rose from hundreds of chimneys, and probably out some open windows, for *Messieurs* were constantly making laws to prevent people setting fires in rooms without fireplaces and chimneys (in fact, the constant lawmaking indicates an endemic lawbreaking).[1] In many respects Geneva was a typical city of its day, crowded, busy, and dirty.

But in one respect Geneva was unique. Although not in France, it was the center for the Protestant Reformation in that nation. Or perhaps Protestant *infiltration* would be a more descriptive term, for disguised pastors and bookdealers trekking from Geneva were spreading throughout France that new regard for the gospel that would soon launch France into internal wars that would bring an end to the royal house of Anjou-Valois; the enthronement of Henry IV of Navarre, the first of the Bourbon rulers; and a century of religio-political division for the French people. The center of this heretical ferment was the chief pastor of the people of Geneva, John Calvin.

Rough Beginnings (to 1541)

The first mention of Calvin in the *Registres du Conseil* (the still-unpublished city Council's minutes) identifies him merely as *ille Gallus*, "that Frenchman," who had begun lecturing at St. Pierre's.[2] In order to clarify Calvin's role in Geneva from the autumn of 1536 to Easter 1538, when he, Farel, and a blind preacher named Corault were expelled, it will be necessary to begin with a review of Geneva's struggle for independence.

During the Middle Ages, Geneva was an episcopal village, theoretically governed by its bishop, but actually under the rule of the Duke of Savoy. Duke Charles III began his rule in

1504, and from the beginning his demands were onerous to
many in the city. Among their complaints was Charles's med-
ling in the choice of bishop, persuading the pope that the bas-
tard son of a former bishop (and a relative of Charles's) should
be bishop even though the ecclesiastical chapter of Geneva had
elected another man. Opposition to the new bishop's attempt
to take over the adjudication of criminal cases (a lucrative office
which belonged to the city Council) finally resulted in several
citizens' seeking help from neighboring Swiss cities. The first
such confederacy with Fribourg came to naught, as Duke
Charles escorted the bishop back into his obstreperous city and
executed one Philibert Berthelier, a leader of the Eidgenots.[3]

After Bishop Jean died, Duke Charles took more and more
of the city's government into his own hands, including the all-
important rights of coinage and the adjudication of civil cases.
Both these rights had belonged to the bishop. When an episcopal
judge protested, he was seized, arrested, taken to another town,
tortured, and executed. The citizens were angry not only at the
duke for usurping privileges for his own gain, but also at the
new bishop for not defending his rights and the *Franchises* of
the city.[4]

It was at this point that the powerful city of Berne entered
the picture. Although Berne lay more than a day's journey to
the east and north of Geneva and used German as its language, it
became Geneva's most important ally. Europe was dominated
by two powerful rulers, Francis I of France and Charles V,
Emperor of the Holy Roman Empire, the Low Countries, and
Spain. Berne considered Charles the dangerous one, for the
Hapsburg rulers continued to claim authority in Switzerland,
even though they actually had had no power there for many
years. When Duke Charles of Savoy switched from the side of
France to that of his relative Charles V, Berne entered the lists
on the side of the little city that wanted to be free. On 8 February 1526, Berne's Council received Geneva as its confederate;
the bishop immediately vetoed any Genevan participation, so the
citizens, in order to bypass the pro-episcopal Small Council,
called the first meeting of a new Council, the Two Hundred.

The new Council, packed with Eidgenots, overwhelmingly approved the confederation, and the bishop fled the city with fifty of his supporters.

For several years there was a stalemate. The duke was afraid to attack because of the power of Berne and Fribourg. The city had declared its independence from his control and confiscated the property of the fleeing Mamelukes, the term used for Christian converts to Islam in the Middle East and here derisively attached to Genevan converts to Duke Charles. But the only action was the bandit warfare some of the duke's noble vassals in the Pays de Vaud carried on against goods entering and leaving the beleaguered city.

This intolerable situation was not completely relieved till the year Calvin entered the city. But the events leading up to full emancipation can be recited quickly. Duke Charles mobilized an army in 1530, but failed to attack when Berne and Fribourg also mobilized. They forced the Treaty of St. Julien upon him in October 1530, which stipulated that an attack upon Geneva by the duke would be met by arms from its two confederate cities, and the duke would forfeit the rich Pays de Vaud to Berne. But in practice there was no change: the banditry of Savoy's supporters continued to place an immense burden upon the city Council to find food for the city. A siege mentality developed in Geneva that would not be fully dissipated till 1602. Although they called on Berne for help, the latter wanted to avoid an outright conflict that might bring into Switzerland the armies of the emperor.

Finally the prudent Bernese decided to act, not so much out of concern for Geneva as because it decided Savoy was ripe for plucking and feared France might invade and enjoy the harvest alone. Duke Charles did not help his cause by refusing to call off the harassment outside the city walls. In January of 1536, the Bernese army, 6,000 strong, began to move. Within a few days all resistance had ended in the neighboring regions of the Pays de Vaud and Pays de Gex (whence the bishop had removed his seat), the roads to Geneva were unblocked, and the city was finally free from fear. The small war continued for about two months, with Berne taking forts and towns, and by the end of March Berne's troops had taken the Castle of Chillon —freeing the Genevan Bonnivard, the famous "Prisoner of Chillon," after his imprisonment of six years—and had captured Lausanne.

Duke Charles had made the tactical mistake of entering into a treaty with Charles V against Francis I, so France now entered the fray, invaded Savoy proper, and reduced Charles to helplessness within a week. The final treaty gave the unhappy duke only a fraction of his former power. It would be a generation before Savoy would again frighten the city watch at Geneva.

During this decade of struggle the growing strength of Protestantism became gradually entwined with the fight for freedom. The bishop became a symbol of reaction and of Savoyard tyranny; when he left the city many of his canons and lesser ecclesiastics left with him. Berne, Geneva's protector, had become Protestant in 1528 through the efforts of Berthold Haller, later to be both good friend and strong critic of Calvin. Protestantism entered Geneva gradually—brought by merchants from Nuremberg, by soldiers from Berne with their chaplain, Megander, and then boldly by men like Antoine Froment and Guillaume Farel. Froment's preaching against the Roman clergy late in 1532 was so inflammatory that the city Council had to outlaw unauthorized preaching.[5] In April 1533, the Protestant Lord's Supper was celebrated for the first time, and the bishop's brief return in July did nothing to strengthen his church. He stayed but a few days, then left, never to return.

The religious trend made Fribourg, Geneva's first confederate, back out of their old alliance. Despite its proximity to powerful Protestant Berne, Fribourg remained Catholic, and when open Protestant preaching was permitted early in 1534, it withdrew from the federation (*combourgeoisie*). But the Protestant wave continued. On 1 October 1534 the Council voted that the episcopal see must be considered vacant.[6] Although Mass continued to be said, the outflow of ecclesiastics grew, the nuns at the ancient convent of Saint Clair departing in August of

1535. Money from ecclesiastical goods and properties went to endow the newly unified hospital located in the abandoned nunnery, and the bishop's residence became the prison. On 10 August, the saying of Mass was prohibited. But the city did not become officially Protestant until the final defeat of Savoy.

It was on 21 May 1536, that the General Council (i.e., all the *bourgeoisie*—those men who had the right to vote) voted unanimously "to live according to the Gospel and the Word of God."

> According to the resolution of the Ordinary [i.e., Small] Council, the General Council was assembled at the sound of the bell and the trumpet as is customary, and in front of the first syndic Claude Savoye the edict of the Ordinary Council and the Council of Two Hundred was proposed concerning the mode of life; and then in a loud voice the inquiry is made that if anyone knows and wishes to say something against the word and the doctrine which has been preached to us in this city, that he say it; and if all do not wish to live according to the gospel and the Word of God, as since the abolition of Masses has been and is preached to us every day, without ever again aiming at or wishing Masses, images, idols, nor other papal abuses of whatever kind. Consequently, with unanimous voice it is generally ordered, concluded, promised, and sworn to God by the elevation of hands into the air that all, unanimously, with the help of God, wish to live in this holy evangelical law and Word of God, as it has been announced to us, wishing [also] to give up all Masses and other papal ceremonies and abuses, images, idols, and all that this may involve, to live in union and obedience of justice.[7]

Two months later, in July, Calvin made his first, fateful visit to the city. It was at that time that he was threatened with divine wrath by Farel if he did not return to help build again the church in the city. In August "that Frenchman" returned and began his life work. But his first attempt was to prove abortive, concluding with defeat and exile.

The bone of contention was the attempt made by Calvin and Farel to force the citizens of Geneva to swear to a Confession of Faith, written by Farel. A moral code had been adopted by the Council prior to Calvin's coming, which prohibited blasphemy, playing at cards or dice, giving protection to thieves, adulterers, and vagabonds; it contained a note against selling bread and wine at unreasonable prices, and forbade the unauthorized holding of taverns. Attendance at sermon was also enforced, and private baptism proscribed.[8] But Calvin and Farel wanted a fuller reformation, and so presented to the Council a memorial asking for monthly celebration of the Supper (*Cène*), the necessity for excommunication (though who pronounced excommunication is not clear), surveillance by the government over morals, the need for the Confession of Faith, new marriage laws, and catechizing the young.[9] This memorial was approved except that the frequency of Communion was reduced to once per quarter.

But the citizens simply refused to subscribe to the Confession. Over and over one reads in the Council *Registres* that new efforts must be made to persuade the people to swear. One has the impression that perhaps the Council was not nearly so concerned as the preachers! Finally, on 3 January 1538, the preachers announced that they wanted to refuse the *Cène* to those "ununited" (*disunys*), but the Council refused to allow them to fence anyone from the Table.[10]

Support for the French preachers dissolved rapidly during the winter and spring of 1538. The annual February election of the four syndics who would guide the Small Council that year boosted into leadership men who opposed the ecclesiastical freedom demanded by Calvin and Farel. Three of the four, Jean Philippe, Jean Lullin, and Ami de Chapeaurouge, had been on Farel's side in 1532 when he wanted to preach the gospel in Geneva. But they were not in favor of the citizenry signing the Confession of Faith. If one can believe the Council minutes, the preachers immediately began to mix politics with religion. In March, Calvin was called on the carpet for describing "the Council to be a Council of the Devil." And in the same meeting a warning was made: "M. G. Farel and M. Calvinus are not to mix themselves in magistracy."[11] It all sounds remarkably modern!

Berne then got into the religious business. Wanting churchly uniformity in the cities and towns under its control, Berne called a council at Lausanne to decide on a number of matters. While Berne exercised no legal control over the affairs of Geneva, the Genevan Council decided that Geneva's churches would also follow Bernese uniformity in matters ecclesiastical whether its own freedom-driven preachers wanted that uniformity or not. The particular measures taken by the little ecclesiastical council were not important—use of the font when baptizing, unleavened bread in the *Cène*, and observance of the four festivals of Christmas, Easter, Ascension Day, and Pentecost. But Calvin and Farel were not informed of this decision until two days before Easter when the council demanded that they follow the Bernese observance. Although they pleaded for more time, it was refused them. Further, they were prohibited from preaching Easter morning if they would not celebrate the sacrament in the manner prescribed. They did refuse to celebrate, and they also preached, explaining that to administer the sacrament under the prevailing conditions would be to profane it.[12] The Small Council met in special session that same afternoon, the Two Hundred the next day, the General Council on Tuesday. All were in agreement—they had no need of the preachers:

> It has also been proposed concerning Farel and Calvin and the other preacher [Corault, the blind, whom the Council had jailed over Easter], who did not wish to obey the command of the magistracy, to see if they should be granted permission to leave or not, as the Small and Large [200] Council(s) have resolved. By acclamation it is ordered that they shall leave the city within the next three days.[13]

Whether Calvin, Farel, and Corault were right in their attempt to persuade the citizens to subscribe to the Confession is a difficult question. But the final conflict over worship and sacraments was clearly over the question of whether the Council or the pastors ran the church. We can see why the Council would opt for itself—it had taken into its hands everything else that had once belonged to the bishop. And we can see the weakness in the pastors' position—they wanted the church to control the church; but without any lay representation this meant simply the preachers' running affairs without hindrance. The magistrates voted for themselves and the three nerviest pastors moved on.

One is tempted to dwell on the three years Calvin spent in

Strasbourg, his pastorate there of French refugees, and his friendship with Martin Bucer, who certainly wielded considerable influence upon Calvin's thought. It was in Strasbourg that he met and married Idelette de Bure, the widow of a former Anabaptist. From there he journeyed to Hagenau, Worms, and finally Ratisbon (Regensburg) to engage in discussion with other Protestants and with Catholic theologians about the unity of Christendom. In these councils he made the acquaintance that began a life-long friendship with Philip Melanchthon, Luther's younger friend and fellow reformer. At Strasbourg he came into contact with the marvelous school of Johannes Sturm, an ideal which he was finally able to reduplicate in the College of Geneva. And there he first saw the local church governing itself through a council made up of ministers and laymen, which council in Geneva would soon be known as the Consistory. Finally, anyone who wants to study Calvin's liturgical theory and practice must turn to the Strasbourg liturgy of Bucer, much of which Calvin borrowed and turned into French. Suffice it to say, Calvin lived, taught, preached, and published there for about three years before he succumbed to the prayers of his friends and the Council at Geneva to return to the site of his first defeat.

Why was Calvin wanted back in the city where, as he wrote to Farel, he "should have to die a thousand times a day"? Partly because the political climate had changed. His opponents in the Council managed to conclude a treaty with Berne so unsatisfactory with that protector that, when the citizens learned of it, they branded the three men (including de Chapeaurouge and Lullin) "Artichauds" (Artichokes) and forced them to flee to Berne for their lives. And partly, it would seem, because the city fathers saw the need for a firm hand at the helm of a demoralized church. After the departure of the treaty-makers, one reads in the minutes constant references to efforts to have "M. Calvin as preacher" so that the "honor and glory of God be advanced." [14] Finally, against the wishes of the Council at Strasbourg and against his own better judgment, Calvin allowed the pleas of his friends Pierre Viret, Farel (who stayed the rest of his life in Neuchâtel), and the Genevan Council to win him over. His life's work began again on 13 September 1541.

Calvin and the Power Elite (to 1555)

From September of 1541 until the riotous defeat of his opponents in May of 1555, much of Calvin's energy was expended in his attempt to guarantee the church its right to excommunicate unworthy persons. For Calvin it was blasphemy of the body and blood of Christ to allow fornicators, adulterers, blasphemers, usurers, dancers, wife-beaters, and other notorious sinners to partake of the bread and wine. But who was to pronounce excommunication? His earlier failure in Geneva and his Strasbourg experience convinced him that the church must have its own disciplinary arm made up of both pastors and laymen. So the new Ecclesiastical Ordinances provided for the election of a Consistory whose chief task was to ferret out and try church members whose activities (usually nocturnal) polluted the Christian fellowship. But—and this was to be the bone of contention for fourteen troubled years—the ordinances did not make it clear to whom the actual excommunication and readmission belonged, to the Consistory or to the Council. A typical case might proceed something like this: A young man and woman would be brought before the Consistory accused of having sexual relations (*paillardise*) before marriage. After hearing their defense or confession, the Consistory would find them guilty, deny them the Supper, and remand them to the next Council meeting for punishment. The Council (which included several Consistory members) would hear the Consistory's report and sentence the couple to bread and water for several days, plus assessing a fine. After the sentence came the point of confusion. The couple would again appear before the Council, be warned and freed. The Council thought that the sentence and the warning terminated the case and admitted the couple back into full communion with the church. Not so Calvin and the other pastors. They demanded that the Consistory hear the couple again to see if their repentance was genuine. If it was, then they were

readmitted to the *Cène*. But if not, they were still excommunicate even if the civic legalities had been served.

To modern eyes there is a hopeless muddling of civil and
ecclesiastical discipline in sixteenth-century Geneva. Most of
the sins that required church censure were written into the
city's law code. This was in line with the Council's assumption
of the rights of the bishop. In earlier days it was the episcopal
court which decided civil cases (many of which would require
ecclesiastical censure and even excommunication), and the
Council tried only serious criminal cases. Now the Council was
doing the work of both courts, but was sharing the "moral" cases
with the church's Consistory, and the two were squabbling over
their mixed jurisdictions.

While there were early attempts on the part of the city
government to show the church that it was merely a department
of state, the really hard struggle began in 1547 and brought
Calvin toe-to-toe with Ami Perrin, notable heir of one of the
oldest families in Geneva. Perrin had early favored Calvin. He
had been sent to Strasbourg to plead with him to return. Calvin
had rewarded his confidence in many ways: he had stabilized the
church and several of its unstable pastors; he had recodified the
laws of Geneva, and had worked with Perrin to renegotiate a
livable treaty with Berne. In all of these efforts Calvin's gifts
—his ability to work hard, to reason with opponents and win
support for usually moderate views, and his obvious intellectual
resources—had been used to Geneva's profit. But Perrin had a
wife and a father-in-law, and thereon hangs the tale.

Perrin's father-in-law, François Favre, had been arrested for
dancing, excommunicated by the Consistory, sent to jail by the
Council (despite his son-in-law's presence thereon), and released. But the Consistory demanded his appearance to see if the
ban of excommunication should be lifted, and because at the
earlier trial he had had an altercation with pastor Abel Poupin.
Perrin argued that his wife's father need not reappear and need
not be sent before the Consistory to be lectured. The Council
tried to dodge the issue by telling Favre to try whatever means
possible to reconcile himself with the ministers.[15] But it also

jumped on pastor Poupin because he belittled the *princeps* (civic leaders) in his sermons, and because he had called Favre a dog! Several days later the Council warned the Consistory that it was overstepping its bounds. Often the charges for which it sent people to the Council were found to be false; it should treat people more graciously; and, more to the point, the Council asserted that the ordinances did not oblige it to send delinquents back to the ecclesiastical body, but that the decision to remand persons for "good remonstrances" by the ministers was always at the discretion of the *Seigneurie*.[16] When Calvin appeared to defend the Consistory's right to know the attitude of the ones sentenced, the Council declared to his face that it would send back those who were rebellious and obstinate but those who were penitent would be allowed to go in peace.[17] And yet, strangely enough, in this particular instance it did send back Favre for the inevitable harangue.

The Favre affair is quite amusing to read from a distance. It was perhaps less amusing for pastor Poupin when Mrs. Perrin (Françoise Favre) tried to ride him down with her horse as she escaped jail by fleeing to her country estate. And perhaps Perrin, Favre, and Favre's son Gaspard did not enjoy the former bishop's residence (the jail), when a friend of Calvin's, a refugee from France named Laurence Maigret and called "le magnifique," accused Perrin as a conspirator with the King of France against Geneva's liberties. Nothing came of that except that Maigret lost his voting rights, being removed from the list of bourgeoisie.

The bitterness grew as 1547 became 1548. Calvin himself was called on the carpet because "with great choler [he] preached that the magistracy permits many insolences. Ordered that he should be called before the Council in order to know why he has so preached, and that if there is some insolence in the city, the lieutenant should be commanded to look into it and to do justice concerning it." [18] To add to Calvin's problems at this difficult time, he was plagued by the fairly obvious adultery going on in his own household. Calvin, his wife, and her daughter, Judith, by her former marriage lived in the same house with his

brother Antoine and family. Antoine's wife, Anne, was suspected
of committing adultery with one Jean Chautemps, son of
a Council member. She escaped this time by admitting that
Chautemps had been in her bedroom of a night but insisting
virtuously that she had repulsed his advances. The day after her
release from prison on this charge, Chautemps (who agreed with
her version) was put out of the way for a time when his father
swore out a warrant for his arrest because he was a *vaccabun.*
Although it gets ahead of our story here, we might note that
Anne was eventually caught in the act early in 1557 with
Daguet, Calvin's own hunchbacked servant. Antoine was given
a divorce. In 1562, Calvin's stepdaughter, Judith, made the same
mistake, causing Calvin to leave the city for a period while the
scandal died down.[19]

The case that lingered, however, was not that of the Favre
family, but of a friend and supporter of Perrin, Philibert Berthelier. Berthelier had unimpeachable credentials—his father had
been executed by Duke Charles of Savoy during the early agi-
tation for independence. (A statue of Philibert, Senior, "defender of the city's liberties," stands grim and arrogant on the
Ile in the Rhone today.) He was brought before the Consistory
initially for breaking a marriage contract to one Jeanne Pignon
when he discovered that her face was her only fortune. He became irritated at the pastoral counseling he received there and
"used great words against M. Calvin," speaking with words
aspres et arrogantz, and "with great disdain made with his fingers
the sign to the whole assembly of the Consistory." [20] At the
same time Berthelier stormed at the Consistory, Calvin was in
hot water over letters he had written several years before which
were critical of the Council. The letters had been sent to Pierre
Viret and evidently had been sold by Viret's secretary to an ex-
monk named Trolliet, whom the Council had earlier tried vainly
to install as Geneva's first native pastor. The other pastors turned
him down because of his ignorance, but now Trolliet had his revenge. The proud chief pastor was severely admonished by the
Council, given to understand that "there are no tares in the
church," and had to respond point by point about what he had

written. Calvin received what most fair observers would have to call a taste of his own medicine.

What with his brother cuckolded in Calvin's house and Calvin himself called before the Council to answer for harsh words, we can imagine with what bitterness he appeared before the Council, 14 December 1548, to complain that some people were shortening his name to *Cayn* (Cain) and others were calling their dogs "Calvin." [21]

The Council's churchly authority was occasionally asserted even in the service of worship, the very area Calvin had been exiled for defending in 1538. In October of 1549, Calvin complained to the Council about the burden of daily preaching, from which we can infer that the original Monday, Wednesday, Friday, and Sunday schedule of services had grown to one a day. The Council received his complaint calmly, made no effort to reduce the number of services, but merely ordered that the preachers should shorten their sermons. [22] It even appointed four of its members to see that its order was obeyed! At the same time the Council tried to persuade Calvin to change the recitation of the commandments. Later Louis Bourgeois, the composer of many of the Genevan Psalm-tunes (including "Old Hundredth," which modern Protestants often speed up for the Doxology, "Praise God from Whom All Blessings Flow"), was tossed in jail for printing the songs differently, and had to be rescued by the intervention of Calvin. [23] So went Calvin's dictatorial powers in Geneva!

But the great test of church freedom continued to revolve about the person of Philibert Berthelier. He was brought before the Consistory again in March of 1551 for absenting himself from worship and from the Supper, and for overfamiliarity with the widow of a former Council secretary, Ruffi. When asked if he intended to marry her, Berthelier told the Consistory that "when he wanted to marry, he would not counsel with M. Calvin"! [24] After Berthelier bounced back and forth between Council and Consistory for several weeks, the exasperated Council decided to go to the sources—to examine the *Ordonnances* of 1541 to see what they said on the matter of excommunication.

Then Berthelier's friends grew vocal. Philibert Bonna, a Council member and syndic, stormed out of a Consistory meeting and returned wearing a flower in his hat, to the chagrin of the pastors; the Sept brothers, Jean Baptiste and Balthasar, complained that Calvin had disturbed their tennis game (Calvin argued that they were playing loudly just outside St. Peter's in order to disturb his lectures); on one occasion Berthelier's brother François lectured the Consistory so vehemently on pastoral tyranny that he was excommunicated.[25] In the meantime, the Council had completed its research into the 1541 ordinances, and by "la plus grand voix" (i.e., unanimously) decided that no changes were to be made—the Council did not have to return persons to the Consistory to have the ban lifted.[26] As Roget puts it: "Calvin had not advanced further on this point which was so close to his heart than the day of his arrival at Geneva." [27]

So Calvin resigned. The year 1553 marked the low point in Calvin's influence. The February election had been a decided victory for the Perrinists, with Ami himself elected the first syndic. This meant that the man Calvin had grown to scorn as "our comic Caesar" was director of the powerful Small Council for the year, setting the agenda, calling the meetings, appointing committees, and delegating responsibilities. In addition, he had been for a long time captain-general of the city's militia. Three of the new members of the Small Council were enemies of Calvin—Gaspard Favre, Jean Baptiste Sept, and Claude Vandel. The first shot fired by the anti-Calvinist Council was to refuse to the pastors the right to attend meetings of the General Council, despite the fact that all of the clergy except Calvin were *bourgeoisie*, i.e., had purchased or been granted the right to vote. Calvin's response was reasoned, but he lost.[28] Then a visitation of refugees was ordered by the Council. This was a direct slap at Calvin, for it was due to his fame that most of them were in Geneva, and they were extremely loyal to their pastor. So Calvin quit. The Council record is laconic:

M. Calvin has prayed that there be no displeasure if, since he sees that, because some wish him ill, many murmuring and turning away from following the Word, he would rather retire somewhere without serving further; nevertheless he prays that one wish to hear the Word of God and to let them [the ministers or the people?] serve in the name of God.[29]

We cannot know his real reason. Did he really wish to resign? Or was he simply trying to force the Council's hand? In either case, he lost. His resignation was not accepted, and the Council went out of its way to insult its chief pastor by ordering his close associate, Nicholas des Gallars, to the pastorate of the insignificant village parish at Jussy, against Calvin's fervent pleas.

But the flood of refugees finally won the victory for Calvin over his opponents. We saw earlier that the Council ordered a visitation when the flood of Frenchmen (for most were French) grew to alarming proportions. The immigration had begun as early as 1542, and by 1549 the ranks were swelling so fast that the Council ordered a book opened in which new *habitants* were to enter their names, swearing "to live according to the Holy Reformation and to be obedient and subject to us, and to observe our commandments and contributions throughout the time they may be habitants of our city." [30] However, it was only when these refugees were wealthy enough to pay their way into the *bourgeoisie* that they became politically important. At first this was no problem. Only eight were received in 1545, and in 1546 only nine, one of whom was Antoine Calvin.[31]

After the Perrinist victory at the polls in 1553, the swelling ranks of the refugees invited repressive measures. They were visited by some of the Council members and militia, warned not to take up new quarters without advising the captain of the quarter, nor to entertain guests, bear arms in the streets, or take part in the city watch—normally a duty of all *habitants*. In 1554 the flood grew as life became riskier in Catholic France. The *Livre des Habitants* shows 78 names in 1553 and 356 in 1554. In the spring of 1554, inhabitants of a whole French village from Provence appeared at the door of Geneva. They were later given unused land near the villages of Jussy and Peney, but for a time they worked on the city's fortifications and were lodged in the pestilential hospital.[32] Opposition to the newcomers was not con-

fined to the *Seigneurie*. One man was brought in for wishing out
loud that all the French be thrown in the Rhone.

In addition to some natural fear of outsiders and the flood-
ing of the labor market, which no doubt caused some bitter
statements by common people, there is some evidence that Perrinist leaders encouraged a species of gangsterism against the
French. Bonnivard, the former Prior of St. Victor and prisoner
of Chillon, an early chronicler of this period in Geneva (who
was not usually square with the Consistory himself, but was in
complete disharmony with Perrin), tells us that the city's rough-
necks would have dinner with Perrin or, more likely, Pierre
Vandel (who was more generous), and would from dinner sally
forth to outrage or beat up some foreigner. After reporting back
to their leader, he would promise them rewards: "Since you
know how to beat and outrage, you will have at this election an
office of assistant, you of chatelain . . ." [33]

If it was true that the *citoyens* (native-born) were sniping
at the French, the latter had their revenge. The 1555 election resulted in four syndics elected favorable to Calvin. Perrin's rather
cocky, strutting leadership must have cost his side valuable votes
in the Two Hundred. The four old syndics, of course, remained on the Council but with diminished responsibility and
authority. The Calvinist leaders then began to "pack" the General Council by admitting many of the French refugees as *bourgeoisie*. (Because they were not native-born, they could never
serve on the Small Council, however.) In an eight-day period in
April, thirty-one were admitted, when in the previous year only
seven had been received.[34] Perrin and his friends did not realize
what was being done to them. They considered these admis-
sions simply as more money in the treasury, the better able to
pay off the city's war debts to Basel.

But by May the Perrinists were fully alarmed and sent the
Lieutenant (prosecutor and keeper of the peace) to the Council
to complain that too many *bourgeoisie* were coming from one
nation. The Council turned a deaf ear and continued to build
both the treasury and the Calvinist majority by admitting those
who could pay the fee. Finally, the fears and grievances of the

Perrinists spilled over into the famous riot the evening of 16 May 1555.

The riot really amounted to very little. A few liquored-up ruffians made a noisy attack on the home of a Council member known to be favorable to the French. No one was hurt badly, and perhaps only one man hurt at all. But the anti-Perrinists on the Council interpreted the riot as an attempted coup d'etat, and Perrin and several of his friends left the city just in time to escape death for treason.[35] They were condemned to decapitation *in absentia*, but were already safe in Bernese territory which lay near at hand. Two other Perrinists met that unhappy fate the hard way—in person—and before the year was out François Berthelier had had his head removed, though Philibert escaped.

One can only be saddened by this debacle and by Calvin's approval of it. It seems to have been axiomatic in Genevan politics that when emotions ran high enough someone would be on the receiving end of sharp and summary justice. Ordinarily Geneva's brand of law was on a high level, but occasionally emotions built up to a kangaroo court. At one turn it was the Eidgenots, then the Mamelukes, followed by the Artichauds, and now the Perrinists. It crops up again in the eighteenth and early nineteenth centuries. Had the Calvinists lost, we can assume a similar fate for them. Regardless, however, of the cause of the Calvinist victory—and it must be remembered that the majority of the leaders were now on his side, from no force except his personal charisma—the victory was sewed up tight in the 1556 elections. Calvin can be considered the victor. His struggle with the ancient families of Perrin, Favre, Sept, Berthelier, and a few others was over. It is only from this point that Calvin can be said to hold any sort of command in the little city.

Before we turn to his decade of power, however, let us look very briefly at two significant theological crises within the city during the years of Calvin's struggle. The condemnations of two medical men—Jérôme Bolsec and Michael Servetus—show us that even when Calvin's intense desire for the church's freedom did not prevail, the rest of his theology was impregnable. Bolsec was a Carmelite monk who became Protestant, settled near the

city, and began the practice of medicine. Unlike most of the refugees, who supported Calvin wholeheartedly, Bolsec was critical of Calvin's view of double predestination, which he thought
made God the author of human sin. Theologically, he was in
deep waters; politically, he had no rescuer. In October 1551 he
argued this publicly, as he had done previously in private with
several friends and a second-string pastor named Philip de Ecclesia. Calvin replied hotly, quoting especially from St. Augustine,
and Bolsec was arrested. Strangely enough, the theological decision was left up to the Council. The Genevan entente between
church and state was such that there was no other tribunal which
could make adequate theological judgment. After much discussion and the sending of letters to other Swiss churches (only
Neuchâtel, where Farel served, supported Calvin very strongly),
the issue was decided against Bolsec and he was banished from
Geneva for life.[36] The obvious point to note in all this is that—
in accord with the times—theological heresy had to be treated as
political treason. There was no other way to deal with it. Calvin
wanted both church freedom from the state and state support of
the church. It's no wonder that he encountered some difficulty
eating his cake and having it too.

In 1903, 350 years after his fiery death at the stake in Geneva, followers of Calvin erected an expiatory monument to
"Michel Servet de Villeneuve & Aragon." In a way, it is quite
odd that of all the murders performed in the name of Jesus by
Catholics and Protestants alike in the age of the Reformation,
this one death—the only one we can put to Calvin's charge—has
caused more controversy than all the rest. And yet, when he was
killed, both Catholics and Protestants alike agreed that of all
the world's dangerous men, this one most deserved to die. Only
Sébastien Castellio, pastor and teacher at Basel who had also
locked horns theologically and temperamentally with Calvin, said
such a death was to turn Christ into a Moloch who required that
men should be offered and burned alive.[37]

The Spanish physician and amateur theologian, as is commonly known, had treated the doctrine of the Trinity with
some brashness, comparing the God so defined with Cer-

berus, the three-headed hound of Hell. In addition, he opposed infant baptism—two heresies for which ancient Roman law prescribed death as the penalty. He had been in correspondence with Calvin, and there is some reason to think that Calvin had a hand in Servetus' arrest by the Catholic Inquisition in southern France, he being imprisoned at Vienne. Servetus escaped from prison there through a window and, making his way to Italy (perhaps), stopped over in Geneva and was apprehended on Sunday at worship in the Madeleine and put in prison on 13 August 1553. His trial for his heretical views began two days later. His defender for a time was none other than Philibert Berthelier, connoisseur, lawyer, and enemy of the Consistory, who was himself excommunicate. Indeed, Calvin's greatest test over the denial of the sacrament to the unworthy came during the trial, when the Council agreed that the Consistory had no right to refuse the Supper to Berthelier. But the latter had not the stomach to face up to his pastor at St. Peter's on Sunday morning.

The Servetus trial was a double-pronged one—the official prosecutor, Claude Rigot (a Perrinist), argued that he was a public menace who wanted to take the sword of justice from the magistrate; and then Calvin engaged in the theological prosecution, for which Servetus was finally immolated. The Swiss cities were polled, as they had been two years earlier for Bolsec, and were this time more stern in their condemnation. Perhaps they feared that to turn free such an obvious heretic would indicate that the Reformation had torn down every doctrinal standard. We recite here only the last lines of the Council's verdict:

> . . . you have had neither shame nor horror of setting yourself against the divine Majesty and the Holy Trinity, and so you have obstinately tried to infect the world with your stinking heretical poison. . . . [therefore] having God and the Holy Scriptures before our eyes, speaking in the name of the Father, Son and Holy Spirit, we now in writing give final sentence and condemn you, Michael Servetus, to be bound and taken to Champel and there attached to a stake and burned with your book to ashes. And so you shall finish your days and give an example to others who would commit the like.[38]

The Council, not the Consistory, delivered the sentence, though the verdict makes it clear that Servetus was burned not for political reasons but for heresy and blasphemy. Twenty of the twenty-five members of the Council were present at the voting, including anti-Calvinists Perrin, P. Bonna, and J. B. Sept. So even the extirpation of heresy escaped official ecclesiastical discipline.

Bainton is surely right about the burning of Servetus. The severity of Calvin came from his zeal for truth and the majesty of God. "Today any of us would be the first to cast a stone against Calvin's intolerance; [but] seldom do we reflect that we who are aghast at the burning of one man to ashes for religion do not hesitate for the preservation of our culture to reduce whole cities to cinders." [39]

A Decade of Strength

From his victory over the Perrinists in 1555 till his death in 1564, Calvin engaged himself in behalf of his city on two non-churchly fronts. On the one hand, there was the constant hostility from Berne, which continued to press for amnesty for the Perrinists. On the other hand, Geneva found itself involved more and more in the shifting fortunes of the French Protestants.

Within the city we find the Consistory now exercising without conciliar hindrance its right to excommunicate. The definitive decision was made 24 January 1556 by the Councils of Sixty and Two Hundred. After Calvin appeared to answer the objections of those who wanted to diminish the authority of the Consistory, and argued from Scripture and from the practice "in the church when it was in its purity what was the true usage of excommunication," the Councils declared:

> Concerning this, despite all the efforts of Satan to reverse such holy and useful order, nevertheless it was by M. the first syndic, S[R] Amblard Corne, in full council declared to the said ministers that God had been victorious, and that it had been ordered both in the Council of Sixty and in the Two Hundred,

that the Consistory would remain in its estate, and would have its accustomed authority, just as the Word of God conveys it, and that the ordinances already passed concerning this contained that.[40]

It was quite fitting that the old ordinances should simply be interpreted according to Calvin and that the definitive interpretation should be pronounced by Amblard Corne, one of the first of the Council members to go to jail with Ami Perrin for the sin of dancing!

It should not be assumed that Calvin always got his way. No longer did ruffians jeer him when he walked from his home and presumably the dogs named Calvin were renamed Ami. But when he and the other ministers tried to get the Council to increase the "bread and water" penalty for adultery and fornication, the Two Hundred decided the proposed edicts were "too rude and should be moderated and then reviewed." [41] So it would be wrong to interpret the defeat of the "Libertines" as a total triumph for Puritanism. Many a Calvinist burgher danced despite the law and sometimes paid the penalty; *paillardise et adultaire* were facts of life not to be eliminated by eliminating the practitioners.

The renewal of the confederation with Berne was slated for 1556. But the eastern "Bear" wanted conditions detrimental to Geneva's economy, as well as full pardon for Perrin and his company. Calvin and three others were appointed by the Council to work out the new treaty, and when Berne's demands were finally judged to be unacceptable to a free city, it was Calvin who was commissioned to respond to the city Council at Berne. The historian Roget, who criticizes Calvin severely for his part in the death of Servetus and the condemnation of the Perrinists (although Calvin's part in the latter was limited to some letters written to his friends), is lavish in his praise for the Reformer's diplomatic acumen in this crisis. But finally the treaty was renewed, and barely in time. For Savoy rose from the dead. In April 1559, Philip II of Spain and Henry II of France ended the long struggle between their royal houses by the Treaty of Cateau-Cambrésis. Among the provisions of the treaty was that Duke Philibert-Emmanuel of Savoy would be given back the lands taken by Francis I in 1536. This meant trouble for Geneva, faced for the first time in over twenty years with a Savoy anxious to re-establish its profitable control over the city. For Geneva it meant expensive preparations for fortifications, shaping up the militia, and preparing stores of food in case of siege.

In France, however, the Huguenot fortunes took a turn for the better. Scores of pastors had infiltrated that country, most of them from Geneva, and the Protestant growth was fantastically swift.[42] Before Henry II could turn his efforts from fighting Spain to fighting his own Protestant subjects, he was killed in a joust. Marriage to young Mary, Queen of Scots, proved too strenuous for his son Francis II, whose short reign was followed by efforts on the part of the queen mother, Catherine de' Medici, to find religious peace. She called a Colloquy at Poissy (1561), and asked Geneva for someone to espouse the Reformed cause. The city Council decreed that Calvin could not go unless some "notable and great persons" would come to Geneva as *ostages*.[43] So Theodore Beza was sent with a herald. The cessation of religious persecution during the Colloquy and following the resulting Edict of January (1562) encouraged many of the refugees to succumb to nostalgia and return home. At first the city Council was outraged to find some of those received into the *bourgeoisie* leaving the city, and complained that those people had sworn to live and die in Geneva and, by abandoning the city, showed disloyalty and perjured themselves. But finally they had to let them go "so no one can say that we keep people here by force, understanding that this city is *franche et libre*." [44]

But this relief was quickly ended by the infamous Massacre of Vassy by Duke Francis de Guise, when more than a hundred Protestants were trapped in a barn where they had been worshiping and cruelly put to death. This catapulted France into the first of the horrible religious wars which kept it in a state of turmoil for more than thirty years and was to continue to make Geneva the home of the oppressed. But most of this struggle and Geneva's part in its lies outside our present view. Calvin did make suggestions on how to help the Protestants of Lyons without committing the city so greatly it could not defend itself against Savoy. And it was Calvin who agonized with the Council over the request from Condé, the Huguenot prince-general in France, for a loan of more than 60,000 *écus*, which Calvin thought could neither be refused nor paid without ruining the city.

At the time of Calvin's death the future held many crises for his beloved city. There would be panic caused by the close passage of the troops of the Spanish Duke of Alva on their way to inflict a "council of blood" on the Low Countries; in 1572 the city would welcome its greatest flood of refugees following the massacre of St. Bartholomew's Day; the outbreak of an exhausting war with Savoy would occur in 1589. Still farther in the future was Savoy's final attempt to scale the city's walls by night—the unsuccessful "Escalade" of December 1603—the defeat of Savoy, and the treaty of St. Julien in 1603, which gave final peace with Geneva's great enemy.

But when 27 May 1564 had ended, the two struggles Calvin had been entangled in were over for him. The city's struggle for freedom still had a long way to go, all the way to 1603. But the other struggle—the church's fight for freedom in its own realm—was finished. Calvin had been victor. From our vantage point we may argue that it should never have been entered upon, that had the sword of the magistrate never been used to punish moral and religious delinquency, the Council would not have been forced to fight the church over its discipline. Indeed, the Anabaptists in the sixteenth century could see that clearly enough. But for Calvin the church could never be a cell in society whose influence was inward and merely spiritual. The church and society were as one, so that the former, wielding the Word of God, could transform the latter for the betterment of the human condition and for the greater glory of God.

CHAPTER III

Calvin's Critique
of Human Society

IN GENEVA the Consistory was the church's arm of discipline. Made up of an equal number of pastors and laymen (six of each) and presided over by the first syndic (each year one of the twenty-five members of Geneva's Small Council was elected to this office), the Consistory dealt with all the ills of human society. It was the Consistory which had to decide how to deal with an alarming number of women "pregnant by fornication" (*femmes grosses par paillardises*), who couldn't be sent to jail while in that condition, and certainly not after they had produced the fruit of their labors. Also to the Consistory, one wintry afternoon, came a resentful native-born Genevan named Pierre Frochat, who was disturbed by the influx of French who had left their native land because of religious persecution. Perhaps he saw them taking jobs from people like himself or maybe he just disliked foreigners. Anyway, the Consistory had to admonish him to watch his language because he had been overheard to say that "these _____ French don't come here for the gospel, but to beat other people." [1] Modern Geneva has a political party with roughly the same slogan.

The existence of the Consistory illustrates concretely Calvin's understanding of human society. Put in a nutshell it was this: the Fall of man has broken the original tie of love and equality among men, but in Christ God has begun the restoration of right relations between men. And since the church is the visible society of those united again to one another in Christ, the church must see to it that its life exhibits wholeness, justice, and love. The Consistory's task was mainly to admonish Christians to be Christian.

Before we examine Calvin's understanding of society more carefully, let us pause to give credit to the research of the Swiss pastor and economist who has finally opened up Calvin's social and economic thought, André Biéler, and his magnificent *La pensée économique et sociale de Calvin*, published in 1961. Before this publication Calvin's thought in these crucial areas had barely been touched by such writers as Williston Walker and Georgia Harkness. Particularly do we owe to Biéler the debt of calling to our attention the social and political emphases of Calvin in his sermons preached Sundays and weekdays in Geneva. In these sermons we see Calvin confronted both by the Word which he sought to explain and by the people of Geneva for whom the Word was intended. To them—the housewives, laborers, refugees, and *bourgeoisie*—he explained carefully what he considered to be God's plan for mankind, and launched bitter attacks against those who trampled human love and perverted simple justice in their scramble through life.

The Basic Unity of Man

"The name 'neighbor' extends indiscriminately to every man, because the whole human race is united by a sacred bond of fellowship. . . . To make any person our neighbor, therefore, it is enough that he be a man." [2] This basic solidarity is, of course, not readily apparent in society, and the inequalities that we see Calvin did not hesitate to blame on human sin. "Any inequality which is contrary to this arrangement is nothing else than a corruption of nature which proceeds from sin. In the meantime, however, the benediction of God so prevails that the earth everywhere lies open that it may have its inhabitants, and that an immense multitude of men may find, in some part of the globe, their home." [3] This pre-population explosion statement about the openness of the earth to a multitude of inhabitants simply means Calvin believed God's benediction goes further than man's capacity to spoil it.

But spoil it, man will. And the result is that men take God's bounty and grab it for themselves, hoarding, monopolizing, speculating, so that the original order of nature is perverted. Imagine how this preaching must have sounded to the burgher who has just made a killing in wheat, stored till the supply was scarce and the price at its peak:

> There will be those who would rather that the wheat spoil in the granary so that it will be eaten by vermin, so that it can be sold when there is want (for they only wish to starve the poor people). . . . See the wheat collected; how well our Lord has poured out his grace and his benediction so that the poor world would be nourished. But the speculator will gather it in granaries and lock it up securely, till finally the cry of famine is heard and that's no longer possible. What will happen? It will be spoiled and rotten. How true it is that our Lord is mocked by those who want to have much profit. . . . These people entomb the grace of God, as if they warred against his bounty and against the paternal love which he displays toward everyone.[4]

The basic solidarity of man cannot be broken. But human avarice goes a long way toward obscuring God's order. This same note will be echoed by Rousseau two centuries later when he remarks in *Émile* that "everything is good when it leaves the hands of the Author of things, but degenerates in the hands of man."

The Partial Redemption of Society in the Church

But God has not been content to allow the original order to rest in its present perverted form. He has begun the restoration of nature and the universe in Jesus Christ, and the new life united with others in Christ's church.

But there are those who seem not to be cut out to live this life wrapped up with others. One such was the oft-mentioned wealthy young Genevan Philibert Berthelier. Berthelier was originally brought before the Consistory when his bride-to-be, Jeanne Pignon, complained that he had reneged on his promise to marry her after he discovered that her face was her only fortune. In the Consistory meeting his temper got the better of him when Calvin was admonishing him about such breach of promise, and he reacted with words "bitter and arrogant," and finally "with great disdain made with his fingers the sign to the whole assembly of the Consistory." [5] Beyond assuring ourselves that "the sign" was not the sign of the cross, we're not sure what motion Berthelier made with his fingers, but the implication is plain. He was aggravated at the restrictions implied in his membership in that community of Christians whose allegiance is to Christ. In short, he was not cut out to be a saint.

But that, Calvin would have said, was his calling. "The Communion of the Saints . . . very well expresses what the church is. It is as if one said that the saints are gathered into the society of Christ on the principle that whatever benefits God confers upon them, they should in turn share with one another." In other words, the original solidarity of mankind, ruined by the Fall, is now expressed in the church. We shall examine later in some detail (see Chapter IX) some indication that the disciplinary arm, the Consistory, itself overstepped Christian love in its attempt to enforce solidarity and sainthood on the likes of Berthelier. Certainly the rigid enforcement of that law on Christians was hard in a society like that of Geneva where every inhabitant was considered a member of the church. But the theory was egalitarian and, at least in principle, absolutely just.

However, Calvin did not mean that Christian brotherhood implied the end of all the inequalities of society, any more than the professor who teaches equality among men means to imply that the distinction between undergraduates and professors with Ph.D.'s should be erased. What he did insist was that in Christ there can be authority without oppression and subordination without shame. He preaches, "Whoever has some superiority over others ought to abstain from all tyranny—we ought to be humane toward those whom God has subjected to us, so not to dominate them in cruelty, nor to extract from them all that we are able; but to remember to treat them humanely as our brothers." He went on to remind the crowd at St. Pierre's that we all have one Father and Master, and concluded with a fairly typical warning: "If we wish to obtain mercy from our God and to be supported by his grace, let us be advised to do the same toward those who are subject to us." [6]

This simply means that the restoration of man to his original state begun by God in Christ is not yet complete. Human society still contains a hierarchy of social relations which Calvin, like Luther, spoke of as the political order. For example, the normal order between men and women, which is fundamentally a relation of equality,[7] remains in this present provisory society an unequal relationship. The church cannot try to suppress this external or political order under pretext of Christian liberty. But it can, in this and all other hierarchical human relationships, plead for mercy and mutual regard.

An almost classic expression of this conservatism toward the structures of society coupled with the clarion call for Christian concern is found in his discussion of the master-slave relationship in Ephesians. After noting that civil codes always give masters too much power, he points out that "God allows to masters no power over them beyond what is consistent with the law of love." Philosophers, he says, attempt to guarantee that slaves will not be harshly treated by pointing to the usefulness of well-kept servants or slaves. But Paul goes much further, showing masters that they are actually obligated to their slaves. "Masters and servants are not indeed on the same level; but there is a mutual law which binds them. By this law, servants are placed under the authority of their masters; and by the same law, due regard being had to the difference of these stations, masters lie under certain obligations to their servants. This analogy is the only true standard. . . . for we are ready enough to demand what is due to ourselves; but, when our own duty comes to be performed, everyone attempts to plead exemption. It is chiefly, however, among persons of authority and rank that injustice of this sort prevails."[8]

Perhaps there is some connection between Calvin's distrust of those with authority and rank and the battle which we have seen him fighting with such highborn *bourgeoisie* as the Berthelier and Sept brothers, the Perrin and Favre families, and others of power and importance in mid-sixteenth-century Geneva.

The legitimate strata of society, then, are never absolute. These social distinctions are a provisory arrangement that has fundamentally been set aside by the new human community reestablished by Jesus Christ. This, plus the obvious reluctance of men to take the rule of love seriously when their own interests are involved, means that the church must preserve its liberty and authority to speak God's Word to a sinful society. This goes a long way toward explaining the bitter battle that Calvin fought with the civil authorities in Geneva from 1536 to 1555 over the independence of the church.

Unlike some modern Calvinists, for whom the sacraments are mere pointers or reminders of God's gracious action, Calvin saw them actually aiding the process of mutual love.

> For since we are made members of Jesus Christ, being incorporated in him and united with him as to our head [*chef*], there is good reason that we have together such charity and concord as the members of the same body ought to have. Wherefore, insofar as the power of the Holy Spirit is joined with sacraments, when one receives them properly, we have by this means hope of a good means and aid to make us grow and profit in holiness of life, and especially in charity.[9]

Not that Calvin was very optimistic about human nature—even partially redeemed human nature; nor did he regard the sacraments as magic tablets which if taken regularly would automatically promote Christian growth. But to partake of the *Cène* is to enter into a real communion with Christ that includes all those within that communion.

> We shall benefit very much from the Sacrament if this thought is impressed and engraved upon our minds: that none of the brethren can be injured, despised, rejected, abused, or in any way offended by us, without at the same time, injuring, despising, and abusing Christ by the wrongs we do; that we cannot disagree with our brethren without at the same time disagreeing with Christ; that we cannot love Christ without loving him in the brethren; that we ought to take the same care of our brethren's bodies as we take of our own; for they are members of our body; and that, as no part of our body is touched by any feeling of pain which is not spread among all the rest, so we ought not to allow a brother to be affected by any evil, without being touched with compassion for him.[10]

One Sunday morning when everyone was supposed to be at worship, a Genevan dandy out for a stroll was accosted by a policeman who asked him sarcastically if he knew where the fellowship of Christians was. "Of course," he responded, "out here." We smile at his cavalier individualism, but Calvin did not. For the solitary Christian was unknown to Calvin, for whom to be in Christ meant to live with and for that great multitude (many of them unwashed) for whom Christ had died and who were members of his Body. The sin of the Sunday morning stroller was not his stroll but his rejection of Christian communion, the tie of mutual love and regard.

Church and State: A Mutual Concern for Society

Perhaps the clearest way of illustrating the relationship of church and state in Geneva is to pick out several incidents which show the tension between the church, led by Calvin, and the state, directed by the equally obdurate Small Council. The first incident followed the first election after Calvin came to town in September of 1536. The election was held on February of the next year, and the majority of those elected to the Council and to the four highest posts within the Council (the syndics) were opposed to Calvin's aim to get the people to swear to a Confession of Faith. Almost immediately Calvin and his associate, Guillaume Farel, were called on the carpet—Calvin for calling the Council "a Council of the Devil," and both of them in order to be admonished "not to mix themselves in magistracy." [11]

But the Council itself was not above some mixing in ecclesiastical affairs. Twelve years after the incident cited, the Twenty-Five elected themselves a liturgical commission by commanding the pastors to have the Lord's Prayer more often, "to say the commands of the Lord as it was in the beginning," and then celebrated by throwing Louis Bourgeois, the composer of many of the Genevan Psalm-tunes, into jail for printing the songs differently.[12]

As we have seen, the events in sixteenth-century Genevan life make it clear that both church and state were not above elbowing a little for freedom from the demands of the other. At first the civic authorities tried to operate the church as one of the departments of the city's uplift program. On the other side, the church, led by Calvin, tried to guarantee its freedom in matters ecclesiastical and disciplinary, and in the process often overstepped the hazy boundary line between sacred and secular. In theory, of course, the two were separate, but in practice absolute separation is clearly impossible. Let us examine the relationship between the two in Calvin's thought.

In Geneva, as in all of Europe, church and state were coterminous. That is, all citizens were by birth members of both societies. There were Anabaptists around who disputed this time-honored arrangement, who were convinced that only by a new birth could anyone truly join Christ's church. But they were negligible as a power (indeed, they generally regarded the political arena as dominated by Satan), were regarded by all reasonable men as inimical to social order, and therefore were drowned in Zurich, cursed by Luther, burned in France, and ushered hastily out of town by the upright Genevans. On its side of this theoretical separation, the church, in Calvin's view, had four tasks vis-à-vis the state.

In the first place, the church must pray for the political authorities. "Since God appointed magistrates and princes for the preservation of mankind, however much they fall short of the divine appointment, yet we must not on that account cease to love what belongs to God, and to desire their preservation. That is why believers, in whatever country they live, must not only obey the laws and the government of magistrates, but likewise in their prayers supplicate God for their salvation." [13] It is well known that Calvin would countenance rebellion against even the most repressive government only in extreme circumstances and then only when led by lower magistrates.[14] But in practice Calvin would allow no rebellion at all, not once advising anyone to raise the sword against a monarch. Hence I have called Calvin a revolutionary—but one who did not wish to rip asunder the fabric of society.

Secondly, the church must encourage the state to defend the poor and weak against the rich and powerful. This is an impor-

tant point for us because it places the church squarely against
all economic injustice and makes it quite clear that preaching the
gospel is linked with the demand for social justice. Commenting
on Psalm 82:3, "Give justice to the weak and the fatherless;
maintain the right of the afflicted and the destitute," Calvin
wrote: ". . . a just and well-regulated government will be distinguished for maintaining the rights of the poor and afflicted."
Noting that it is the duty of magistrates to observe justice for
all men, Calvin points out that it is the weak and poor who are
in real need. "It is rare that rich men resort to magistrates for
help, except when they happen to fall out among themselves.
From these remarks, it is obvious why the cause of the poor and
needy is here chiefly commended to rulers; for those who are exposed an easy prey to the cruelty and wrongs of the rich have no
less need of the assistance and protection of magistrates than the
sick have of the aid of the physician." [15]

Indeed, for Calvin it was the treatment of the weak in society that really determined the value of a political regime. He
was not the sort of pastor to be impressed with the outward,
superficial morality of either the wealthy or those in responsible
positions. His was the critique which pierced below superficial
standards of right and wrong (such as the pietistic commenda-
tion: he must be a fine person—he doesn't smoke or drink!).
We shall see that his critique led the church in Geneva to battle
about interest rates, employment opportunities, and all that pertains to a humane secular society.

The third task of the church is that of ensuring its own
status by calling on the political authorities for help in promoting true religion and even enforcing ecclesiastical discipline. Of
course, this is really the state's obligation to Christ's church.
"Holy kings," Calvin writes, "are greatly praised in Scripture
because they restored the worship of God when it was corrupted
or destroyed, or took care of religion that under them it might
flourish pure and unblemished. . . . This proves the folly of
those who would neglect the concern for God and would give
attention only to rendering justice among men." [16] In this, Calvin
was certainly a man of his age, reflecting over one thousand

years of *res publica christiana* and not one iota of the New Testament.

We must not, however, interpret Calvin by the pluralism existing in today's Western world and the quasi separation of religious and secular which now prevails. It seems obvious to the American Christian that if the church does not want the state to usurp spiritual powers, then it should not call on the state to enforce its religious decrees. But twelve centuries of intimacy between the two "swords" made that relationship as unassailable for Calvin as our constitutional provision for separation is unassailable for most of us today. A Genevan pastor at the turn of this century applied the term *theocracy* to this close relationship between church and state in Geneva. But by "theocracy" he meant only to show the close relationship between the two powers. If by "theocracy" one means "the domination of the church over the state, or in the sense of the domination of the clergy over the political government, it is completely impossible not to recognize that *there had not been* a theocracy in Geneva." [17]

The fourth task of the church is to warn the authorities when they are at fault. Commenting on Amos 8:4, Calvin writes: "Because there is often great blame to lay at the feet of rulers is the reason the prophets address themselves so sharply and rigorously against them. For the common people often fail, either by default or by common error or even because of the example of others. But those who rule are ordinarily the ones who also pervert all law and equity. . . . So it is not to be marvelled at if our Lord by his prophets attacks them so sharply." [18] So the minister, the "mouth of God," has the duty of speaking out sharply against all injustice, all neglect of duty, all ungodliness in high places. A theory like this is seldom popular with rulers, and much of the revolutionary ferment of Calvinism must be laid at the feet of this doctrine.

Everyone who writes on Calvin includes something on his theory of the relationship between church and state. Clearly Calvin was opposed to those who would place the church under the control of the state, the situation prevailing then in England and Germany. Rulers were *nutritios ecclesiae*, supporters and nourishers of the church, but they must also consult the "mouth of God," and in Geneva if they didn't, the mouth of God (i.e., Calvin) would consult them. It would seem that H. Richard Niebuhr, who regards Calvin as one intent on having Christian faith *transform* culture, is close to the heart of the matter.[19] In his *Protestant Concepts of Church and State*, Thomas G. Sanders follows Niebuhr's analysis and labels as transformationist that "moderate and pragmatic" theory of many modern churchmen who want to assert the church's competency to criticize and influence the state.[20] For Calvin there was an undeniable separation between the two powers. But since both were under the Lordship of Christ, the church's task was always an active one toward the state, and we shall see that activity at work more than once.

CHAPTER IV

Wealth and Poverty

LIKE ALL CITIES in all times and all places, Geneva had its haves and its have-nots. That normal situation was made abnormal from about the middle of the 1540's onward as refugees fled Catholic persecution and flocked into the little city. To handle a bad situation made worse, a public *bourse* (purse) was set up to take care of the most striking examples of poverty, and the work of the public hospital was expanded to provide shelter, medical care, and work for the indigent and the refugee. A key figure in the war on poverty was the head of the hospital, known as the *hospitaller*. His task was a formidable one, demanding time and patience and competency in several professions. He not only had to account for all the orphans, the old, and the sick, all of whom were housed, fed, taught, and tended at city expense, but also had to oversee vineyards, hemp, grain, and turnip fields, keep an eye out for the dozen cows, the horses, pigs, and other livestock, and be foreman for the weaving and jug-making industries at the hospital. All this he must do, and then make a weekly accounting to the *procureurs* who oversaw the whole operation for the church (they were also deacons) and for *Messieurs* of the city Council.[1] The church and city of Geneva were not so spiritually oriented that human bodies were deemed to be unimportant to the plan and purposes of God. Let us look at Calvin's own thinking in this vital area.

From Each According to His Ability . . .

Like almost all Christian thinkers, Calvin ascribed material blessing to the bounty of God. Commenting on Christ's petition in the Lord's Prayer, "Give us this day our daily bread," Calvin flails the teaching of Erasmus that in the presence of God it would be wrong to ask for something as common as food. For God's "fatherly kindness extends to the smallest matters, so that he does not disdain to take care even of our flesh." [2]

But unlike some modern Christians, Calvin never saw poverty and misfortune as evidence of God's disfavor of the individual afflicted, nor did he regard prosperity as a sign of God's blessing for personal merit, nor as evidence of one's election to salvation. In fact, Calvin was much closer to Jesus' teaching about the impossibility of the rich getting into heaven than he was to any glib equation of prosperity with goodness.

> It is an error which is by far too common among men, to look upon those who are oppressed with afflictions as condemned and reprobate. . . . Most men, making judgments about the favor of God from an uncertain and transitory state of prosperity, applaud the rich, and those upon whom, as they say, fortune smiles; so, on the other hand, they insult contemptuously the wretched and miserable, and foolishly imagine that God hates them, because he does not exercise so much forbearance toward them as he does toward the reprobate. The error of which I speak . . . is one which has prevailed in all ages of the world. [3]

The author was raised in precisely this erroneous way of thinking. Not that the Calvinists of central Ohio regarded the rich as blessed—far from that; we weren't rich! But we were taught that the slum-dweller of Columbus would not be there if he were not shiftless and lazy, and we learned to look askance at those who could find no jobs during the late Depression and had to work on the WPA. Max Weber is not right in asserting that the Calvinist Puritan tended to find evidence of God's election in personal prosperity—we shall examine this in Chapter XI. But social Darwinism—the biological doctrine of survival of the fittest applied to economic advancement—though certainly non-

Christian in any recognizable way, has had a great influence on the large Protestant American middle classes. Calvin would have had none of that sort of peeping into the secret counsels of the Almighty!

It would not be too strong to say that for Calvin both wealth and poverty were sacramental—that is, they were channels of grace from God, and means of evidencing faith on the part of man. "Why is it then that God permits the existence of poverty here below, except because he wishes to give us occasion for doing good," he preached. "Thus we do not attribute it to fortune when we see that one is rich and another poor. . . . God distributes unequally the frail goods of this world in order to investigate the goodwill of men; he is examining man. . . . If a man is liberal when he has means, seeking to do good to those in need of his help, this is good proof. If the other, being poor, takes patiently what it is pleasing to God to send him, not being solicitous of fraud nor other malice although he is suffering and his condition is hard—this is also a good and useful test." [4]

But Calvin was no fool. He was under no illusion that the rich were apt to pass such an examination. A few might (God softens a few hearts), but the great majority refuse Christ and idolize their possessions. "They entertain," he writes, "a firm and deep-seated conviction that the rich are happy, and that there is nothing better than to increase their wealth by every possible method, and to brood jealously over whatever they have acquired, rejecting as foolish paradoxes all the sayings of Christ which have a contrary tendency." [5]

Nor had Calvin any great trust in the well-to-do who had declared themselves for the Reformation. Imagine how the wealthy among his flock must have reacted to these words from the pulpit of St. Pierre's:

> What is the Christianity of this world? It is true that there will be enough who will protest they follow the Gospel. And even the word "Reformation" will run about in the mouth of many who are like ravening wolves just the same. Nor is it a question of how much to grab for themselves, since if they were able they would swallow everything. They are not content to have three

times what they need, but are sorry that anything at all escapes them.

After charging that such people delight in seeing the poor go hungry, he returned to the attack:

> If they were able they would have a sun all to themselves in order to say that the others have nothing in common with them. If they were able, indeed, it is certain that they would change the whole order of God and nature so they could swallow everything. *And yet what Christians!* Yes, if one wants to believe them![6]

This bitterness of Calvin against the misuse of God's blessings was not simply a Reformation asceticism. It was not a question of giving up the legitimate blessings of God as a necessary duty. Calvin was not a Manichee. But he was concerned that God's gifts be used for the relief of the whole community of God's people. It was not asceticism to which Calvin called Geneva's monied, but the rule of love. Indeed, if there is any central theme in Calvin's social and economic thought, it is that wealth comes from God in order to be used to aid our brethren. The solidarity of the human community is such that it is inexcusable for some to have plenty and others to be in need. Commenting on Paul's use of the story of the manna in the wilderness as illustrative of the true Christian's concern for the brother in need, Calvin brought the message home:

> Let those, then, that have riches, whether they have been left by inheritance, or procured by industry and efforts, consider that their abundance was not intended to be laid out in intemperance or excess, but in relieving the necessities of the brethren.[7]

It should be noted that there was no legalism involved. A few pages earlier, commenting on 2 Corinthians 8:8, he writes, "God everywhere charges us to help the necessities of our brethren, but he nowhere specifies the sum, that, after making a calculation, we might divide between ourselves and the poor. He nowhere binds us to circumstances of times, or persons, but calls us to take the rule of love as our guide." [8]

But Calvin did not stop with the rich. Not being a wealthy man himself, he understood that the poor also hold an office from God. They are God's *procureurs* or *receveurs*, God's messengers to check on the faith and charity of their neighbors. "God sends us the poor as his receivers. And although the alms are given to mortal creatures, yet God accepts and approves them and puts them to one's account, as if we had placed in his hands that which we give to the poor." [9] Nor is this an obligation which we can discharge in merely legalistic fashion. The poor are brothers and must be treated as such. There is no coldhearted giving in the Calvinist plan; giving must be done with compassion. "No act of kindness, except when joined with compassion, is pleasing to God," he writes. "There are many apparently liberal, who yet do not feel for the miseries of their brothers." [10]

Perhaps it was the scholar with little property of his own speaking, but Calvin thought that such sharing of goods had to go as far as there was need, even if it meant real hardship on the part of the giver. Commenting on Matthew 6:19–20, "Do not lay up for yourselves treasures on earth," Calvin writes:

> The command to sell possessions must not be literally interpreted, as if a Christian were not at liberty to retain anything for himself. He only intended to show that we must not be satisfied with bestowing on the poor what we can easily spare, but that we must not refuse to part with our estates, if their revenue does not supply the wants of the poor. As if he said, "Let your liberality go so far as to lessen your patrimony, and dispose of your lands." [11]

And none of this liberality on the part of those who have received an abundance of God's material bounty is at all dependent on the goodwill of the poor. Several generations ago the wealthier classes were disturbed by the lack of gratitude shown by the poorer classes at offers of genteel largess. Today we exhibit the same concern as a nation for those impoverished nations which are ungrateful despite our material and technical assistance. But Calvin did not see the personal character of the needy, nor his response, as in any way affecting his position as God's ambassador to receive what the rich owe to God. "Although the poor acquit themselves badly of their duty," he preached, "and though having been helped they do not bless us, yet despite that we ought not to cease doing what God commands us, knowing that the alms which go from us will serve as adequate benediction when those whom we have helped are silent." [12]

Perhaps the most refreshing dictate of Calvin in the economic area was his assertion that God's design provides for an equitable distribution of goods among all men. From the pulpit he implored the good burghers and poor refugees in Geneva:

> We must recognize that God has wanted to make us like members of a body. When we regard each other in this way, each will then conclude: "I see my neighbor who has need of me and if I were in such extremity, I would wish to be helped; I must therefore do just that." In short, this communication of which St. Paul speaks here is the fraternal affection which proceeds from the regard that we have when God has joined us together and united us in one body, because he wants each to employ himself for his neighbors, so that no one is addicted to his own person, but that we serve all in common.[13]

Although Calvin specifically condemned Communism, as we shall see, so harmonious did he believe the life in human society ought to be that André Biéler says it can be defined according to the famous Marxist formula "from each according to his ability, to each according to his need." [14] Certainly that is not a strained interpretation of Calvin's words in his Commentary on 2 Corinthians:

> Thus the Lord recommends to us a proportion of this nature, that we may, in so far as every one's resources admit, afford help to the needy, so that there may not be some in affluence, and others in need.[15]

This adds up to a social and economic ethic of concern. Human solidarity is such that anything which contributes to the impoverishment of part of society is *ipso facto* evil. Whether this brands Calvin as a social revolutionary depends on the definition of the term. But clearly he is a Christian who has read in his Bible both the Hebrew concern for the poor, the orphan, the widow, and the sojourner, and the concern of Christ for all oppressed. And certainly the situation of little Geneva, surrounded by enemies and possessing a small and uncertain harvest from her rural possessions, demanded such practical social concern within the sometimes-beleaguered city. Perhaps because of the lack of abundance in basic grains, Calvin was particularly incensed at those who engaged in monopoly and speculation. Note his pointed explication of the prophet Amos' thunder against those who bought the poor for silver and the needy for a pair of shoes:

> Here he [Amos] speaks of the avarice of the rich, who in time of scarcity held the poor subject to their obnoxious selves and reduced them to slavery. . . . We indeed know what is the influence of poverty and pressing want, when men are oppressed with famine; they would rather a hundred times sell their lives than not to rescue themselves even by an invaluable price. For what else is food but the support of life? The rich . . . saw that wheat was high in price; "Now is the time for the poor to come into our possession . . ." But the other circumstance increases this iniquity—that they sold the refuse of the wheat; and when they reduced to bondage the poor, they did not feed them; they mingled filth and offscourings with the wheat, as it is wont to be done.

Perhaps recalling some of the wheat offered to the pastors as part of their pay and coupling with that the complaints of the common people of Geneva when wheat was scarcely to be had, Calvin finished with acid on his pen: ". . . for we know that such robbers usually do this, when want presses upon the common people; they sell barley for wheat, and for barley they sell chaff and refuse. This kind of wrong is not new or unusual . . ." [16] And in a sermon he went so far as to call such wheat-cornering operators "murderers, savage beasts, biting and eating up the poor, sucking up their blood." [17]

But despite the thunder from St. Pierre's against those among the saints who were really blood-sucking murderers, Calvin had a horror of social turmoil that gave his thought a conservative twist. Just as he could not bring himself to countenance armed rebellion even for the sake of the gospel, neither could he give the poor and oppressed any theological support for open rebellion. Commenting on the Epistle of James 5:4, where the wages of the poor laborer are withheld, Calvin's anger boils over. He calls such action "monstrous barbarity," and lashes out at those who "think that the rest of mankind exist only for their benefit." But the vindication for such economic abuse should not come from the laborer, but from God: "We ought to notice . . . that the cries of the poor come to the ears of God, so that we may know that the wrong done to them shall not be unpunished. They, therefore, who are oppressed by the unjust ought resignedly to sustain their evils, because they will have God as their avenger [*vindex*]." [18] While there is undoubtedly something theologically correct about such advice, there will usually come a time when the poor are no longer willing to wait on God and will try their own hand at avenging. Calvin could lobby, preach, and legislate for the poor, but for him, as for Luther, armed rebellion by common people without magisterial leadership was always beyond the pale.

This conservatism is also evident in Calvin's understanding of the "Christian communism" passages of the New Testament, particularly the Acts account of the early Christians having all things in common. That Scripture had been used by some "frenetic and fantastic spirits" among the Anabaptists as proof that Christians should have all things in common. Calvin thought of the Acts situation as a temporary measure made necessary for the relief of the poor in the early Jerusalem community, not as the model for Christian economic theory. "Truly," he writes, "this place needs a sane exposition, because of fanatic spirits who imagine a *koinonia* of goods, in which all civil government is taken away; as in this age the Anabaptists have raged, because they taught there was no church unless all men's goods were gathered together in one heap, in order that everyone might lay hold on it." [19]

Here, as with all of Calvin's thought on practical matters, there is a balance between extremes. Modern rugged individualists can get no comfort at all from his harsh treatment of the avarice of the wealthy, his belief that wealth is almost always built on the blood of the poor, and the strict industrial and economic regulation which we shall see Calvin approving of in the Genevan marketplace. But on the other hand, neither is there any evidence that Calvin had the slightest disposition to do away with private property. Indeed, in his *Institutes*, IV, i, 3, he writes: ". . . it is necessary to keep peace among men that the ownership of property should be distinct and personal among them." What we do have, as Biéler remarks, is a middle way between communism and individualism. Private property is really private—it does not belong to the state. But it is private property meant to be used for the common good of society. In other words, Calvin hoped by dint of explanation and persuasion to make the social and economic code conform more closely with the law of love.

The Role of Government in Economic Life

Our last concern in this chapter will be to pinpoint Calvin's view of the economic role of the state. Since the Weber thesis holds that laissez-faire capitalism came about because of the moral climate created by later Calvinists, it should be instructive to see if Calvin himself believed that government should keep hands off the labors of the businessman. A problem arises, however, because Calvin simply does not discuss this matter very fully. When we turn to actual Genevan practice, and Calvin's own influence upon this practice, we shall find a state ordering all sorts of regulations in business life, with Calvin cheering on the sidelines and occasionally giving the magistrates a bit of advice on how to regulate better. But he writes little and speaks little in his sermons about such regulation. Of course, Calvin had not had opportunity to read Adam Smith's massive explanation of laissez-faire capitalism, *Wealth of Nations* (which appeared in 1776), and the fact that such regulation was accepted everywhere in western Europe in Calvin's day probably accounts for his lack of comment.

Certain items are clear, however. First, the practice of civil government embraces not only the establishment and protection of true religion, but also was to see that "men breathe, eat, drink and are kept warm," that the public peace is preserved, that "each man may keep his property safe and sound," and "that honesty and modesty may be preserved among men." [20] While the references to peace and the safety of ownership are not exceptional, the concern for eating, drinking, and warmth, as well as public honesty, bids fair to mean some intervention by government for the protection of the common good. This is clarified by Calvin's contention that proper governmental interference extends to weights, measures, and money—which puts the state directly in the marketplace.

> We note that if men seek to enrich themselves by bad and illicit means, that it is like ripping up the landmarks or terminals (as people say); and that is like falsehood. What should be done? That everything should be protected in the same way as weights and measures, and also money; for there would no longer be communication among men if there were not some fidelity in such things. . . . And so we note that it is not without cause that God has commanded that they [the ancient landmarks] should be retained; for under one specie he has comprised the whole, showing that we must carefully guard that which we know to be necessary for maintaining the public weal and humanity among men.[21]

Calvin was a pragmatist in search of the common good of society. Whatever promoted the happiness of men in society was good; whatever harmed human existence was bad. The reader who knows something of Calvin's theology will know that this pragmatism extended into other areas—for example, the system of church government, where his own predilection was for what has come to be called the presbyterian form, but in his correspondence he made it clear he believed England should continue its government by bishops.

So when Calvin talked about the value of ancient landmarks, that is, laws and mores, he was thinking only of "maintaining the public weal and humanity among men." But not all ancient landmarks preserved what was humane. In the sermon quoted above, Calvin went on to say that ancient laws ought not to be changed "out of frivolous curiosity or in a flighty way." He thought the ancient laws should be maintained as often as possible for the good of society. "But when necessity shows that it is necessary to change, then our Lord wishes that the means that he shows are used, the ones he places in our hands. And if one is stubborn for the ancient here, it is pure absurdity." So the common weal was the real test of the adequacy of the government to interfere in the marketplace or anywhere else. Here the Calvinist disregard for tradition per se is quite clear. In Geneva we shall find the state openly involved in the economic enterprise, as it regulated buying and selling and making contracts. Furthermore, we shall see that for the most part that regulation did promote the humane society for which Calvin labored.

One last point should be noted: Not only must the state guard against business interests milking the life of the people by unjust methods, but the state itself must not be an economic liability to its citizens. Calvin affirmed the right and necessity of the state to tax its subjects for "public necessity," and went further to say that those in office will, of course, benefit from their position. But this is not carte blanche; the obligations of rulers and people are mutual. ". . . princes themselves will in turn remember that their revenues are not so much their private chests as the treasuries of the entire people . . . which cannot be squandered or despoiled without manifest injustice. Or rather, that these are almost the very blood of the people, which it would be the harshest inhumanity not to spare. Moreover, let them consider that their imposts and levies, and other kinds of tributes are nothing but supports of public necessity; but that to impose them upon the common folk without cause is tyrannical extortion." [22]

Biéler's summary is helpful. "As for the economic role of the state, the Calvinist ideal conforms to Christian teaching of all times and joins with that of the scholastics as well as that of the other reformers. All are in accord in recognizing that it is the province of the state to maintain among men a certain economic harmony, to defend the poor against the rich and to remove from money its oppressive power. . . . The Christian doctrine of the state is equally distant from state-socialist theories which would almost entirely abolish private property, and from liberal doctrines [i.e., defending laissez-faire] which deny in principle the intervention of the state. . . . The liberty of Christians is verified in that being strictly under the headings of faith and obedience, they are very supple and mobile in affairs of state." [23]

In the face of Calvin's insistence in sermon and Scripture commentary on the solidarity of mankind, his concern to make the law of love the Christian's social and economic ethic, and his acceptance of the right of the state to interfere in business practices to keep human life human—in the face of all this, is it sufficient that one be able to affirm the theological gargoyles of limited atonement (Christ died only for the elect) and predestination for one to be called a Calvinist? Those so-called Five Points of Calvinism, erected by the Dutch Synod of Dort in 1618–19 against those who wanted to whittle away at Election and Reprobation, merely hardened one aspect of Calvin's thought and helped erect Predestination as the shibboleth by which one could quickly take the measure of a churchman. The author would insist that Calvin's social and economic teachings were clearly just as important to Calvin himself, and might just as well be used as the yardstick of Calvinist orthodoxy. Certainly they place Christ's church on the side of the poor—and in our day when the revolting poor of the world are generally found outside the church, this is a sobering thought. Will we who are rich continue to support our pastors and teachers when they march at the side of the poor?

CHAPTER V

Economic Activities

A STRANGER entering the city of Geneva in Calvin's day would have found himself in a city that was frankly and openly commercial. Antony Babel, the dean of Genevan economic historians, says that sixteenth-century Geneva had an amazingly diverse number of small industries for a city of its size. Shops lined the streets and even the bridge, which joined the main city with the section across the Rhone River to the north, known as St. Gervais.

Spotlight on Commerce and the City

What distinguishes Calvin's economic thought from the medieval theologians and from Luther is that he approved of commerce. For him it was the natural way for men to commune with each other, and he saw the exchange of goods as necessary for the spread of God's bounty throughout society. It was as natural for him to use commercial illustrations to underline man's economic solidarity as it would have been unnatural for Thomas Aquinas, Martin Luther, or Thomas Jefferson. Discussing the parable of the talents, Calvin wrote:

> Those who employ usefully whatever God has committed to them are said to be engaged in trading [*negotiari*]. The life of the godly is justly compared to trading, for they ought naturally to exchange and barter with each other, in order to maintain intercourse; and the industry with which every man discharges the office assigned him, the calling itself, the power of acting properly, and other gifts, are reckoned to be so many kinds of mer-

chandise; because the use and end which they have in view is to promote mutual intercourse among men.[1]

The author of this book must shake himself from time to time in order to appreciate Calvin's uniqueness here. For neither in his day nor in ours have the better theologians, philosophers, and humanists had anything but scorn for commerce. John Baldwin, in his studies of the medieval writers and their economic views, underlines the suspicion with which all the intelligentsia regarded the world of trade. The twelfth-century decretists (codifiers of Roman law) were so suspicious of buying and selling—with the omnipresent evils of greed and usury—that their theories on the subject of commerce were prefaced with a vigorous attack against the position of the merchant. The medieval theologians theoretically justified the role of merchant as necessary to society, but found in practice that this was so hard to do that the profession of trade remained for them an extremely sordid business.[2]

Luther had an abiding dislike for commerce, as over against agriculture. "I do not see that many good customs have ever come to a land through commerce, and in ancient times God made his people of Israel dwell away from the sea on this account, and did not let them engage much in commerce." "This I know well," he continued, "that it would be much more pleasing to God if we increased agriculture and diminished commerce, and that they do much better who, according to the Scriptures, till the soil and seek their living from it. . . . There is still much land lying untilled." [3] We shall not quote Emerson or Thoreau.

The author has spent more than two-thirds of his adult life in academe, either studying or teaching, and must report that the situation has not changed. Conversations over coffee sometimes get around to the grubby businessmen who control the state legislature or to the amount of "low cunning" it takes to operate in the outside world of business and trade. (The amount of low cunning it takes to rise in the university is accepted with better grace.) The College of Business is regarded as a late imposition into the academic world, and one has the impression that the College of Business itself is full of people who would shudder at making a living that way. And, to make it worse, those of the writing class today who do take up the cudgel for business often antagonize the academic community by the gauche way in which they try to defend outworn economic systems or to recall us to the eighteenth and nineteenth centuries with stories about rags to riches, poor but honest youngsters, and the glories of unhindered private enterprise. Usually ignored or played down are the savage methods and stupid self-righteousness of some of our early industrial barons.

But the simple truth is that the Western world no longer depends on whether all the soil is tilled or not; it is a world of industry and trade, and even the great universities owe their present affluence to the solid understructure laid by those who manufacture, buy and sell, and pay their taxes. Most of our large universities have buildings named for five-and-dime entrepreneurs, chemical companies, automotive manufacturers, and breakfast cereals. A rural theology of economic ethics may be nice, but it is not very helpful.

So when we commend Calvin for his acceptance of commerce in his day, we are not making a virtue of our present necessity. It was simply that for Calvin the real world was to be taken seriously, and for him the real world involved shoemakers, printers, and clockmakers, as well as farmers, scholars, knights, and clergymen. Calvin's world-affirming theology is quite apparent. Where Luther views with alarm the evidences of evil in the commerce he sees, Calvin grimly assumes that *all* human enterprise is tainted with evil—a safe assumption—and sets about to make the gospel relevant to the city of commerce in which he lived and labored. Robert Lee, writing in 1965, warns us that a "religion that does not take seriously urban civilization—the focal point of economic and social organization—is surely one that weakens itself. The place of religion should be at the heart of the city." [4] In other words, true religion not only visits the sick and takes care of widows and orphans, but also tries to see the relevance of the gospel in the rest of the world that is. Calvin was more serious about this than others of his day.

Wages: The Gift of God

Calvin was fond of quoting the Psalm (127:2) which flagellates the man who rises up early and goes late to rest, eating the bread of anxiety, whereas the "children of God, though not without work and solicitude . . . supported by the providence of God repose in tranquillity." [5] For Calvin, work was not a thing apart, but one of the good gifts of God. It, like everything else in life, is a fallen good; but for the Christian it nevertheless has its joys. Writing of Adam's demotion from the Garden of Eden and the curse placed upon his labors, Calvin writes: "Whereas in that labor [in the Garden] there had been sweet delight, now servile work is enjoined him as if he were condemned to the mines. And yet the asperity of this punishment is mitigated by the clemency of God, because something of enjoyment is blended with the labors of men, lest they should be altogether ungrateful." [6]

One's work is assigned to him by God. And yet the choice of vocation is one that each man must make for himself. It turns out, of course, that man's choice is not always the same as God's. Yet Calvin's guidance in this matter does not seem to have been very exact. He did, indeed, point out that one's proper vocation "is not to be employed at that which God condemns by his Word." [7] There are those occupations which serve only for corrupting society, those which are only money traps (*attrape-deniers*), invented by people who continually endeavor to discover new ways to pick the pockets (*crocheter les bourses*) of fools and others given to vanity. As in the rest of his social and economic thought, the touchstone for evaluating a profession is whether it serves the common good. From his pulpit, perhaps at St. Pierre's, he spoke:

> It is not enough when one can say, "Oh, I work, I have my trade, I set the pace." This is not enough; for one must be concerned whether it is good and profitable to the community and if it is able to serve our neighbors. . . . And this is why we are compared to members of a body. But now, if one's hand be employed

to give some sport to another member and that even to his damage, the whole body will by this means fall into ruin. . . . It is certain that no occupation will be approved by him which is not useful and that does not serve the common good and that also redounds to the profit of everyone.[8]

This is in harmony with his constant concern for the solidarity of mankind, so that what one does must be of benefit to the whole church and the community of mankind. We might disagree with Calvin that merely to entertain one's fellowman is unuseful and therefore not a Christian calling, yet we would certainly have to agree that Calvin was attempting to apply the rule of love to this situation as to all others. His attempts may turn out to be legalistic in our eyes—we can see a direct line from this to the Puritans' dislike for the theater—but the legalism comes after the rule and not before it. Calvin had St. Paul as his tutor.

Not to work meant to refuse to listen to God's Word. This was not only true of those who were simply parasites on society —we shall see later that beggars were put to work in Geneva— but also true of those who holed up in monasteries and refused to live except on public charity. Like other reformers, there was no mercy in Calvin's inkwell for those people who, not having anything to nourish them at home, go into monasteries, as into "pigsties well garnished," where they "fatten themselves at the expense of others without working." He accused them of reversing Christ's commands. "A rare exchange you may be sure, when those who are ordered to give to the poor what they justly possess are not satisfied with their own, but seize on the property of others."[9] The rich and decadent condition of the monasteries of the sixteenth century drew the wrath of most sensitive writers of the period, whether religious reformers like Calvin and Luther, or more socially oriented analysts such as Rabelais, Thomas More, or Erasmus.

But more biting than his satire of the monks was his anger at those who prevented others from working. If one were to harvest another man's field, he writes, everyone would condemn that as simple robbery. But it is much worse to deprive a poor man of the work of his hands.[10] Evidently Calvin had in mind a situation where the labor market was glutted, and there was not enough work to go around. Not to provide work, when one is able, is like cutting the laborer's throat.

> We know that all artisans and workingmen [*gens de mestier*] have their livelihood, for they do not have fixed rents in fields or meadows. So since God has put their lives in their hands, that is to say, in their labor, when they are deprived of necessary means, it is as if one cut their throat. . . . He has ordained that we work. But, is work denied someone? Behold, the man's life is stamped out.[11]

We shall not be surprised, then, to find that the city, swollen to perhaps twice its former size by the influx of refugees, will try to provide public work for those in need.

Perhaps another hint about the refugee problem can be detected in Calvin's concern that nothing be allowed to deprive the artisan of the tools of his trade. We shall see that most of the refugees were artisans, who simply picked up their tools and headed for the city of refuge when persecution became too hot in France or Italy. "God prohibits," Calvin preached, "taking as security all that is necessary to the poor to gain their livelihood and to maintain themselves. . . . The one, then, who takes as security that which sustains the life of a poor man is cruel. It is as if he grabbed the bread from a starving man, and his life itself which is, as it were, cut off in denying the means of maintaining himself." [12]

All of this is pretty clear: work is only good work which benefits the community. Commerce is as good as any form of labor. Whenever work is denied a person, or the means to pursue his livelihood is taken away, then the individual and the common welfare suffer. Therefore society must struggle against anything which corrupts the labor of men. All that pertains to work must be instruments of commonweal and not social oppression. ". . . no manner of life is more praiseworthy to the heart of God, than that which yields some advantage to human society." [13]

This means that man's work must be conducted under proper conditions. Anything which renders work oppressive

should be condemned. The Bible does not allow one to abuse
the work of another. For example, in the Timothy reference to
the pay owed to presbyters who do double service (which involves a not-too-fortunate juxtaposition of Old Testament texts
about not muzzling the ox which is treading out the grain and
the laborer who is worthy of his hire), Calvin remarks:

> This is a political precept, which recommends to us equity and
> humanity in general. . . . For if he forbids us to be unkind to
> brute animals, how much greater humanity does he demand
> toward men! The meaning of this statement, then, is the same as
> if it had been said in general terms that they must not make a
> wrong use of the labor of others.[14]

Lashing out in a sermon, he cried that some people would
be content to kill a poor worker in three days, their only concern being for their own profit. But God wants human labor to
be such that the worker can render thanks to God in the midst
of his service. "For there is no doubt that God wishes to chas-
tize the cruelty which the rich display who would employ the
poor in their service and yet not recompense them for their
labor." [15]

This brings us to the fruit of work, the wage, pay, or salary
which one receives from his labor. Before God, man has no
right to expect to be remunerated for his labor. There is no
merit to what man does, for he is bound in simple obedience
to his Creator and Master. Therefore the pay that everyone receives—master and servant alike—is a sign of the unmerited
grace of God. "It is by his own undeserved favor, and not by
the value of our work, that God is induced to reward it," he
wrote, commenting on the Lucan (17:7) parable of the unprofit-
able servant. This means literally that wages are paid to rich and
poor alike by God, that no one is "worth" what he gets, and,
consequently, for the employer to withhold from his worker
what he owes is really to withhold from him what God pays to
him. The man who pays the wages is really paying out what
does not, in fact, belong to him at all. The master is simply
"paymaster" for the heavenly Master. Calvin rambles a bit as

he preaches, but bear with him as he portrays God checking out
the estate of a rich man:

> God comes, as it were, to make an inventory because men will
> always complain: "Oh, I do not have enough to give, and I may
> be in need myself." But our Lord makes the inventory . . . and
> says: "What's this? This one has wheat in his granary, but is not
> able to give to the one who has served him and from whom he
> has drawn blood and labor? Should he not at least notice the
> wheat that he has in his granary? He [the worker] has ploughed
> the earth, he has cultivated it . . . should he not savor some
> sweetness and some fruit?" Afterwards he comes to the wine-
> press and to the stables, as if he said: "Let each of you take note
> of what he has, for according to your faculty you are required to
> recompense those who have worked for you and who have been
> the instruments of such benediction." For if we bless God with
> our mouth, confessing that he it is who has blessed us, and if he
> has sent us people who have served to augment us, there is only
> fakery in us when we render thanks with the tip of our tongue
> and yet despise those whom God has sent to work for us.[16]

Bloodsucking is one of Calvin's favorite, albeit pre-Dracu-
lean, ways of expressing his regard for those who pay poor
wages or withhold wages from the workingman. "When a robber
kills a man, his object is the spoil; but he who extorts labor from
a poor man and sucks, so to speak, his blood, afterwards sends
him away naked and needy; this is more atrocious than if he
violently killed a stranger." [17]

Calvin did not try to find some mathematical basis for the
just wage, for the problem is first of all a spiritual one—because
men in paying wages are dealing with the grace of God which
goes from person to person within the human community.
Human solidarity, especially in Christ, provides the clue to man-
agement-labor relations. He imagines from the pulpit a master
withholding wages and saying, "He is my subject; I will command him as I wish." But, says Calvin, the master should remember who is the real Master, and say instead: "I am master, but
not in tyranny; I am master, but on this condition, that I am
also brother; I am master, but there is a common Master in
heaven, both for me and for those who are subject to me. We
are all here like one family." [18]

The only thing Calvin had to say about a quantitative measurement was that the legal minimum wage was not sufficient for the Christian employer. For it is always equity before God that ought to be taken into account, and this equity can only be measured by the gospel norm: "Do unto others as you would have them do unto you."

A master will have a servant; but if he draws from him all the labor that he is able without having any concern for him, he shows himself to be cruel. If he says, "But I feed him and pay him his salary." Indeed, but it is necessary to have regard also for his capacity and the service which we are able to receive from that; and especially that we regard that natural equity of not doing to another what we would not wish to be done to us. When, thus, a man has someone in his service, he ought to ask himself: "If I were in his place, how would I want to be treated? I would want to be supported." When it is a question of *our* profit or loss, we are very able judges; but when it is a question of others', we are blind.[19]

Defenders of classical economic theory have made much of the "invisible hand" (invented, or first observed, by Adam Smith) of the market, which determines prices, wages, and shifts in industry according to actual need, if only outside, non-economic forces keep hands off the marketplace. According to this theory, wages are determined solely by the need for laborers. When an industry needs laborers and can find few, the wages will rise, and this will produce an influx of new laborers anxious to receive these higher wages, thus producing a labor glut, which automatically drives the wages down. Now, Weber may be right—it may be that the descendants of Calvin were responsible for the attitude toward work which produced this theory of laissez-faire capitalism. Regardless of that, it is certain that Calvin himself would have regarded such a state of affairs as unchristian, inhuman, and to be redressed as quickly as possible by all the outside influences (mainly, the state) that could be brought to bear. Obviously that condition obtained even in Calvin's day; just as obviously, he thought it unjust. In a sermon on Deuteronomy 24:14—"You shall not oppress a hired servant who is poor and needy, whether he is one of your brethren or one of the so-

journers who are in your land"—Calvin recognized that sometimes the day's wage is really only a half-wage, leaving the
worker so little he cannot even feed himself. He represents the
greedy employer as saying, "I see that this man has only here
to work, he has no other means of working, so he is in my
power, and therefore I can have him for whatever I wish."
Angrily Calvin preaches,

> See how often the rich, in so doing, are on the watch for occa-
> sions so that they can subtract half the wages of the poor, when
> the latter do not know at what to be employed. Indeed, they of-
> fer themselves, they demand only to earn a living on condition
> that they find it there. A rich man will notice that: "That one is
> destitute of everything, so I will have him for a morsel of bread,
> for it is necessary for his belly's sake [lit., "in spite of his teeth"]
> that he give himself to me; I shall pay him half a wage and he
> will have to be content." . . . It is necessary to know if the poor
> man is content.[20]

Human labor is simply not a piece of merchandise that can
be speculated on. Here Calvin gives cold comfort to some who
so proudly own his name. It comes from the sweat, or as Calvin
would say, the blood of the working person. The ultimate wages
come from God, and those who defraud the poor unmercifully
will in the end find mercy denied to them. And so he hurled his
cannonballs at the employers in his congregation:

> When the poor whom you have employed at work, and who put
> their work, their sweat, and their blood for you, have not been
> paid as is right, when you do not give them comfort and support;
> if they demand vengeance from God against you; who will be
> your lawyer, or your advocate, so that you will be able to
> escape? [21]

But Calvin was no dreamer; he recognized that self-interest
blinds men to the needs of their fellowmen; he knew that the
opportunity to take advantage of another is well-nigh irresistible to some. So in order to guarantee a certain order about wages
and working conditions, he thought legal contracts could express
agreements arrived at, and thus level some inequalities and in-
justices.

> God has engraven in man's nature a law of equity. . . . so men seldom err in general principles, and therefore, with one mouth, confess that every man ought to receive what is his due; but as soon as they descend to their own affairs, perverse self-love blinds them, or at least envelops them in such clouds that they are carried in an opposite direction. . . . The ancient saying is known, "We should deal lawfully with our friends, that we need not afterwards be obliged to go to law with them." For whence arises so many legal broils except that every one is more liberal toward himself and more niggardly toward others than he ought to be? Therefore, for the purpose of cherishing concord, firm compacts are necessary which may prevent injustice on one side or the other.[22]

Looking ahead, then, we can expect to see Calvin's influence felt on the Genevan labor scene, and felt in a way beneficial to the artisans who worked for someone else. We can expect the church to be concerned about working conditions and wages. And, since people are indeed blinded when their own interests are at stake, we can expect to see outside arbitration at work to settle disputes between management and labor. Again, there is no such thing as a gospel divorced from the concerns of this world.

Usury: Calvin Against the World

One of the least imposing pastors in Geneva was Philip de Ecclesia. He came to the city soon after Calvin returned from exile in 1541. There were complaints that he could not be heard in church, so de Ecclesia was demoted to the small country parish of Vandoeuvre. Perhaps he was irked when thus farmed out or perhaps he was simply a person with easy moral standards. Whatever the reason, de Ecclesia immediately became a stench in the nostrils of the other pastors. He was accused of many things—friendship with the banished doctor Bolsec, neglect of pastoral duties, wife-beating, heresy. For four years the Company of Pastors tried to get the Council to depose de Ecclesia (indicating that the state had the chief say in ecclesiastical appointment and preferment). They were finally successful in 1553, but not until they could add the lending of money at usurious rates to his other crimes. *Usura* was a species of moral turpitude so heinous that *Messieurs* of the Council could not ignore it, even if it meant finding another pastor to hire for only 240 florins per year.[23]

It is necessary to conclude our study of Calvin's social and economic doctrine with a glance at his radical evaluation of the practice of lending money at interest, known generally as usury. Here with startling clarity we see Calvin's recognition of the real world and his most shocking break with medieval tradition. It is to his credit that Calvin handled this, not as did Luther, with equivocal remarks hard to organize, but with a clear analysis of the economic realities of his day and a head-on tackling of the biblical and Aristotelian bases for the medieval condemnation of the practice. Let us begin by posting the two biblical passages most commonly used to condemn lending at interest:

> You shall not lend upon interest to your brother, interest on money, interest on victuals, interest on anything that is lent for interest. To a foreigner you may lend upon interest, but to your brother you shall not lend upon interest . . . [Deut. 23:19–20.]

> But love your enemies, and do good, and lend, expecting nothing in return . . . [Luke 6:35.]

Ambrose in the fourth century interpreted the usury passage in Deuteronomy to mean that one could not extract usury from another Christian ("your brother"), but could extract it from an infidel. But this exegesis was attacked throughout the Middle Ages by theologians who argued that all are brothers and any usury was illegal. This was true despite the fact that in many lands Jews were protected by princes for their value as moneylenders, since they could lend money to Christians, who were not their brothers. It was practice, not theory, that led Pope Innocent III (1215) to demand the cessation of all interest exactions by Jewish moneylenders from Christians during the period of time they marched on crusades.

As a matter of fact, usury, though prohibited in the whole of the Roman Empire as early as the Synod of Aachen by

Charlemagne (789), was actually practiced through a series of evasions.[24] And although the church's theologians inveighed against such practices, they were used as readily by the church as by the banking houses of Medici or Fugger. Even the popes availed themselves of the obvious advantages of interest in a world becoming more and more commercial. R. H. Tawney points out that the status of the borrower or lender was important. "The distinction between pawnbroking, which is disreputable, and high finance, which is eminently honorable, was as familiar in the Age of Faith as in the twentieth century; and no reasonable judgment of the medieval denunciation of usury is possible, unless it is remembered that whole ranges of financial business escaped from it almost altogether." [25] The historian of the fabulous Medici family, Florentine and international bankers during the fifteenth century, observes that "the best customer of the Italian banking and mercantile companies was the church." [26] Indeed, high finance was not only lucrative—if one could avoid lending to princes who went bankrupt—but also quite respectable. "A banker's social standing in thirteenth-century Florence was probably at least as good as in twentieth-century New York." [27]

But it should be remembered that *theologically* no one had yet come to the defense of lending money at interest. It was practiced, yes, but never defended. The Franciscan Order in Italy had set up small banks and pawnshops to lend money to the poor, so that cities could rid themselves of Jewish pawnshops which had been licensed to take from 20 to 50 percent interest on petty loans. But the Franciscans failed to attack the usury prohibition directly, affirming (against the Dominicans) that the 5 to 10 percent they charged was not interest but simply the cost of operation, especially to pay the salaries of the officials of their *monti di pieta* (banks for the pious).[28] Just before the Reformation, one noted theologian, John Eck, was hired by the wealthy Fugger family (the papal bankers) to debate at Bologne and elsewhere that the 5 percent triple contract was legal. This complicated lending arrangement guaranteed a fixed interest return to the lender.[29] But even Eck, more famous for his debate with Luther, did not attack the usury argument itself, but only argued that the *contractus trinus* did not come under its condemnation.

Luther gave attention to usury in several tracts, commentaries, and letters, but it is difficult to state with any assurance just what he thought ought to be done. His dislike for commerce, which we have already noted, coupled with his belief that the last days were at hand, probably made clear analysis a species of adiaphoron for Luther. In his *Open Letter to the Christian Nobility of the German Nation* (1520), he wonders how "one gulden . . . can make another; and that, too, by another way than agriculture or cattle-raising." And in the same context he lashed out against *Zinskauf*, a form of interest-taking. But four years later in a letter to Duke John Frederick of Saxony, he called instead for regulation by the magistrate, saying that "it can be made just," but limiting the interest rate to 5 percent.[30]

It would be unfair to accuse Luther of vacillation or contradiction, as Benjamin Nelson has done. For Luther this problem was one for the prince, not the churchman, and his concern was practical—the protection of the poor against the *stul reuber* (swivel-chair robbers), who were ". . . not men at all, but wolves and irrational beasts, who do not believe there is a God." [31]

But with Calvin we get a systematic study of the biblical passages involved, as well as the morality of *usura* in his day. It is instructive that the two scholars who have devoted the most energy to the study of usury, Benjamin Nelson and John T. Noonan, both agree that Calvin made the strongest and first major contribution to the overthrow of the scholastic analysis of usury. According to Noonan, Calvin "abandons completely the detailed analysis of the scholastics in order to urge one general principle: follow the Golden Rule." [32] This is correct, essentially, but it is nevertheless true that Calvin was forced to examine the biblical passages, to examine the scholastic assumption that money is barren (an assumption borrowed from Aristotle), and to relate his analysis to the world in which he lived. It is his attempt to relate the gospel to the actual world that will decide again how penetrating his analysis shall be. As we have so far done, we shall let Calvin speak for himself. In 1545 he tackled the problem in a letter to Sachinus.[33]

> While I have had no experience myself, I have learned from the example of others how dangerous it is to give an answer to the question on which you ask my advice. For if we wholly condemn usury [*les usures*], we impose tighter fetters on the conscience than God himself. Yet if we permit it in the least, many under this pretext will take an unbridled liberty which can then be held in bounds by no restriction. . . .

> In the first place, by no testimony of the Scriptures is usury wholly condemned. For the meaning of the saying of Christ, commonly thought to be very clear, i.e., "Lend, hoping for nothing again" (Luke 6:35), has been perverted [*faulsement destournee en ce sens*]. As elsewhere in speaking of the sumptuous feasts and ambitious social rivalry of the rich he commands rather that they invite in the blind, the lame and the poor from the streets who cannot make a like return, so here, wishing to curb abuses in lending, he directs us to loan chiefly to those from whom there is no hope of receiving anything. . . . The words of Christ mean that he commends serving the poor rather than the rich. Thus we do not find all usury forbidden.

> The law of Moses (Deut. 23:19) was political, and should not influence us beyond what justice and philanthropy will bear. It could be wished that all usury, and even the name, were banished from the earth. But since this is impossible, it is necessary to concede to the common good. . . .

> Now it is said that today, too, usury should be forbidden on the same grounds as among the Jews, since there is a bond of brotherhood among us. To this I reply, that in the civil state there is some difference; for the situation in which the Lord had placed the Jews, and many other circumstances, made it easy for them to engage in business among themselves without usury. Our relationship is not at all the same. Therefore I do not consider that usury is wholly forbidden among us, except it be repugnant to justice and charity.

Calvin was not a biblical literalist, of course, and saw that justice and charity were the real Christian norms here, as in all social and economic issues. Then, turning from the Bible, he attacked the second fort thrown up against usury, the Aristotelian notion that money is barren.

> The reasoning of Saint Ambrose and of Chrysostom, that money does not beget money, is in my judgment too superficial.

What does the sea beget? What does the land? I receive income from the rental of a house. Is it because the money grows there? The earth produces things from which money is made, and the use of a house can be bought for money. And is not money more fruitful in trade than in any other form of possession one can mention? Is it lawful to let a farm, requiring a payment in return, and unlawful to receive any profit [*fruict*] from the use of money? . . .

How do merchants derive their profit? [Lit., "increase their goods."] By their industry, you will say. Certainly if money is shut up in a strong-box, it will be barren—a child can see that. But whoever asks a loan of me does not intend to keep this money idle and gain nothing. The profit is not in the money itself, but in the return that comes from its use. It is necessary then to draw the conclusion that while such subtle distinctions appear on the surface to have some weight, they vanish on closer scrutiny, for they have no substance. I therefore conclude that usury must be judged, not by any particular passage of Scripture, but simply by the rules of equity.

After an illustration showing that borrowing money to buy a farm and paying interest to the lender is no worse than renting a farm and paying rent, Calvin proceeds to lay down some exceptions to the permission to lend or borrow money at interest. (1) One must take no interest when lending to the poor. (2) One must not neglect charity in order to have money to lend. (3) Nothing should take place which is not in accord with the Golden Rule. (4) The borrower should make at least as much on the money as the lender. (5) We must not measure our practices by what is *licit par l'iniquité du monde*, but by the Word of God. (6) What is good for the public takes precedence over our private benefit. (7) What is legal may be unchristian and prohibited to the Christian.

Throughout this discussion and in his commentary on Deuteronomy 23:10, 20, and its parallels, there are two main points to notice. First, that the law in the Bible is political and is not meant to apply to all persons at all times, else there would not be the permission to lend at interest to a foreigner. Secondly, that there is a gospel "law" which always applies, and that is the law of love, the rule of charity. Here Calvin brilliantly cut through the whole medieval tangle and opened the way to a legitimate use of capital, but clung sternly to the obligation here, as in every area of life, to make the rule of love the economic norm. This does not mean that Calvin could see much good in the practice; like Luther, he was sharp in his denunciation of the one who makes moneylending his business, for it is hard to find a usurer who is not also "rapacious and lewd," one who hurts the poor rather than the rich.[34]

We have often spoken of Calvin as a revolutionary leader, but at this juncture it may be well for us to anticipate later discussion by pointing out the obvious, that the whole Western world was in a period of transition. Revolutions come only when a "boiling point" has been reached, when man has so altered the structures of his communal life that the future becomes radically open. Such periods are never quiet, nor do they automatically produce good. They may well cause man to lose more than he gains. Sixteenth-century man's literary output showed his awareness of the revolutionary character of his times, and strong men (like Henry IV) seized the situation boldly and turned it to their own advantage.

In this period there was tension between the old economics of the soil, tied to land, where money was weak and man's dependence on nature strong, and the new denatured money economics. In the latter, Western man's increasing ability to rationalize and compartmentalize life had begun to exert its influence. Production and consumption were separated, as they had not been on the feudal manor. Impersonal forces were at work. Barely understood economic "truths" were beginning to appear, and to appear mainly as problems. One of these was the problem of the use of this increasingly plentiful money supply.

The old world of feudal, manorial agriculture and the new one of money, banking, and trade could not understand each other. Calvin, however, understood the old world while living in and approving the new. It was for this reason that he was able to make the necessary distinction between lending to one who needed to subsist until harvest and lending to someone of the new breed (perhaps a printer) who used the money to increase his productivity and who knew it bore fruit despite Aristotle and a distinguished corps of medieval theologians.

Calvin's contribution, then, does not lie in his hatred for the profession of moneylender, nor in his belief that usury was here to stay and must therefore be allowed. These were common property in the sixteenth century, nay, in the thirteenth as well. Rather, it was his willingness to wrestle with the Word as well as the world that distinguishes his writing on the subject. He saw too clearly that neither Old Testament legalism nor Aristotelian axioms (*la subtilité d'Aristote; ratio Aristotelis*) covered the real world in which he lived. There was a species of profit-making on money that was neither base nor rapacious. Late medieval commerce had operated on this assumption for a good many generations, but Calvin was the first to see the positive side in the light of theology.

This does not mean that Calvin was a modern man. We shall see later that his repugnance for the practice overcame his appreciation for its occasional value to society, and the stringent rules he helped write caused some trouble in the Genevan marketplace.

. . . . .

So we finish this overview of Calvin's social and economic thought. He was not a legalist in any Roman or biblical sense, but regarded the rule of love as the Christian norm and human laws as attempts to regulate with some measure of justice sinful men in their social existence.

In the second part of this book we shall be concerned with the practical application of this social and economic philosophy in his city in the sixteenth century.

PART II
Calvin's Influence on Genevan Life

CHAPTER VI

Geneva's Struggle for a
Decent Life

GENEVA was a small city. Anyone who has visited the modern city will remember how the "old city"—with St. Pierre's, the Hôtel de Ville (city hall), and the Palais de Justice on the Bourg-de-Four—stands high above the shopping district which lies toward the lake. That elevated old city, the shopping district below, and a few hundred yards of land across the Rhone constituted the sixteenth-century city. Any citizen could march à pied to the open area in front of St. Pierre's within fifteen minutes. Thanks to our technological world of automated wheels, any modern driver can make it in twenty minutes but cannot, unfortunately, find a place to park.

Calvin, the city's head pastor, was first a theologian. But his understanding of the Christian faith went much further than churchly concerns. Witness the following:

> Calvin has proposed that a problem has raised itself among the citizens because some have sworn the "mode of life," others not. Also some children are in papal schools, and their doctrine must be investigated. Also concerning the hospital, which is very badly furnished, so that the poor are suffering.[1]

Here, in his perplexity because the *citoyens* of Geneva would not subscribe to the Confession of Faith during his first stay, Calvin began to address the Council about faith, continued through education, and finished his bill of concerns with the hospital and the poor. We shall find that this concern for the impoverished comes up again and again during his lifetime in Geneva. We shall study this struggle against poverty under two major headings: the Diaconate, with its assigned surveillance over the hospitals, medicine, and refugees; and the so-called Sumptuary Laws, which have been generally misunderstood by some modern inattentive writers.

The Diaconate

In his Psalm commentary Calvin began with a salutation to "faithful and meek [*debonnaires*] readers," in which he included a view of Geneva at the time of his arrival, and the sad state of the church there. Among the problems that gnawed at him was "that there were also many pursued by poverty and hunger, others driven to insatiable ambition by avarice and greed for dishonest gain." [2] After his return in 1541, concern for the poor and ill became an official concern of both church and state through the newly-created office of deacon. This was in marked contrast to the situation in France where the same condition called for all-out war, not on poverty, but on the poor themselves. Gaston Zeller says that in France the number of poor without jobs grew rapidly during the second quarter of the century, ". . . probably in connection with the development of permanent or semi-permanent armies, which uprooted quantities of young men and only temporarily furnished them with a livelihood." [3] Whatever the reason, these vagabonds became a veritable army, and in the first years of the reign of Francis I Paris declared war on "rascals, vagabonds, and other beggars," and forcibly employed them on public works, carrying off filth and rubbish, cleaning sewers, repairing ramparts, and such activities, and often ". . . being transformed into veritable galley-slaves [*forçats*]: they worked chained two by two, under the threat of whip or prison." [4] From time to time *parlement* kicked out those who had been Parisians less than two years, and the king declared in August of 1536 that being out of work and begging were offenses punishable by whip, thus effectively ending mendicancy in Paris. Those officially exempt from work were marked with a special sign, a cross of red and yellow on the right shoulder. [5]

How different was Geneva's concern for the poor and the

refugee. Perhaps our best tack will be to reproduce selected sections of that part of the Church Ordinances, drafted by Calvin in 1541, which dealt with the "fourth order of ecclesiastical government, that is, the Deacons." [6]

There were always two kinds in the ancient Church, the one deputed to receive, dispense and hold goods for the poor, not only daily alms, but also possessions, rents and pensions; the other to tend and care for the sick and administer allowances to the poor. This custom we follow again now for we have *procureurs* and hospitallers. [And in order to avoid confusion . . . one of the four *procureurs* is to be receptionist at the said hospital for all its goods, and is to have a suitable wage, in order that he discharge his office properly.]

The [number of four *procureurs* is to remain as it is, of whom one will have charge of reception, as has been said, so that the] number of *procureurs* appointed for this hospital seems to us to be proper; but we wish that there be also a separate reception office, so that not only provisions be in time made better, but that those who wish to do some charity may be more certain that the gift will not be employed otherwise than they intend. And if the revenue assigned by their Lordships be insufficient, or should extraordinary necessity arise, the Seigneury will advise about adjustment, according to the need they see.

. . . .

It will be their duty to watch diligently that the public hospital is well maintained, and that this be so both for the sick and the old people unable to work, widowed women, orphaned children and other poor creatures. The sick are always to be lodged in a set of rooms separate from the other people who are unable to work, old men, widowed women, orphaned children and the other poor.

Moreover, care for the poor dispersed through the city should be revived, as the *procureurs* may arrange it.

Moreover, besides the hospital for those passing through which must be maintained, there should be some attention given to any recognized as worthy of special charity. For this purpose, a special room should be set aside to receive those who ought to be assisted by the *procureurs,* which is to be reserved for this business.

. . . .

The ministers must on their side enquire whether there be any lack or want of anything, in order to ask and desire the Seigneury to put it in order. To do this, some of their company with the *procureurs* should visit the hospital every three months, to ascertain if all is in order.

It would also be good, not only for the poor of the hospital, but also for those of the city who cannot help themselves, that they have a doctor and a surgeon of their own [at the expense of the city] who should still practise in the city, but meanwhile be required to have care of the hospital and to visit the other poor.

As for the hospital for plague, it should be wholly separate and apart, and especially if it happen that the city be visited by this scourge of God.

For the rest, to discourage mendicancy which is contrary to good order, it would be well, and we have so ordered it, that there be one of our officials at the entrance of the churches to remove from the place those who loiter; and if there be any who give offence or offer insolence to bring them to one of the Lords Syndic. Similarly for the rest of the time, let the Overseers of Tens take care that the total prohibition of begging be well observed.

The diaconate was organized, then, to handle money, to order and supervise the hospital, and to aid the poor of the city; it was lay in its membership, though the ministers were bidden to inquire about the work of the deacons and to make quarterly visits to the hospital to see that the people there were given proper attention.

The deacons or *procureurs* had four sources of income: moneys appropriated by the Council for the hospital and the wages of the hospitaller and surgeon, revenue from fines, gifts or alms, and the sale of items devoted to charity. Each source shows something of the city's concern.

Part of the yearly budgeted expenditure of the city treasurer was for the public almshouse, i.e., the hospital. In 1544 the fifth largest public expenditure was the 1,477 florins devoted to this purpose, plus the 100-florin wage of the hospitaller, and 82½ florins for heralds and surgeon.[7] Fines were a regular source of income. For example, in the Ordinances for the Country Parishes, written by Calvin and passed in 1546, all fines levied were divided so that one-third of the receipts went to the poor of the parish and place, and another third to the deacons.[8] And this is the rule, not the exception; one constantly finds references to the fact that one-third of the income of fines went to the *procureurs* or to the hospital.

The third way of obtaining money for the work of the diaconate was to solicit gifts. For example, on 24 May 1547, the pastors carried a complaint to the Council that the hospital for the poor lacked wine, wood, and other things, because the income from church properties and goods given for the hospital were used elsewhere, and this, in turn, made people hesitate to give their money for the hospital. This was a direct slam at a Council that was robbing Peter to pay Paul, for they complained that the Council was taking such donations and using them for some other public need.[9]

The fourth source of revenue for the work of the diaconate —the sale of items devoted to charity—is illustrated well by the Psalm translation of pastor and university rector Theodore Beza, which he had given to the deacons to help finance their work. On 30 June 1561, we read of their request to be allowed to print Beza's new metrical work:

> The deacons charged with the dispensation to the poor refugees have presented their request that they be permitted to print the rest of the Psalms composed by Theodore Beza, minister, which he has given for the relief of the said impoverished—to grant them the privilege for ten years. It is agreed to consult Calvin and Beza, ministers.[10]

Unfortunately we must report that the printers were not always prompt in paying the royalties. In 1563 the deacons had to appear before the Council to get them to pay, in 1565 printer Jean Crespin had to be ordered to pay the author's percentage to the deacons, and two years later Beza himself had to step in to make them pay their "debvoir aux paouvres pour l'impression des pseaumes . . ."[11]

Here, then, we have seen that the church under Calvin was not content to have its weight felt in the social arena solely through the efforts of good men acting as individuals. Instead church and state cooperated as one in concern for the poor. Gustave Weigel, S.J., has remarked somewhere that Protestant

charity lacks the heart of Catholic charity but is better organized.
The first part of his statement we cannot document (nor do we
wish to!); but that Genevan charity was well organized was in-
sured by the work of the deacons and the pastors' concern for
that work. Certainly that refugee-crowded city needed such
organization and, thanks to the genius of Calvin, received it.

The Hospitals

The work of the deacons was not limited to the city's two
hospitals, but certainly centered about these institutions. Prior
to the Reformation there had been several small hospitals in
Geneva—one for travelers, one for the sick, another for the
indigent, etc. On 29 November 1535, upon the departure of
the ecclesiastics with their bishop but before Calvin came to the
city, the Council founded a new inclusive hospital in the ancient
convent of Sainte Claire, remodeling and stocking it with revenues from ecclesiastical goods and properties abandoned by the
departed clergy. (Today the Palais de Justice occupies the site
of the convent-turned-hospital.) It is clear from the Church Ordinances that this hospital, sometimes called the Hospital of the
Holy Spirit, was a refuge for the ill, the aged, widows, orphans,
and those without means of subsistence, as well as a haven for
the traveler. In addition to this all-purpose sanctuary, there was
also provided just west of the city walls a plague hospital which
was used from time to time. It is unclear just what that building
was formerly used for, but it was evidently the only building
left standing when the city's *faubourgs*, or suburbs, were torn
down as a measure of defense in 1534. From the thirteenth century on, the dread of plague had prompted a periodic exodus
from cities all over Europe. This, of course, was impossible for
almost all Genevans.

During the Middle Ages hospitals of various types were
usually associated with religious groups. But by the Reformation
era that pattern was no longer true in France; the hospitals in
larger cities had been or were being secularized. According to
Zeller, the transfer of such hospitals from religious orders to lay
control was due to the relaxation of standards in the charitable

orders, which led to *l'anarchie grandissante* in many hospitals. In Paris the *parlement* had been called in to arbitrate between the religious order and the chapter at l'Hôtel-Dieu in 1495, and had totally reorganized the work, putting in eight *proviseurs* responsible to the city rather than the cathedral chapter. Of course, religious decline was not the only reason. The increase in the number of poor, which we have already noted, the debasement of chapter revenues based on land holdings—these also contributed to this secularization. By 1547 all hospital administrations had to render account to the king, and after 1560 ordinances were passed which stipulated that in France all hospitals were to be administered by laymen.[12] One glimpse of this can be seen at Lyons, where in 1486 the city council took over from the church the supervision of the Hôtel-Dieu and other hospitals originally founded by religious orders.[13] The Genevan hospital seems to have been better run: in Lyons, orphans who were not apprenticed early were sent out to beg! In Geneva begging, of course, was illegal, and we know that children there had a schoolmaster of their own,[14] and were brought before the deacons every week so that those ready for apprenticeship or service (the girls) could be assigned.[15]

Calvin's own concern for the hospital is occasionally seen in the pages of the ancient records. On 29 August 1544, it was he who reported to the Council about the mismanagement of the present hospitaller.

> M. Calvin, minister, has reported that he has heard that Justin, the hospitaller of the hospital of the Holy Spirit, is a thief, and has tried to take an *écu* from a foreigner, and moreover, sells the bread that is taken to the poor sick, and takes their allowance from them, and ransacks what they carry on them. He believes these reports. Ordered that this should be looked into diligently, and if it is so, he should be chastized and removed from his office. [He was removed that day.] [16]

And Calvin was one of five commissioned by the city Council to establish at the hospital a cloth-making or fustian business, so that with the times dear and the poor indigent many, none would need to be idle.[17] Whether this should be listed as WPA or War on Poverty or a government-sponsored training program is unclear. What is clear is that the government of the city with the aid of Calvin, the chief pastor, took a firm grip at a time of economic necessity and set up a new industry to be overseen by the deacons of the church. Here, church and state made a holy alliance with industry.

"Socialized medicine" was also in vogue in Geneva, as the Ecclesiastical Ordinances have shown us. The doctor and surgeon who served the hospital did so at the city's expense. This arrangement was continued after the death of Calvin, and even extended. On 11 May 1569, "Ordinances Concerning the Estate of Medicine, Pharmacy, and Surgery" were passed, which made it the duty of each doctor to visit without charge the poor in his area:

> Besides the doctors appointed for the large hospital and for the poor refugees, each doctor is required to visit the poor sick in the quarter in which he lives, being required by charity.[18]

It should not be forgotten that the hospitaller was also a deacon. His was a full-time job which netted him a small salary, but full living expenses. Once a week, on Sunday, he had to report to the other deacons, the three *procureurs*, about the state of the hospital. We learn from the updated hospital edict of May 1553 that this was a job requiring a man of diverse knowledge, skilled in several *métiers*, and demanding almost limitless patience. He not only had to account for all the orphans, the poor, the old, the ill, and overnight guests who were housed, fed, taught, and tended at city expense, but also had to oversee vineyards, hemp, grain, and turnip fields, keep an eye out for the dozen cows, horses, pigs, and other livestock, be foreman for the weaving and jug-making industries at the hospital—all this, and make a weekly account to the *procureurs*.[19] No wonder that the next entry has to do with the hiring of a new hospitaller!

The church, with Calvin as undeclared bishop, was vitally concerned with the bodies, as well as the souls, of its members. Nothing in Geneva bears this out more clearly than the diaconate, and that body's chief arena of action, the hospitals. Here Calvin's influence permeated with a vengeance.

The Refugees

A strong contributor to the ranks of the impoverished at Geneva was the steady growth in population caused by the immigration of refugees, especially from France. It should be borne in mind that this increase in the city's population from about 1542 to 1561 was almost entirely within the city's walls; the destruction of the *faubourgs* meant that there was to be no building outside the walls, lest the enemy be encouraged to approach the city under cover of such structures.

How large was Geneva? The best estimates tell us simply that there were about 10,300 souls in the city when a house count was made in 1537.[20]

In 1542 the influx began, according to Michel Roset.[21] By 1549 it was large enough that the *Book of Habitants* was opened and kept open till 1560. In this ledger the names of incoming family heads were enrolled, usually with the place from which they came and the occupation of the breadwinner noted. There were 4,776 such names inscribed in that first book.[22] This means that between 1542 and 1560 almost 5,000 workers legally entered the city of Geneva, a city of perhaps 10,300, many of them accompanied by families. Doumergue adds to this list those "more or less resident who for diverse reasons did not seek to regularize their situation, and who were tolerated, except by accident." [23] Doumergue is probably wrong. The city was very conscious of the strangers within its gates; constant efforts were made to see that everyone signed up or left town. I think that there were not too many who stayed any length of time who escaped the eyes of the captains of quarters and thus escaped enrollment.

How many had families and how large these families were is impossible to say. On 26 November 1554, it was proposed in Council,

> that daily there come many foreigners to live who are unknown people, and that many may be of evil life or poor and overburdened with children, concerning which it should be necessary to give some order, so that the good should be received and the bad rejected.[24]

That many were poor and overburdened with children sounds quite reasonable. The Perrinists, in power at the time, were unhappy; the deacons and the hospital must have been busy.

If we could assume that births and deaths balanced each other, then we could simply add to 10,300 (itself an educated guess) a figure of about 10,000 (figuring for each refugee an average of only one dependent) and arrive at a figure of 20,000 in 1559, the peak year for the refugee. But of course, some people must have come only to leave again when some immediate danger was over. A good deal of guesswork makes any projection hazardous.

Quite frankly, the population explosion in Geneva during the 1550's seems to the writer to have been quite serious—more serious than those scholars who settle for 10,300 in 1537 and 13,000 in 1589, but allow the interim to go undiscussed, indicate. Those figures are probably accurate enough. But during this interim a good 10,000 people must have entered the city, and some must have stayed throughout the period. One indication of the seriousness of the problem is the opening of two new churches in 1559, "because a large part of the people who enter St. Peter's are not able to hear." [25]

Although inconclusive as to numbers, this discussion throws light on the terrific task facing church and state in Geneva to take care of the waves of people inundating the city. Even providing subsistence living must have strained the resources of the tiny republic. In this light, the work of *procureurs* and hospitallers—deacons all—is now seen as nothing short of heroic.

The Cost of Living

What effect did refugees and changing times have on the cost of living in Geneva during this period? Certainly times got harder in the early 1550's, and occasionally the French were blamed for the rise. In 1551 one Pernette, wife of Pierre Bertet called Tallabard, was convicted of having blamed the French refugees for the rising dearness in prices, and was excluded from the Lord's Table. It was probably about this time that another disgruntled native proclaimed in his cups that all the French should be thrown in the Rhone. Lewis Mumford has pointed out that the village—despite all its good qualities—passed to the city such narrow traits as isolation, jealousy, parochialism, and suspicion of the stranger.[26] Certainly sixteenth-century Genevan citizens exhibited all these traits, and even today there is a "vigilantes" (*sic*) political party whose professed aims are as xenophobic as poor Pernette. The irony of this is that all authorities agree that much of the later wealth of the city was directly attributable to the despised refugee, no matter how disastrous the short-term effects of his entry.[27] Today's vigilante may well be the descendant of a sixteenth-century refugee.

Most of these refugees were not nobility, although some were. Nor were they wealthy *bourgeoisie*. Of the 4,776 names inscribed in the *Livre des Habitants*, 2,247 have a profession indicated. Of these the predominance of artisans is overwhelming, 1,536 of them being *gens mécaniques*—those whom Professor Davis in her Lyons study calls the *menu peuple*, the little people of the lower classes.[28] Of the remainder, there were 275 from the liberal professions (74 in some aspect of medicine, 50 scholars, plus notaries, lawyers, judges, teachers, ministers), 180 merchants and commercial people, 70 of the nobility, 77 peasants, and 100 hard to classify. Of the artisans, there were 699 textile workers of various kinds, 264 who worked in leather (mainly shoemakers), 249 in the building trades, 228 metalworkers, and 67 goldsmiths. Geisendorf thinks that of the unclassified even more would have been "average" people, since it is unlikely that anyone of importance had his trade or degree neglected when he swore loyalty to the city and the gospel.[29] The shortage of both nobility and peasantry shows that the man tied to the soil either did not infect readily with heretical views or was in an unfavorable moving situation. One can pick up his shoemaker's tools and travel to Geneva; one cannot take his farm.

These immigrants were sometimes put on relief (rather like WPA) when they came to the city without places to work. In 1545, before the flood was strong enough to warrant opening a special book of newcomers, Calvin and Farel were sent to Berne, Basel, Zurich, and Strasbourg to arrange help for refugees es-

caping the wrath of Francis I after the affair of the placards.[30]
And Viret came to the Council two weeks later requesting work
"for the poor persecuted faithful," who did not wish to remain
idle. The Council "ordered that they should be put to work for
the city, each according to his ability." [31] Roget reports that for
the most part this meant working on construction of the ramparts of the city.[32] This same plan was followed in 1554.

Evidently this system also included a certain amount of
practice of "from each according to his ability, to each according
to his need" among the refugees. The contemporary chronicler
Councilman Roset reports it this way:

> That was the first occasion that a little after the foreigners came
> for the Word of God, they established a system of contribution
> among themselves in order to give alms to the poor, and ap-
> pointed deacons and receivers from each nation or country, who
> were to collect everything into one purse and administer it to
> the needy and ill, and were to teach trades to the young people
> and others who had no means of livelihood. Many good person-
> ages of France sent good sums, so that this system has been main-
> tained to this day [June 1562] with great fruit and solace for
> those who have been destitute of all other human means in the
> extremity of persecution.

And later, in the spring of 1554, when about four hundred families came at once, Roset relates how they were put to work
digging ditches, being paid by the work, not the day, so that
they could work as much or as little as they wanted.[33]

That inflation grew as the 1550's began is quite evident.
Wages probably did not drop, probably even rose. But as industry began to move with the new influx of workers, as new industries began or grew larger, and as housing became dearer,
there is no doubt that the cost of living must have risen. Most
of the refugees were artisans, but enough of them must have
been wealthy enough "to provide a needed influx of new capital
and new industry." [34] Finally, to halt the rise in prices perhaps,
or perhaps because the city treasury was nearing bankruptcy—it
is not clear which—the city's employees' wages were lowered.
This took place in May 1551, before the hardest influx of refugees
had yet taken place. The syndics reduced their own wages from

125 florins to 100 to 50. So these magistrates decided to start where few politicians today would even think of beginning— with their own salaries.[35]

Probably the hardest blow for the Geneva economy was the sudden fluctuation apt to come in wheat prices. In the spring of 1544, for example, wheat was seven florins per *coupe*, 233 percent higher than the three florins that it brought in 1536.[36] When it reached that same level in 1557, the Council opened the city's granaries and sold wheat in the city and country for five florins, and then, because this good price caused it to disappear too quickly and the Council feared hoarding, it raised the price to six.[37]

There is no indication that the civic leaders knew what to do about the rise in cost of living. To lower their own salaries was of no value, and of course, none of them lived solely on his wages as syndic or secretary. A later attempt was made to put a ceiling on wages—which we shall discuss in the next chapter— but this probably did not work either. All we can say is that though the Geneva-minted florin became more plentiful, it was worth less. The *écu d'or au soleil* of Savoy was worth four and one-half florins in 1536, more than five florins in 1557, and five and one-half florins in 1568. So, by the gold standard, the florin had devalued 22 percent in thirty years. At the same time, money was more plentiful. The city's revenues were 21,790 florins in 1540; 34,400 florins in 1550; and 52,454 florins in 1555.[38] The city was definitely richer.

This fragmentary and uncertain information has little practical value for our study. What it does is indicate how inadequate our knowledge is and how shaky any generalizations we make from it. But certain things one dares to state: prices did rise, and wages rose with them; sometimes the fluctuation was quite sharp, a situation true in any fairly simple economic system when a basic commodity (here, wheat primarily, though wine also) becomes scarce; the city stepped in at least once to alleviate the gouging prices being asked on stored or hoarded wheat; the devaluation of the florin was not as sharp as the rise in city income, which surely reflected a rise in money circulation in Geneva.

Sumptuary Laws

Although not usually recognized as such by humanities instructors, the infamous "Sumptuary Laws" enacted by the Council in 1558 were actually part of the war on poverty, or at least against the sort of "conspicuous consumption" that highlights the difference between rich and poor. This is quite clear from the testimony of the Consistory's representative, the minister Nicholas des Gallars, when he presented the request for such laws to the Council.

> M. Nic. des Gallars, representing the Consistory, has proposed that inasmuch as superfluity and excess increase among us in place of diminishing, so that great scandal is given to others who, thinking us to be Christians, and seeing such excess, are scandalized.

The Council's decision to draw up such laws contains the same reasoning:

> Ordered that there be provided by means of public proclamations which will be made, but that first there be conference with the ministers in order to make them, in order to find some good means of stopping such superfluities which engender many evils and nourish gluttonous pride, then bring poverty, high cost of living, and are the cause of the destruction of many; moreover the principle is that God is greatly offended.[39]

While the edicts themselves have been lost, the preface to the "Ordonnance somptuaire" hits only at dress and food, the two things des Gallars complained about in his request to *Messieurs*. After defining certain hair arrangements and types of adornment that were considered overdone, the principle is stated: "and generally all excess in dress both for men and woman." Then the question of banqueting is answered so that banquets cannot feature more than three courses or more than four dishes per course.[40]

Today we might mock the paternalism of a Council concerned because people who worked by the day spent their money in taverns and thus lived in poverty, but there is no mistaking the concern on the part of both pastors and Council. (It should be noted that this took place after the victory of the Calvinists.) The poor were not poor by some divine fiat that made the concern of the state irrelevant. Everything was done to give man opportunity to rise out of impoverishment to a more comfortable station in life. This is even illustrated by the laws concerning games. It is true that there are constant references in the Council records about the prohibition of cards, dice, and certain other games, but the concern was not for games in themselves, but always the evils of gambling. No doubt it was as evident then as it is today that gambling hits the poor hardest. Games were not frowned upon, and Sunday games were permitted also, except for the four Sundays per year when the Supper was celebrated.[41]

These laws, like all laws in Geneva, were enforced upon rich and poor alike; in fact, only the rich could reasonably be expected to overeat, though from time to time there were complaints about even chambermaids dressing in such manner that their social status was obscured. Many laws began with words of warning, "that no one, of whatever state or condition he may be, should dare or be so bold . . ." The sumptuary laws were applied to rich and poor, *habitant* and members of the Council —with refreshing blindness. Monter remarks: "The point which does emerge clearly from the available evidence is that the Genevan sumptuary laws were enforced with commendable impartiality; the hand of justice fell on those of high and low estate alike."[42]

Nor were they enforced as harshly as similar laws in France at the same period. The French *parlement* in 1559 had the same concern, but more draconic means of enforcement:

> It denied to artisans the wearing of "slashed hose and puffed taffeta on pain of being taken and strangled."[43]

Nor was this law unique.

However, there is a darker side to this sumptuary legislation which should not be ignored. The one-sided calumny which Calvin has often received from later students is not rectified by an application of whitewash over the darker areas. Calvin was a man of his time, and Geneva existed in the sixteenth century, and not all was well on the shores of Lac Leman. Some of the efforts to curtail conspicuous consumption for the sake of the poor were both helpless and hopeless; some were obviously ignored; others probably produced more hardship, rather than alleviating bad conditions.

The sumptuary legislation on food and apparel was not so much pernicious as it was hopeless. Such legislation either depends upon consensus or hopes to bull its way to consensus, and there is little or no indication that such agreement either existed or was obtained. The creation of the ephemeral *abbayes*, which were to take the place of honest-to-goodness taverns, was the first attempt to control overeating and drinking. Brought into being by an edict on 28 May 1546, these five *abbayes* were located in diverse parts of town, and had for presidents the four syndics and the lieutenant. The host was to allow no improper language, dice playing, dancing, or dishonest songs, nor was anyone allowed to enter after 9 P.M. Each person who ate or drank had to pray first; a French Bible was required on the premises so that anyone could read who wished, and conversation about the Word of God was to be encouraged.[44] These *abbayes* lasted less than a month, for by 22 June the complaints had reached such a pitch that the Two Hundred gave license to feed and serve drinks back to the original purveyors.

Some of the gaming legislation, which was not strictly sumptuary legislation, was not the creation of Calvin but had existed long before. For example, the anti-dancing regulation of 1549, wherein one was "not to sing dishonest songs nor dance in any manner," was simply a restatement of laws passed both in Catholic days and while the city was under anti-Calvinist control.[45] It is interesting to see that Councillors passed such laws even if they were among those to break them. Perrin, first syndic when the 1549 ordinance was made law, had spent some time on bread and water in 1546—so had his wife and father-in-law—for breaking that same rule. Amblard Corne was first syndic the next year, when the same edict was reissued, and he too had been arrested and had spent three days dieting because of the same caper with

Perrin and company.[46] And he was presiding officer at the Consistory! So the evidence leads one to suspect that habit and custom were stronger than regard for civic sobriety. While not a central issue by any means, and not the creation of Calvin or the pastors, the continuation of dancing regulations (along with card playing, dicing, etc., for money) with stiff monetary fines contains a note of desperation.

Nor did the real sumptuary legislation—at least in sartorial matters—fare any better. The laws passed in 1558 are not extant, but from the preamble (as we have seen) we know they had mainly to do with matters of dress and banqueting. But six years later, on 8 June 1564, a new edict was passed which admitted, in effect, that the hope that all would live in "sobriety and honest *mediocrité*" had been shattered; instead, new clothing fashions had been introduced to get around the details of the code, and other excesses had been introduced from the outside world. Among the restrictions were the old ones about gold chains, precious stones, embroideries, and other items of feminine splendor, but there were also restrictions meant to keep the wives of *gens de métier* and serving girls dressing according to their social rank.[47] In other words, there was a certain unreality about these codes that precluded their being taken very seriously by ordinary men and women. We should say that they show a tendency on the part of Calvin and the Council to overlegislate —a weakness of medieval and contemporary society as well.

The criticism of Berthold Haller, chief pastor in Berne and friend to Calvin, is instructive. Writing to Heinrich Bullinger in 1559, he said of Calvin and Viret: "If they had had the governance of the church of Corinth, they would have excommunicated not only the incestuous, but almost the whole community." [48]

To attempt to evaluate the success of the type of legislation considered here involves an egregious measurement of presumptuousness. No one can take exception to the pastors' basic concern—to eliminate the conspicuous consumption so detrimental to a small society with many have-nots. But the methods used were ones modern people would regard as inconsistent with the right of a person to be himself, at least at home. Then, of course, there is always the problem of putting oneself into another century or another culture. For example, I find it easy to sympathize with the Council when it forbade (and forbade and forbade) mixed bathing in the public bathhouses (*les estuves*). But a Swede or a Polynesian might regard such a view as prudish in the extreme.[49]

Perhaps the rather obvious observations we can make confidently are two: First, much of the sumptuary and gaming regulation shows that the pastors and Council were unaware of the limits of legislation without community agreement in areas not essential to the gospel proclamation. We may extol their courage or their concern, but not their wisdom. We have shown that Calvin spoke much of the church being a community of saints; but they were not in sixteenth-century Geneva that saintly.

A second observation is that the application of such laws demanded the cultivation of a climate of thrift, if they were to be paid even lip service. And thrift involves a certain "rationalization" of life. That is, one can only be thrifty if one's life is taken seriously. And we shall see in Chapters XI and XII that there are strong reasons for noting a connection between Calvinism and this revolutionary rationalizing of human endeavor which came to be characteristic of Western society in the next few centuries. One is also reminded here of Wesley's famous dictum that thrift leads to wealth, and wealth leads to irreligion.[50] So perhaps we can see in the sumptuary legislation the emphasizing of a virtue which will lead to capital savings, and by extension to capitalism. I would not, however, push the argument this far.

In Geneva Christian concern for the poor, the sick, the orphan, the widow, the refugee, was institutionalized in the diaconate and legislated by law. Because the problems were great, the effort to solve these human problems was prodigious, using up a fair portion of the budget and the time at the disposal of the city Council. Every effort was made to plan in such ways that human needs were met. Later Christians lost the urgency of this need to plan so that suffering be met by rational methods of alleviation. Lewis Mumford has written that the city of the Victorian nineteenth century was a "new species of town, a blasted, de-natured man-heap adapted, not to the needs of life, but to the mythic [Darwinian] 'struggle for existence' . . . There was no room for planning . . . Chaos does not have to be planned." [51] Not so Calvin's Geneva. There a revolutionary people supporting a flood of refugees struggled with success to bring order out of chaos. That their efforts were successful and that they were pursued so vigorously was due to the iron will and careful concern of their chief pastor. In this concern he showed himself not only to be a leader of revolution, but a revolutionary statesman as well.

CHAPTER VII

Business and Finance

LEWIS MUMFORD has argued that one of the failures of the Greek city-states was to "moralize trade," to bring it under restraint by considering it within the orbit of legitimate human enterprise. Because Athens, and to a lesser extent the medieval city, considered trade outside the pale, it was largely unregulated and left in the control of social and religious untouchables. So when Calvin dared compare trade with the life of the godly (see above) he was, in effect, bringing the Genevan bourgeois under the influence of restraint by blessing his activity. It is only when religious and social restraints are later weakened under the combined influence of Adam Smith's economic determinism and Darwinian (or Spencerian) "survival of the fittest" that the nineteenth-century industrial merchant—capitalism's version of the feudal robber baron—wins society's blessing without suffering society's regulation.

Calvin's brand of revolutionary doctrine was in no fashion nihilistic. He could bless the new without either cursing the old or granting the new untrammeled freedom. He felt himself free both to be traditional and to deny tradition. We see this clearly in Calvin's involvement in two important business problems in sixteenth-century Geneva: the regulation of interest rates, and the regulation of wages and industry.

Usury

> [In his analysis of usury] Calvin did not vault the barriers raised against the spirit of lucre, but vaulted a barrier set up against the knowledge of economic facts.[1]

In Chapter V, I did not argue that Calvin's fame in regard to the usury controversy lay in his business acumen, but in his willingness to attack Aristotle head-on (as merchants had been doing in practice for a good many centuries) and to read the Bible with new eyes, ignoring prevalent medieval interpretation. But he was never content to be paralyzed by his own analysis. For it is accurate to assert that Calvin was involved in every dispute and edict from 1544 till long after his death, when Theodore Beza applied the *coup de grâce* to the public bank in 1580. The latter action, in a real sense, was as much Calvin's doing as the first edicts after his second arrival in the city.

The city's *Franchises*, authorized by the Bishop of Geneva in 1378—in which were confirmed and explained the liberties, franchises, immunities, ways, and customs of the city—enforced and confirmed articles not only favorable to usury, but even to professional moneylenders.[2] Article XXXIV reads:

> Concerning those who die without making a will: that if any cleric, citizen, juror, or inhabitant of the said city dies without a will, whether he be an open usurer or not, bastard or otherwise, whatever he may be or whatever condition, the children that he may have shall be his heirs.[3]

Article XXXV protected the right of an open usurer to make a will; Article XXXIX prohibited seizing the goods of a usurer, dead or alive, or molesting or disquieting him by making inventory of his goods; and Article LXXVII summed up the protection given to the usurer so completely—no one was allowed even to argue with a usurer about his profession!—that there is little room for doubt about the city's position: moneylending was so important to the economy of fourteenth-century Geneva that the usurer was protected in the statutes for the present and for the future.

In 1444 those parts of Bishop Fabri's city charter which protected bastards, usurers, and their heirs were suppressed by Pope Felix V. However, usury itself was not suppressed, for in 1485—during the period when fairs were still strong in Geneva—there is an example of taking interest on a loan at 5 percent from fair to fair, a real interest of 20 percent.[4] After the Reformation, January 1538, the Council of Two Hundred noted that poor people were borrowing money from *renevoz* (an obscure term used then for usurers) and paying an undefined but oppressive rate of interest, and ordered that all rates be reduced to 5 percent.[5] This took place shortly before the February election which brought the Artichauds to power and led to the dismissal of Calvin and Farel in April of that year. There is no evidence that Calvin had anything to do with this decision.

But in 1543, after his return to Geneva, Calvin plunged head first into the usury problem (this was the same year he wrote his letter to Sachinus). The problem was a serious one from the pastors' point of view.

Usurers. Concerning which the preachers have made good remonstrances that the great usury which reigns in Geneva should be looked into. Ordered that this should be set in order, and that it should be taken up with M. Calvin in order to look into it.[6]

The upshot of the affair was that on 24 December 1543, the Small Council ordered that interest taken in kind—that is, in wheat or wine—must be reduced to 5 percent.[7] This protected the farmer who had to borrow from seedtime to harvest. Thus Calvin's concern was translated into direct appeal to the state, and the state acknowledged that this was a proper sphere of pastoral concern.

But the definitive legal action by the Council, one that would stand for a dozen years, was taken in 1544. This time the decision was made, not by the Small Council and Two Hundred alone, but by all the *bourgeoisie* meeting as the General Council.

. . . concerning which judgment by the said *Seigneurie* [of the Small Council and the Two Hundred], the General Council ratifying that which has been arrived at in the Council of Two Hundred, namely that from this time on none should dare, no matter how bold, to place money at usury nor in any way in order to have a gain of more than five percent per year, and that concerning this there should be made a most ample declaration which ought to be done by *Messieurs* of the Small Council, to make some public proclamations concerning this as they may think expedient.[8]

Martin believes that this definitive action was inspired by the pastors, Calvin *en tête*.[9] Since it came after Calvin had preached through Deuteronomy—sermons full of social and economic concern—his judgment seems reasonable.

The next action of the city government seems to me to have been aimed not so much at the lender as at the borrower. It came in the Ecclesiastical Ordinances for the country parishes written by Calvin and passed by Council on 17 May 1547.

> Let no one lend at usury or for profit higher than five percent, under penalty of confiscation of the principal, and of being assessed an arbitrary fine according to the requirements of the case.[10]

The country parishes were peasant almost entirely. Landowners were more apt to live in Geneva than on their holdings, and the chatelains of the city (since much of the land seems to have been city controlled) ordinarily lived in the city and were therefore already subject to the city's usury laws passed in 1544. Only the pastors lived in the rural areas, and while they may on occasion have lent money at interest—as we shall see—the edict was surely not aimed at them, they having already been forbidden to lend at usurious rates. It seems, then, that either this was merely an attempt to keep the rural areas consistent with the city in legal matters or a warning to peasants not to borrow at usurious rates, as lenders had already been warned not to lend at illegal rates, i.e., over 5 percent.

Except for one case of usury among the clergy, there is a hiatus in the records for ten years. The pastoral culprit was Philip de Ecclesia, whose case was discussed in Chapter V. When the pastors were not able to procure the demission of *Spectable* de Ecclesia by appealing to his heretical views and incorrigible nature, they added to the other charges the one of usury. In the 1541 *Ordonnances* usury is listed as one of "the vices . . . intolerable in a pastor." So in addition to heresy, mistreatment of his wife, and companionship with Jerôme Bolsec, de Ecclesia was removed for usury.[11] Whether it was of equal importance to heresy seems doubtful, but that it was considered important is clear.

Calvin's next brush with usury did not take place until 1 July 1557. That day he appeared before the Council to relate the Consistory's concern that usurers not remain unpunished—which indicates to us that some were able to thumb their noses at the law. The ninth of August he came to complain about one "Pierre Mercier, accused of excessive interest-taking." The latter was judged guilty and fined two weeks later.[12] But all the lawmaking in the world cannot completely ignore the economic facts of life. Obviously lending at interest was going on, as permitted by law; but just as obviously the 5 percent rate was getting cavalier treatment. So the Small Council appointed a committee of *Seigneurie*, seated on the *Chambre des Comptes*,[13] together with *avocats*, *savants*, and *ministres*, "to discuss the matter fully in order to do something right." [14]

The final result was a new edict on usury, 12 November 1557, and its most outstanding advances (if one agrees that they *were* advances) were the raising of the rate of interest to 6.67 per year and a frank recognition that those with money to lend were refusing to lend it at the old rate. Consequently, runs the edict, in order to give some rule and limitation and "to obviate for the future the frauds which are committed by excessive usuries to the ruin and destruction of many," this new ruling was made.[15]

The recognition that some had idle (*oisif et inutile*) money which they had no ability or opportunity to use, which "they may give to others more able and with better means and industry in order to trade for an honest profit," and that such people were not grubbing Shylocks but people who needed such an opportunity "to help in their strong necessities to lend in good conscience"—such recognition was a long step toward the modern world. Martin comments:

> It seems incontestable that in raising the rate of interest, as in authorizing interest on agreed loans—not only to those who have need of it for their affairs, but also to those who give their idle money to other well-off persons who will use it honestly in their commerce and industry—the operations of lending at interest are extended and developed. It does not deal any longer with lending for production or enterprise, but of that which proceeds

from it, of lending money, capital, which will procure a profit
for the lender.[16]

This would seem to be another indication that the real world
will break in from time to time and disturb the status quo. If real
evil is involved, then the intrusion must be fought; but if lending money at interest is not in itself evil (and Calvin had so argued), and if an over-restrictive rate simply creates a black
market for exorbitant loans to those who need it for business ex-
pansion or slow periods (and this seems to have been the case),
then one would have to argue that this was a step forward, not
backward. It was to obviate the subterfuges with which Europe
was plagued at the time, to keep rates within limits, to make sure
that all lending was public and true rates were known,[17] and to
protect the borrowers from financial ruin that the edict was proclaimed. If there be virtue in playing the ostrich, then the ministers were remiss in initiating the study that led to this edict.
What we have here are Calvin's theories in actual practice in the
Genevan marketplace.[18]

There is another indication that Calvin's views were influential in this edict. It is clear from our discussion of his views on
usury that he distinguished the lending of idle money to one who
could use it well (lending for enterprise or production) from
lending money in cases of need, where the return of the loan
ought to be without interest. The first was part of the new economy which had been growing for hundreds of years and which
he was the first theologian to understand with any clarity. The
second was throat-cutting, sucking the blood of the poor—the
evil scored in Deuteronomy, the evil which the *monti di pieta*
tried to overcome in Italy by lending to the poor at low rates.
Most of this edict deals with the former. But one paragraph prohibits the common practice of lending money to one having grain
or fruit yet green, with the agreement that at harvesttime the
farmer will pay back in kind (wheat, wine, etc.) at the harvest
rate. This means that instead of receiving a relatively low amount
of, say, wheat, which was dear in the spring, the lender will receive a large amount in the fall when wheat is cheap. The edict
specifically prohibits this practice and was repeated in December

of that same year, 1557. It stipulates that the value set must be at what the produce will be worth at harvesttime, that these hypothetical prices agreed upon must be reasonable, and expressly notes that if a notable excess is charged it will be reduced.[19] Thus was set up a powerful protective device against anyone who would gouge the peasant who needed money desperately in spring or summer, only to see his produce flow into the hands of the sharper who lent him money in order to harvest his crops. Perhaps this is one of the reasons Monter could write:

> . . . nearly all the local peasants seemed to be far more favorably disposed to the Genevan government than to their own. This seems to be an impressive tribute to the careful and generally honest fashion in which *Messieurs* treated their rural subjects, and perhaps even more a consequence of the comparative lightness of Genevan taxation, which did not burden its peasants with an annual *taille* as did the reorganized Savoyard state after 1560.[20]

Calvin died in May of 1564. But his influence in this area continued, particularly in the person of his friend and successor, Theodore Beza. An extraordinary session of the Council was called on 10 December 1565, which addressed itself to the problem of usury alone. Evidently those whose business made it necessary for them to borrow or lend on occasion in France and Italy were involved in dealings where the interest rate was higher than Geneva's, and a special committee of *savants* had suggested that the legal rate be set at one-twelfth, or 8⅓ percent.[21] Three of the magistrates, among them Michel Roset, were asked to discuss the matter with Beza—although at the session the action had been not to allow such a raise which would enrich merchants, weigh down the poor, and contribute to the dearness of the times. But Beza admitted that those who traded in Lyons and Venice were faced with a separate situation and that their conscience should not be troubled by enforcing the local rate in foreign places where the interest rate was higher. Indeed, lending to merchants "who know very well how to make their profit" could be at a higher rate than the *pour quinze* set in 1557; but lending "for other affairs and for need" was restricted to the old level. (Martin thinks this meant 5 percent.) It is interesting that the final Council discussion specifically mentions Calvin:

> After many long discussions it has been ordered to hold to the preceding edicts, which are reasonable and severe enough, which also the late Monsieur Calvin, when he was asked, had found good, without changing anything. Yet this does not mean to punish those who will exceed by one [percent?] or a little more, especially when they lend to merchants.[22]

The last indication of Calvin's influence came with the establishing of a city-owned bank in Geneva. In 1551 the Council had established a special financial institution, *l'Arche*, which collected certain taxes—e.g., the *gabelle* on wheat and wine—in order to *debasle* the city, to pay off the long-standing debt to Basel. Like Topsy it grew and became a privy treasury and after 1567 expended more funds than the public treasury.[23] Finally, in 1568, the Council established a public bank with new funds borrowed from Basel at 5 percent for the *Arche*, charging 10 percent annual interest, or $2\frac{1}{2}$ percent per quarter.[24] The pastors were never happy with this bank which could charge more than the legal rate, and made numerous complaints about its excessive usury, the debauched to whom it loaned, and the scandalously large sums loaned. In 1571 Beza defended the bank's interest rates by comparing them to a tax, but closed his defense before the Council by noting that all scandals in Geneva soon became "huge as mountains" to the rest of the world and recommended the bank be terminated as soon as possible.[25] It was not, but its rates were lowered to $8\frac{1}{3}$ percent, an amount approved by the pastors at a meeting where the opinions of the "late Monsieur Calvin" were discussed.[26]

The bank went from trouble to more trouble; Pierre Chappuis, the man appointed *changeur*, was better at lending than at recovering the loans, and Monter's discussion makes the bank sound more like a charity than a financial institution. Finally Chappuis was sent to prison by the Council for his mismanagement and misappropriations. An attempt was then made to reestablish the bank, but the pastors, alarmed at the 10 percent rate proposed, managed to get the Two Hundred to bury the proposal on 7 March 1580. A few weeks later Beza gave it the *coup de grâce* by charging that such a bank had produced abuses in such places as Venice, Paris, and Lyons, and that if the bank were re-established, "people would say that at Geneva everyone is a banker, an odious thing." [27] Perhaps to the usual Calvinistic concern for fair regulations, one should add here a parallel concern that someone might be looking. Geneva was, indeed, in Tawney's phrase, a "city of glass."

From the discussion thus far it would seem that Calvin's influence on the usury question was a positive one. Because he was able to distinguish between lending for consumption at interest —a crime akin to murder—and lending for production and enterprise, he was able to sanction low rates of return for the latter. The rule of charity in his hands was more flexible than the Aristotelian natural law which the church had inherited and wielded so clumsily for many centuries. But all was not Christian financial progress in Geneva. There was at least one obvious failure, it seems to me, and several other questionable aspects of Genevan economic practice with regard to moneylending.

The failure lies in the fact that there is no indication that anyone ever loaned money freely "for consumption." Money was given, of course, to the needy by way of the deacons or through the hospital. Probably many poor refugees were helped in this way, and themselves later gave to the hospital that others might be helped. But it is clear that money lent to peasants was generally lent at interest, and this was the sort of lending that rates the term "consumptive," i.e., money lent that the poor might be able to get along till the crops came in. I have argued above that Calvin had something to do with the 1557 edict which prohibited overcharging the farmer in this regard. But that the simple Deuteronomic prohibition which Calvin extolled was ever honored in practice—except as a species of public charity— seems fairly unlikely.

But more interesting is the question raised by two economists about the effect of the 5 percent ceiling that Calvin helped nail down so tightly between 1544 and 1557. J. F. Bergier points out that in the country this was a severe limitation of the rates formerly used between city-dwellers and their country peasants.[28] The other economist, André E. Sayous, argues that the limitation was too restrictive:

> . . . far from facilitating transactions by a breadth of spirit, he [Calvin] established barriers more serious than an interdiction, almost systematically eluded because too absolute: the fixation of a rate of interest not at all high for the epoch (at first 5 percent, then "un pour quinze," that is, 6.66 percent) cramped the capitalists even more than the fact that soon the leader was put to oath, with all its consequences, concerning the size of the sum in fact paid back. . . . Although some isolated operations might escape censure, a professional lender, with exaggerated conditions imposed, would not be able to pursue his activity without exposing himself to grave penalties.[29]

Now, if Calvin realized that in general the standard of living rose as commerce increased, then the over-restriction of commerce by low interests rates—creating a situation where it would not be worth the while of one with idle money to invest it—would be a step backward economically. Geneva depended on commerce for its life. The simple city-country relationship had perhaps never existed for the city, and certainly did not exist at this period. The city needed to produce goods, to sell goods, to create a lively economic climate, in order to live and grow.

I think it is impossible to know if Sayous is right. The raising of rates in 1557 is evidence that the Council was aware of the problem, and since much of that ordinance reflects Calvin's views, it would be possible to argue that Calvin was flexible in this regard and able to protect the peasant at the same time. That Beza, after Calvin's death, permitted a merchant exposed to different conditions in foreign parts to adjust his borrowing and lending to those conditions, and that one might loan at higher rates to merchants "who know quite well how to make their profits," would be further evidence that Sayous is wrong. But the prohibition of the post-Calvin pastors, imbued with his attitudes toward even the city-owned bank, indicate that he may well be right. R. H. Tawney says Calvin's views ". . . can have offered but tepid consolation to the devout money-lender," and, "there have been ages in which such doctrines would have been regarded as an attack on financial enterprise rather than as a defense of it." [30] Hence it is impossible to know whether the future prosperity of Geneva owed much to Calvin's recognition of economic facts or to merchants in a good position who created wealth despite the arguments of Calvin and Beza. Sayous and Tawney see Calvin as too rigorous, "too Jewish," for the good of commerce in Geneva. But I wonder, then, at the paradox or accident that a Reformer (or, counting Beza, *two* Reformers) so implacably hostile to the needs of a developing commerce should have ruled the church and influenced society in the city where commerce did quite well.

Another problem with the usury edicts of Geneva was the failure of several of the pastors to comply with them. Calvin thought it unseemly for a pastor to lend at interest at all—even the legal rate was frowned upon though not legislated against—while usury, as we have seen, was an intolerable vice. Robert M. Kingdon has shown that several of the pastors in Geneva in the middle of the sixteenth century lent at the legal rate of interest (Jean Gerard in 1557 and Jacques Ruffy in 1568), and one of the most influential, Nicholas des Gallars, lent money at a usurious rate and escaped punishment. Des Gallars, until Beza's arrival the most influential pastor after Calvin, lent 300 florins in 1554 and received 447 in repayment in 1560. This was a simple rate of a little over 8 percent per year, or a bit over 6.67 percent if compounded annually. Compounded annually the 6.67 percent would not have been usurious according to the 1557 edict, but the return was a bit higher than that and was clearly not as low as the going rate when the money was loaned. Kingdon's conclusion is worth quoting:

> Just as early Italian capitalism was probably encouraged by the example of the Renaissance papacy in circumventing its own strict canonical regulations by ingenious casuistical arguments that made it possible for it to engage in large-scale banking, so Protestant businessmen may have been encouraged to engage more openly and energetically in capitalistic enterprise by the example of individual Calvinist ministers willing to seek personal financial profit.[31]

I think that the question of illegality is a difficult one to prove and evidently was not brought up by anyone. But the very fact that these pastors were so willing to use their money for profit rather than lending without expecting anything in return may well have encouraged the Genevan bourgeoisie in their pursuit of the treasures of this world.

A long summary to this discussion of usury practices and regulations in Geneva is hardly necessary. There may be some legitimate division over how much Calvin or the other pastors influenced the state, but that the interest and influence were there is incontestable. The pastors had no desire to escape a world of borrowers and lenders; they thought themselves capable of discussing rates of interest, payment in kind, and public lending agencies, and often got quick action. In our day when church financial concern has expressed itself (with a few notable exceptions) in guaranteeing its own tax-exempt status, how impressive to see the pastors argue about and then kill the public bank! The revolution was still religious enough in direction for its leaders to have some success in keeping it within the bounds of charity. We read today that "among the greatest gaps in existing anti-poverty efforts is the failure to provide financial-legal services for people who have neither the education nor the money to protect themselves." [32] The poor of Geneva had part of the answer to that in Calvin and the Consistory.

Regulation of Business and Industry

A brief review of Calvin's social and economic thought leads us to expect certain things in the area of commerce, wages, and industry. We may expect government regulation of prices, wages, and the whole arena of employer-employee relationships; regulation against monopoly; help for industry and commerce; concern for social and economic stability through binding contracts; and church intervention where thought necessary.[33] However, governmental regulation of prices was so common in those days, and was practiced long before, during, and after Calvin's life there, that nothing need be said in that regard. Occasionally the price of a basic commodity would get out of hand—such as we saw happen for wheat in 1557—and the government would step in to do something about reducing prices and stabilizing the economy. What could be sold, who could sell, where it could be sold—these regulations were quite common, and there is no indication that Calvin saw any need to intervene in this aspect of the marketplace. There is available, however, some interesting information about days of labor and wages. Then we shall turn to the important influence of the church as it helped arbitrate differences between masters and journeymen in the Western world's first modern industry, printing. A glance at labor organizations will conclude this study.

Working Days

Calvin, like Luther, wanted to return to the simplicity of the gospel in the matter of feast days. For both there was only one day of rest, Sunday, the day of Resurrection.[34] This meant the loss of about a dozen festival days for a worker who left France and went to Geneva. The definitive rule was first promulgated on 4 June 1537:

> Here it is said that some people are celebrating festivals, and it is ordered that each ought to work as has already been proclaimed without celebrating festivals except on Sunday, and this should be commanded district by district under penalty.[35]

This did not mean, of course, that workers slaved six days a week from dawn to dark without surcease. For one thing, Wednesday morning contained a worship service obligatory enough to merit the day to be called "the day of prayer," and no one was supposed to be working until after worship was over. In 1545 there was a complaint by the pastors that the streets were full of people on the day of prayer and an edict was proclaimed that "Wednesday should be like Sunday until the sermon is over." [36] So a good share of Wednesday morning labor was lost due to worship. And the printing workers were accustomed to receiving all of Wednesday as a holiday, although we cannot tell if this custom was extended to other workers.

Still, there is warrant to extract from the Reformer's views the argument that taking any of God's six working days from labor is lazy, useless, and profitless to the soul. And since pastors and entrepreneurs often share a concern for work— the one from duty, the other for profit—which takes little thought for leisure, we can see the beginnings here of a secularization of the other six days that will reach a horrible nadir in the mines and factories of England and America after the Industrial Revolution.

Wages

Another aspect of labor relations in Geneva was the attempt of the Council to freeze wages. According to Henri Sée, the price climb in neighboring France was not understood as the result of the increase of gold and silver brought from the New World, but was seen as a matter to be handled by price and wage curbs.

> From the beginning to the end of the century, prices tripled or quadrupled. In vain the royal administration tried to apply the brakes to it by laying down *maximums* for prices and salaries, as in 1544, 1567 and 1577.[37]

Nor were measures different in Geneva. In March of 1559, *Messieurs* were worried about sustaining the university, which was about to get fully under way, and it did not help matters that workers were so proud that they could hardly be hired. The Council passed an edict:

> Here there was discussion of workers who are so expensive and proud, a strange thing, so that no one can be found who wants to work in the vineyards. [Of course, most of the immigrants were artisans, not peasants.] Therefore it is ordered to make public edicts that no one may pay masons, hat-makers, nor other workers nor laborers more than six sous per day, and to women ten quarters; and when they are fed, just half that, at a penalty of sixty sous, both for the worker and the master.[38]

This tells us something about the "laborer's market" that obtained at the time, and also something about the price rise which necessitated good wages. But imagine a laborer paying ten days' wages as a fine for receiving too much salary!

Two years later a similar measure was taken, indicating that the earlier edict had failed. This time it was agricultural workers alone who were affected (*Messieurs* owned a good deal of land or, rather, the city did).

> From now on prohibitions should be made against exacting more than six sous and a half for men and three for women, with a penalty of sixty sous payable both by the one demanding more than the rate and by the one who pays the rate.[39]

Here the ceiling on wages was raised a bit for men, but not at all for women (assuming the three sous to be a quarter of a florin, hence the two terms meant the same thing). Nourishment is not mentioned in this release.

Another of the few instances where the Council took a hand in wage-fixing occurred about the same time in 1561 when the ribbon-makers (*rubantiers*) came to complain that the masters "do not want to pay what is reasonable for the making of ribbons, in order that they might support themselves, so that if it weren't remedied they could be forced to leave the city." The Council then listened to management's side: four masters explained that they were paying the going rate and the journeymen ought to be content. So the Council appointed itself a board of arbitration and set two of its members to work out "such a rate for the making of the ribbons that it should be well for everyone." [40] Unfortunately, all we can say here is that the ribbon-makers thought the Council might help them, and the Council did arbitrate the case. As to the justice of their decision, there is not a shred of evidence, except that the *rubantiers* did not leave town.

The failure of the best minds of the sixteenth century to understand the wild rise in prices was shared by the Council and by Calvin. One can imagine that the edicts were generally ignored by workers and masters; indeed, the omission of any but agricultural workers in the second edict probably indicates failure to legislate with any result in the burgeoning industries of Geneva.

The only wages we can talk about with any confidence are those of the pastors. They were almost the only civic employees who earned all their living in their public charge. Others—syndics, treasurers, secretaries, and those concerned with legal matters—were paid, but their wages were not meant to be their subsistence. The pastors continually complained that they were not able to live on their wages—and they no doubt had justice on their side. In the Council records of 1546 we read:

> Calvin, in the name of the others, has requested that it should please *Messieurs* to have regard for their salaries which necessitate their living on such scanty wages, etc. And having listened to him speak decided that it should be theirs.[41]

What the wages were or what increase was granted is not clear—though when Philip de Ecclesia came in 1542 he received a beginning wage of 240 florins per year. Often we read that a certain pastor was given some money or wheat or a robe because of his poverty. But the low point was reached in November 1557, when it came to the Council's attention that the orphans of the deceased pastor, Abel Poupin, were destitute, going vagabonding (*allans vacabondans*).[42] The deacons who had oversight of the hospital were ordered to do something about this, but from then on the pastors banded together on this question and got some action.

On 3 January 1558, Calvin and Jacques Bernard, representing all the ministers of city and country parishes, presented a long plea to the *Seigneurie*. Included in the request were higher wages so that they might live honestly, and a plea that some goods once used by the Roman Church be put to this use—though just what goods is not stipulated. (Perhaps they were referring to the proceeds from land once owned by Bonnivard's Priory of St. Victor, which was torn down when the suburbs were destroyed.[43]) They complained that times were harder than previously and their poverty now quite obvious; the orphans of Poupin were alluded to; the pastors asked not to be enriched, but to be able to live honestly; and Calvin requested, "without sham," that his wages be equal to the other ministers.

The Council resolved to communicate with Calvin, since it wished to be liberal toward the ministers.[44]

On 20 January the wages of the ministers in the city were increased "because of their poverty and the dearness of the times" to 250 florins and 12 coupes of wheat; seven days later the ministers in the country were raised to 240 florins plus the grain.[45] By that fall the city pastors were raised again to 300 florins with no more wheat, much to the rejoicing of the pastors: "God be praised and thanked for this."[46] When Pierre Viret returned as a pastor he was given 400 florins, which placed him below Calvin (receiving 500) and above the other pastors, including Beza, who were receiving 300. This took place in the spring of 1559.[47]

The final raise took place on 23 April 1562, when the Council raised the wages of the city ministers to 400 florins per year, university professors the same, while in the villages wages of 300, 280, and 240 florins were paid. A month later Calvin himself was raised to 600 florins.[48] The modern reader cannot help sympathizing with the pastors of Céligny, Chancy, Neydens, Bossey, and Moing, who were getting only 240. When on 19 June a new minister was received and put directly into the city pastorate without undergoing "trial" in the country, the country pastors howled:

> Some of the ministers in the country were very discontented and even said this might discourage them, and that they would never have accepted the ministry if they had thought they would be left in the country. M. Calvin, very astonished, kept silence, but in his room after the departure of the Company cried out to someone, his hands thrust high together in the air: "What a thing to see before death!"[49]

Frankly, one tends to side with the country pastors and to wonder at the difference in wages, although the suggestion of Professor Kingdon, that living conditions in the villages closer to the food supply might have been lower, may be the explanation sought.

My own attempts to correlate these wages with the prices of wheat and wine are inconclusive. The price evidence, summarized into tables by Bergier, is quite fragmentary and does not tell us much.[50] Suffice it to say that the city did not pay its full-time workers well.

Regulation of the Printing Industry

The establishment of the printing industry divides medieval and modern technology.[51] Nor is this only a recent discovery. Francis Bacon lists printing before gunpowder and the compass as the three inventions which changed the appearance and state of the whole world, and which mark the beginning of man's attempt to regain the rights God has assigned him over nature.[52]

The printing industry is the only one that we have enough information about to study both the concern of the city Council to regulate its way of operating and the concern of the pastors that this be done and done well.

The printing industry in Geneva had been dying out in the early sixteenth century. But the Reformation changed that as the city rapidly became the center for the diffusion of Reformed theology, partly through preachers sent out in increasing numbers and partly through the printing of the literature of the Reformers, especially Calvin. From 1536 to 1550, Jean Girard was the leading printer in the city, and from 1543 till 1549 produced almost all Geneva's printing output. But after 1550, when Girard printed the new Latin edition of the *Institutes*, Jean Crespin, Robert Estienne, Badius, and the Rivery brothers arrived, and the industry flourished in both quantity and quality, the latter being the contribution of the new refugee printers from France.[53]

Although Girard had a virtual monopoly all those years, this does not mean he was given free rein. The Council quickly began to censure his books when in 1539, during Calvin's period of exile, Girard published an anonymous book—probably by the wife of the city's first Protestant preacher, Antoine Froment—which compared the pastors left in the city unfavorably with Calvin and Farel. Girard was thrown into prison for some days—no one was fooled by the false locus of publication, Anvers—and an edict was proclaimed:

Decided that accompanying the sound of the trumpet, it should
be made public that nothing of any sort should be printed in the
city without license of *Messieurs* under penalty of being taken
and punished according to law.[54]

That fall it was ordered that each printer should bring the first
copy of a book to the city hall before the rest of the printing could go on. This hindered operations a great deal—a
printer ran off one book and then waited for the censor to read
it; so in 1540 this was changed to censorship of the signed manuscript, so that type was not set up until after the work was
given its secular imprimatur. Marshall McLuhan has taught us
that print is a "hot medium"; the Council saw to it that the message was not.

In France the development of the printing industry was far
ahead of that in Geneva, and grave troubles between masters and journeymen had already broken out. These *confréries*
of journeymen were really labor unions with their aims quasi-
religious and frankly economic. In 1529 confraternities in Lyons
struck; they did so again in 1539, because of "insufficient salaries, payments in kind, and excessive numbers of apprentices,
as well as the bad division of working hours." In both Lyons
and Paris—for the 1539 strike spread there—the masters called
in the authorities to "pronounce against the pretensions of the
workers, against the principle of coalitions and infractions of the
right [*liberté*] to work." [55] This led to the royal ordinance of
Villers-Cotteret, which laid down prohibitions against coalitions
or monopolies of both masters and journeymen, but without
much success.[56] The historians agree that the royal edicts favored
the masters against the workingmen. Henri Sée says that "with
regard to salaries, fixed in many cases by public authority, establishing a *maximum* but not a *minimum*, they seem to have
been increased in the course of the sixteenth century, but not in
proportion to the depreciation of money from the price rises;
that is, the condition of the salaried was aggravated." [57] Martin,
while noting that the later royal edict of 1572—following printing strikes in Lyons and Paris the year before—contained a few
dispositions favorable to the journeymen, especially in limiting

the number of apprentices, concludes: "the court in general adopted a policy of defiance to the consideration of the workers." [58]

Perhaps the printing industry in Lyons, Geneva, Paris, and other cities in the sixteenth century, more than any other industry, contained in germ the tension between organized labor and cooperative management which we see in Western industrialized society today. The competitive drive of the private entrepreneur was hedged by his need to cooperate with other masters against journeymen increasingly being organized into what resembled modern craft unions. Western civilization would have to pass through a fierce period of almost unlimited avarice on the part of capitalists, and almost unlimited demands on the unorganized labor of men only nominally free, before something of this same corporate balance would exist in its present ubiquity. Both labor and management in the sixteenth century constantly appealed to the state, proclaiming that justice was on their side. In France we have seen that the court elected the side of management. Now let us turn to Geneva.

In 1557 the Genevan Council took action against coalitions of masters at the instigation of Calvin, who denounced the "superstitions and dissolutions of the trades when someone is raised to mastership." [59] The edict written that day prohibited any assemblies for dissolute purposes, nor swearing, nor other things. This is not very clear and was put in a "better mode" the next day.

> No masters or apprentices, regardless of profession, should be so hardy or bold as to make illicit assemblies—even of less than an hour long—before availing themselves of some ordinances or edicts and statutes previously made among them, that they have not previously submitted to the *Seigneurie* and by our very redoubtable Lords looked into and reformed according to reason and in order to prevent all abuses. The penalty for anyone going against this is sixty sous and punishment according to the merit of the case. [60]

What we have, then, is a prohibition of labor organizations and management agreements alike. No doubt this was considered the fair way to proceed and prevent scandal on both sides. For now both sides must either operate *sub rosa* or come to the Council to arbitrate differences and establish rules and regulations. Since this came about by Calvin's intervention, it seems safe to say that he favored the paternalistic features of this edict.

But Council's intervention, when it came, did not arise from either journeymen or masters directly, but from the Geneva Company of Pastors, although the grievances of the journeymen were the basic issue. It was upon the demand of two pastors that on 28 August 1559 the Council decided to establish an overall regulation of the printing industry.

> Printers. Here *spect*. [i.e., *spectable*, term of respect used, as far as I can tell, for ministers only] Jn. Nyco. des Gallars and *spect*. Théodore de Bèze have proposed that although there has already been enough inconvenience because of printers, nevertheless there are some disorders and divisions among them, especially between the masters and journeymen, concerning which they have been minded to make the following remonstrances: namely, that it would seem good that *Messieurs* appoint someone before whom the master printers will be called in order to be heard about what they would like to state about the order that ought to be established in order to prevent the confusions and irritations which are occurring among them; and then the journeymen should also be heard in their grievances, so that with respect to everyone an order might be set up which will be observed from now on, which they have asked to be provided and to advise as to how it could be done. Ordered that that should be done, and Seigneurs Bernard, Syndic Fran. Chevalier, and Jeh. Chautemps appointed.[61]

Up till now Geneva's printing troubles had been between masters—affairs of copyrights, pirated forms, and the like. But now the issues were to be between masters and journeymen, and internal regulation was necessary. It is interesting that the Council did not elect to solve the complex problems by fiat. "Democratically," says Chaix, "it decided first to call together and hear the interested parties, masters and journeymen." It should be noted that this was not in accord with American democratic procedure, which has tried to steer away from government intervention at all. Here the city arbitrators listened to both sides, "democratically," and on the basis of the knowledge gained composed an ordinance which would settle the difficulties. Not for them democratic strikes and lockouts, the hiring of scabs and breaking of heads and windows. They wanted to be fair —and that they were is shown by the longevity of the document they passed—but for them peaceful industry was a right of the commonweal more basic than the right to run one's industry as one's own. It was collective bargaining, in a sense, but compulsory in genesis, and the subsequent "agreement" was binding on both parties.

It will not be necessary to produce and translate the whole ordinance. The regulations were complex, at times obscure to one not acquainted with the inner workings of a printshop in the sixteenth century, and quite detailed.[62] But there were several features of interest to our study.

Masters were prohibited from plotting together to set a wage standard policy, and journeymen were likewise forbidden to band together to agree on a standard wage below which they would not work.

The journeyman was guaranteed job security during the completion of a piece of work unless the work were too heavy or difficult for the journeyman, or he stole from the master of the shop. The journeyman was likewise bound to complete a piece of work, barring sickness or inability, and various rules were laid down to take care of such eventualities.

Every master had to teach his apprentices well so that at the end of apprenticeship the latter would be able to do the work well enough to be a journeyman. In addition, the agreement between the two had to be in writing to obviate quarrels.

Masters were forbidden to overwork their journeymen, and the latter were enjoined not to hurry a piece of work in order "to have time and leisure for gaming." Nor could other journeymen demand anything of a former-apprentice-become-journeyman, such as paying for a banquet, which entailed "corruptions and inhuman constraint."

Days lost from work must be paid for by the offending party. That is, if work was lost by part of the shop because of

unexcused absence by a journeyman, then those wages lost
were to come from his pocket. But if the master caused the
work loss, then he would have to pay the men's wages even if
they could not work.

There were other regulations concerning the relations between compositors and correctors, rules guarding against thefts
of forms or sheets, warnings against bad language in the print-
shops, and even stipulations about the candles for lighting the
way between home and shop, which the workers must provide
but the masters paid for.

Underlying the whole ordinance was the conviction that
there existed a solidarity between journeyman and journeyman
and between worker and master that all must acknowledge and
be governed by. There was, of course, the tacit admission that
things had not worked out that way, else the ordinance would
not have been needed. But that cleavage between labor and management which we are so familiar with today was absent from
the thought and wording of this law.

Chaix's comments are instructive.

> In its entirety it should be recognized that the Genevan edict
> is marked by moderation and humanity. Preserving the rights
> of the masters, it obviously protects the journeymen and ap-
> prentices. The consultation which is at its origin, in accord with
> the evangelical ideal of the epoch, explains the equitable spirit
> of this regulation.[63]

In contrast with the French edicts of the period in which "almost all the prohibitions were imposed upon the journeymen to
the profit of the masters," this one was conceived in a collab-
oration of the interested parties, which ensured a measure of
justice not found in the French edicts which emanated directly
and sovereignly from the royal authority. An example of this
can be seen in the number of apprentices per press: In Lyons
and Paris there were four or even five per press, but in the Genevan ordinance only one, although one of the few changes
made in the ordinance in 1580 allowed two.[64] It was not till 1572,
observes Professor Davis, that the printing workers of Lyons received "some of the concessions which the printing workers of

Geneva had received through the Genevan Ordinances of 1560." [65]

Two other factors are of interest to us: wages and duration of work. About the former, we can say very little. Chaix has discovered only five instances where salaries for the printing industry are mentioned in the *Registres du Conseil,* and concludes that nothing can be established concerning wages from these. Since room and board were sometimes part of the stipend in those days, even if we had salary figures they might help us very little.

Duration of labor is not quite so obscure. Chaix believes the figures show a working day of twelve hours, better than those of the printing workers of Lyons. Concerning the number of working days, we have more information. Although they agitated for two days off per week—Sunday and Wednesday—the workers received just half of the extra day they asked for. So every Sunday was a day of rest and recreation—as we have seen, it bore no resemblance to the Puritan Sabbath—as well as every other Wednesday. It was ordered that any journeyman who took every Wednesday off, or any master who permitted that, would be banished.[66]

Although most of our concern here is with the regulation of journeymen-master relationships, it is also worth pointing out that the ordinance did its best to spread the printing of "best-sellers" throughout the printing industry.

> And so that the privileges should be moderated and that no one should be burdened over much, the *Seigneurie* order for the present that the impressions of catechisms, prayers, and psalms which are for the common use of the church should be common to all.[67]

This meant that those works sure to be purchased could not be monopolized by any influential printer. This was also true of the Scriptures, whether whole or just the New Testament, although a new translation might belong to one printer till his first impression was sold. The latter rule seems to have just the right blend of entrepreneur encouragement and social concern.

The pastors were, of course, much concerned with this industry because it was their voice to the rest of the world. Hence we can expect that the mere making of ordinances would not bring an end to their concern that the industry be well managed. Early in 1562 Calvin went before the Council to complain about the bad printing done in the city and the ease with which men obtained the mastership. He exhorted the Council that those who did not do proper printing should lose their license to print. Roget tells us that seven printers were fined, and we know that one, Étienne Anastaise, lost his license because of faulty Bibles.[68] Poor Anastaise—he had already lost his license once before in 1560, when he got an adverse report from Beza and the other members of the Council's committee on printing and was ordered to stop printing Calvin's Commentaries on the Epistles.[69] This time not only was he criticized for his bad Bibles, but the old affair of the Commentaries was brought up again,

> . . . which are prohibited because they have not done honor to the city nor profit to the readers who have bought them because of the stupid and heinous errors of all sorts, despite the fact that they were sold at great cost and with excessive gain. Ordered that he make satisfaction in prison.[70]

He never seems to have functioned very well. On 25 June 1563, a list of printers and the number of presses was prepared (there were twenty-four printers and thirty-four authorized presses), and Anastaise—for once given his right name, Étienne —was listed as unable to print any further without permission.[71] The last mention of our unhappy printer occurs long after Calvin's death, when on 25 June 1571, a church in France objected to some *alphabets* printed by Anastaise, in which the Apostles' Creed lacked the entire article concerning the resurrection. He later corrected them.[72]

What can we establish from the above discussion? First, that the Venerable Company of Pastors took enough interest in the industrial and economic affairs of the city to regard their own intervention as possible and desirable. This indicates something of the sphere of the gospel that they were supposed to be preaching. It remains true, however, that this must be seen in the whole context of Calvin's thought in this area and in other areas of social justice in which the pastors took a hand. For, by itself, it merely indicates that the ministers were concerned that their propaganda arm function smoothly. But even at this rather low level it is instructive to the modern Christian who thinks he can separate religion and politics, religion and economics, or religion and society to see how impossible it is to disentangle the relationships between an industry (printing) and the propagation of the gospel. If the former had been badly done, the latter would have suffered.

Secondly, in this intervention the workers were helped. This stands in marked contrast with France, where, as Sée, Chaix, Martin, and Davis have all attested, government regulation worked to the benefit of patrons only.

Thirdly, the action of pastors and Council alike was what would today be called paternalistic. It had no observable connection with laissez-faire capitalism, nor was it socialistic. It hinged on the frank recognition that both men and the industry were important and Geneva had better get things straightened out before it had the problems of Lyons or Paris. Arbitration, yes, but an arm-twisting arbitration which sometimes proves necessary even in our land with its long tradition of free bargaining.

All of this indicates a rather positive relationship between Calvin's views and the actual Genevan situation. And, further, shows that the Calvinist influence was salutary. The ordinance remained in effect, with little change, for two and a quarter centuries, until with many other venerable Genevan standards, it was abolished by the edict of Napoleon.

Labor Unions

In order for the edicts limiting wages to have any effect and for the Council's Printing Ordinance to work smoothly, the Council also thought it necessary to ban labor unions, formed by disgruntled workers to pressure the masters to grant higher wages and better working conditions. Geneva had never had the strong guild system worked out in other parts of Europe several centuries earlier. According to Antony Babel, *doyen* of Geneva's economic historians, the associations of workers in Geneva prior to the Reformation had never had the regulative power usually associated with guilds. There were such organizations, of course, which celebrated the conferring of masterships, had masses said for the dead, and functioned in other quasi-religious and social ways. But regulative associations gained no control in Geneva and neighboring French cities till the last half of the sixteenth century.[73] Those that did get a start were promptly banned by *Messieurs* on 23 March 1559. After putting the freeze on wages, the Council added this as an afterthought:

> Item: that no laborer nor other workers may plot together in order to divert the course of the above proclamations and ordinances, under penalty of being chastised according to the exigency of the case.[74]

A similar prohibition had, as we have just seen, been made against both masters and journeymen of the printing industry, and the definitive printing ordinance of 1560 reinforced that ban, especially with regard to uniting together to form a wage scale. The summer of 1561 witnessed a lot of squabbling between masters and journeymen, especially over Wednesdays off, and charges that some workers used pressure tactics to force others to join with them were hurled about.[75]

Perhaps we can say again that the larger solidarity of the community demanded that all lesser solidarities be squelched. This sounds fine in practice, and something like this is what Calvin and the Council had in mind. It worked against employers and employees alike, being equitable in its condemnation of all *complots* that would create a power structure within the community. Unfortunately, as we have learned, such power structures need to be formed by the oppressed and those in sympathy with them to overcome the tendency for those on the top of the economic and social heap to have the ear of the magistrates or to be the magistrates. That this did not happen in Geneva was due to the powerful concern for the poor by the pastors in Geneva, a concern that protected them at least till the death of Beza in 1605.

A brief comparison might be drawn with the situation in Lyons. In that city the printing workers were drawn to the Reformation, according to Natalie A. Z. Davis, because of its emphasis on literacy, especially the reading and interpretation of the Bible, and because these rootless men needed a feeling of religious equality more akin to the democracy of Protestantism than the autocracy of the Catholic Church.[76] This latter was expressed particularly well in the participation urged by the Reformers in the service of worship. So when the city became Protestant in 1562, they were more than willing to go along, having taken an active hand in the revolt. But Catholicism was reestablished by 1564, and many of the printing workers had become disenchanted with Protestantism. Why? She gives several reasons. First, that the printing workers saw the Protestant leaders losing their faith in the ability of the *menu peuple* ("little people") to understand and make decisions on the basis of the Word of God; secondly, that the elders and *surveillants* of the church there under Pierre Viret were of a higher social status and did not seriously consider the workers as potential leaders; finally, that the standards of virtue set by the Reformers were too genteel, not in accord with the boisterous, Epicurean tastes of the workers, who loved to sing both Psalms and bawdy chants on the streets at night.[77] I think she should have mentioned in this connection an important consideration, something she dwells upon for considerable length elsewhere—that the labor reforms they saw made under Reformation leadership in Geneva were not carried out in Lyons. Instead, the confraternities were actually banned (they had only been theoretically banned under Catholic leadership), so that when the workers struck again in in 1570–72 the issues were the same as thirty years before: wages, payment in kind, undue use of apprentices in place of journeymen, and days off—issues already fairly settled by the Geneva ordinance of 1560.[78]

In one city the banning of unions made little difference because the pastors were anxious that the workers be treated well. But in Lyons the short Reformed rule provoked no secular reforms to speak of, and the allegiance of the workers was in great measure lost.

R. H. Tawney speaks of the "cannon balls of Christian Socialism" hurled by the Venerable Company of Pastors at the city Council members. Actually, Calvin was not a socialist, nor doctrinaire at all in his social, political, or economic theories. If we can use a modern term to describe a sixteenth-century theologian--he was a pragmatist, trying to see how the rule of charity could be applied and the common good promoted and protected in the existent situation. The church, Calvin at its head, saw the world as the place where God's people received His blessings and shared it with their brothers. Thus the pastors regarded the world as God's and therefore *their* field. The line which marked the distinction of church and state was acknowledged, but a line between sacred and secular, never.

CHAPTER VIII

The Common Life

IN THIS CHAPTER we shall examine the influence of the Reformer on education and family life. Between the last chapters and this lies no very solid bridge. For one thing, Calvin's influence on the question of usury was a powerful one, his approach one which broke with centuries of tradition. The same can be said about the strength of his influence on education in Geneva, but the tradition-breaking had already been done by Sturm working with Martin Bucer in Strasbourg. In the area of family life, any revolutionary leader must address himself to the question of how the "new day" will affect this traditional social unit. Marx, for example, did this, but very clumsily. Calvin's influence and teachings here were not nearly so great as the example set by Luther and his Katie for Germany, nor, indeed, do we see much more than a slight softening of certain traditional patterns and a tendency toward equalizing the position of the woman. Calvin's influence on the common life was more in the line of modernizing the traditional than in its revolution.

Education

Geneva's respect for the scholar is evident to anyone who visits the university today and is confronted by the busts and portraits of what must surely be everyone who has ever taught in that institution. The modern university lies just outside the ancient walls to the west, not far from the spot where the troops of the Duke of Savoy attempted their famous Escalade. The College of Geneva, on the other hand, almost rests against the city's ancient walls to the south, indicating that the hard-pressed citizens barely had room for its building in 1558. The success of both institutions today makes clear that the city has not lost a zeal for education first made evident on its day of independence, 1536.

The preacher who first sparked a thoroughgoing Reformation in Geneva was Guillaume Farel, an angry young man trained and nourished in the humanist center at Meaux in France, which revolved about the reforming (but never Reformed) Bishop Briçonnet. It was not strange, then, that the meeting of General Council on 21 May 1536, which abolished the mass and established the Reformation, should also include a concern for education.

> Here [at the meeting of the General Council] the article concerning the schools was proposed and on this matter by the same vote it was resolved that we try to have a learned man do that [i.e., teach], and that he be paid so that he might nourish and teach the poor without asking anything of them for salary, and also that each person be bound to send his children to the school and to make them learn [sic!], and all scholars and also pedagogues ought to be obligated to go to make their residence at the great school [i.e., public school] where the rector and his bachelors will be.[1]

There are at least three very interesting items here: first, that the tie between Reformation and education was so close that of all the institutions that might have been mentioned here—the church or the hospital, for instance—only the school is treated; next, that this education was free to the poor at city expense; finally, that it was compulsory. The school itself was directed by rector Antoine Saunier and classes met at the former monastery de Rive. Its aims were quite modest, seeking to inculcate only grammar of the ancient trivium. Saunier was forced to leave the city shortly after Calvin and Farel for refusing to obey Council's wishes in the matter of public worship. After Calvin's return, the "heterodox" Sébastien Castellio was rector from 1541 to 1544.

Upon Calvin's second advent the Church Ordinances were

written and (in the main) passed by the Councils. The copy found in the *Registers of the Company of Pastors* contains an introduction (not found in the official copy of the *Ordonnances Ecclesiastiques*), in which the immediate institutional consequences of the gospel proclamation are seen to be church, school, and hospital.

> So that the doctrine of the Holy Gospel and our Lord should be preserved in its purity and the Christian Church duly maintained, that in the future the youth should be faithfully instructed, [and] the hospital set up in good condition for the support of the poor.[2]

Indeed, such was the importance of education in Geneva that the only major construction in the city during Calvin's life there— except for defensive fortifications and road building—was the college, begun in 1558 and finished in 1563.[3] Monter, who is critical of the republic for taking in more revenue from traditional ecclesiastical sources than it spent on reformed ecclesiastical institutions, admits that this was not true after the founding of the college a few years after the Calvinists defeated the Perrinists.

> Here, too, however, Geneva's situation changed later in the century, principally after the foundation of Calvin's Academy in 1559 had added a large annual charge to the budget which could not be balanced by any substantial additions of revenue.[4]

We saw that in the beginning education was provided for those who could not pay, and that it was compulsory. This continued. Every once in a while there was a notice concerning the appointment of a schoolmaster for the hospital, where were lodged some of the poor and orphans. We note also that it was the job of the hospitaller to work with the other deacons to find apprenticeships for the boys and places of service for the girls— an indication that their education was what we would term elementary.[5] That this education continued to be compulsory can be seen when the compulsion was extended to the villages in the fall of 1561. The pastor at Jussy, Jean Pinaut, complained to the Council

. . . that the children of the subjects at Jussy do not go to cate-
chism nor even to school, so that if there is not a remedy, there
will be a great barbarity and God will call us to account for it.[6]

Councilman Michel Roset and Calvin were appointed to check
into the situation, and after the report Roset was sent to Peney
and Jussy to assemble and harangue the people about their *non-
chalance* and to exhort them to do better. The city offered its
help in increasing the wages of the teachers, and levied a fine of
five sous upon any subject who did not send his child to school,
unless there was some reason known to the chatelain.

An amusing example indicates to us that nothing was too
small for Calvin's attention in this matter of education. In 1551
he came to the Council with the complaint that a scholar named
Collongnies was shooting a peashooter in school, evidently at the
teaching bachelors. The Council solemnly prohibited such ex-
tracurricular activity and appointed the syndic Chamois to separate the scholars.[7]

The main educational enterprise for the small city, however,
came in 1559 with the establishment of the College of Geneva.
This university's genesis (for it then served in place of both college and university today) in Geneva owed its transfer there
from Lausanne to Calvin's concern for freedom of the church
from civil interference in disciplinary matters. Lausanne was
under control of the burghers of Berne, who were concerned to
keep a tight rein on the churches in their territory, and evidently
found the chief pastor in Berne, Haller, sympathetic to their
viewpoint. But the professors at the college in Lausanne and the
chief pastor, Pierre Viret, found Calvin's system of excommunication by Consistory much more satisfactory than leaving such
matters up to the city Council. After long haggling, threats and
counterthreats (in which Viret gave every indication of wanting
to leave, it seems to me), and despite the plea of Bullinger from
Zurich and Peter Martyr from the mountains that the men man
their posts, their dismissal was a *fait accompli* by January of
1559. Theodore Beza had left before that, having been received
24 November 1558 by the Genevan Council to be lecturer in
Greek.[8] By the end of May the roster of professors was com-

plete, and Calvin's statutes for the college were finished. Beza was elected as rector, a task—as we have seen—he labored at between diplomatic trips to France.

We have already quoted Monter to the effect that the expenses of this school had a drastic effect on the finances of the city government. The building was the only public building completed in Geneva during Calvin's stay there. How was education financed? Evidently there were three main sources of income. First, an effort was made to encourage people to give, both while alive and in their wills. For example, in 1559 a little over one thousand florins which had been willed to the school so recently begun was received upon the deaths of the testators.[9] A second source of income was the revenue from fines. In that same year the wife of Antoine Munier was fined twenty-five *écus* for false cloth-measuring (*pour faux aulnage*), which was given to the college.[10] But, though wills might pay the wages of three professors for a year and fines might pay for heat, what about the construction? Interestingly enough, the Perrinists paid for the buildings! Over 30,000 florins went into construction in 1559 and again in 1560, money the city government realized from the sale of goods and properties belonging to the condemned who had been decapitated or who had fled from the city. "Thus, ironically, the financial pillars of Calvin's new school turned out to be none other than his declared enemies: Perrin, Sept, Vandel, Berthelier, and their cronies." [11]

This, by the way, throws some interesting light on city government and the growth of industry during Calvin's period. Almost no construction went on, and when something was built, it was only possible because of confiscation. Evidently there were either sufficient buildings in the city to absorb the influx of refugee industries—especially printing—or times were so hard they made do with what they had, remodeling rather than building. The school construction was not finished till 1562, and even then we might not have thought it finished. For in November of 1564, after icy winds were blowing, Beza solicited the Council to provide glass windows for the lower grades. The decision of the penurious Council was that such a frill could wait, and that in the meantime the scholars could make windows out of paper.[12]

Quirinius Breen has demonstrated that Calvin's humanism was so ingrained that conversion did not rid him of the mental set he had acquired as a humanist scholar.[13] Humanism and Reformation had a great deal in common, as has been demonstrated over and over, and the humanists' delight in the classical Greek and Latin writers is as evident in Calvin's program of study as in the writings of a Hooker or a Mather. Among the ancient authors Calvin mentions specifically in L'ordre for the college are Vergil, Cicero, Ovid, Seneca, Isocrates, Livy, Xenophon, Polybius, Herodian, and Homer. In addition to their works being studied, the professors are warned that "they are not to make invectives against the authors whom they expound, but that they apply themselves to explicate their sense faithfully." [14]

And perhaps one can see something of Calvin's humanity—as well as a rejection of some of the grimness of his own study in Montague College at the University of Paris—in his description of the office of principal, who was in charge of discipline and served as dean under the rector:

> He must be of a *debonnaire* spirit, having neither a rude nor a bitter disposition, so that his whole life may give the scholars a good example, and must carry the vexations of his charge quite peaceably [*doulcement*].[15]

There must have been a few saints in the last half of the sixteenth century in Geneva, else this office would never have been filled.

The college was successful far beyond the dreams of those who began it. Beza wrote to Bullinger on 1 May 1564, just prior to the death of Calvin: "We have counted nearly 1,200 scholars [in the *schola privata*] and their number increases daily." [16] Add to these pupils the 300 in the *schola publica*. What strain this number of students—many of whom were probably not residents of the city—must have put on a city the size of Geneva! Of course, the students began to immigrate about the same time refugees began to leave, so perhaps the difficulties encountered were somewhat different, but no greater. At least most of them did not bring their families along! Probably the greatest expense to the city—apart from the building costs—was the salaries of ten professors only partly recovered by tuition.

Here, in an area at least tangentially related to social thought, we see the genius of Calvin at work again. Education was made cheap and compulsory, theoretically within the range of all. No one could escape at least a brush with learning in sixteenth-century Geneva. When the opportunity came, higher education was introduced and a hard-pressed Council without demur undertook the difficult task of financing it from a budget that, as Monter has shown, was usually barely balanced. This expense was added to the constant struggle to pay off the perpetual obligation to *debasle*, sometimes only paying the interest. The education itself was humanist and Christian and lasting. It had an incalculable effect upon scholars who attended from France, Germany, the Low Countries, Scotland, and England, and who went back home to immerse themselves in church reformation and political revolution. It, like the other social institutions in Geneva—church and hospital—bears the indelible imprint of a man whose relationship with the world of men was formative. How apt that today Calvin's old homesite houses the Office of Youth, Department of Public Instruction.

Family Life

Marriage in the Western world has usually been an amphibian institution, the concern of both the state and the church. In this area, as in others, we see in Geneva a movement from almost total state control to one where church and state shared concern in a complex arrangement. The 1541 Ecclesiastical Ordinances make clear that the Council believed marriage to be its concern.

> With regard to differences in matrimonial cases, because it is not a spiritual matter but involved with civil affairs, we remit these to their Lordships [*Messieurs*], desiring them nevertheless to be willing to set up a Consistory without delay to judge in such matters, to which, if it seem good to them, there could be joined some ministers as counsellors.[17]

But Calvin was not satisfied, and by the end of 1545 he had worked out a marriage ordinance, although there is indication that the Council was not willing to be bound by this project.[18] While this project does not clearly distinguish the spiritual and temporal realms in the case of marriage, it does admit that there is some distinction. At the very end, Calvin wrote:

> All matrimonial causes concerning the union of persons and not of goods should be carried first to the Consistory, and there, if some amiable agreement is able to be made, it will be made in the name of God. If it be necessary to pronounce some juridical sentence, the parties should then be sent to the Council with a declaration of the Consistory's recommendation, in order to give a definitive sentence there.[19]

The fact that Calvin was knowledgeable in law makes the problem of the separation of the two realms even stickier than had he been merely a pastor with a passion for social righteousness. But here Calvin the "lawyer" and pastor showed that he distinguished the two areas—the concern of the church and the concern of the state. That one advised and influenced the other is undeniable. He would not have considered this wrong.

In the later *Ordonnances sur les Mariages* we see again Calvin's concern not only for decency and order but also for the Word of God, and for that basic equality between men and women which has been partially restored in Christ.[20] The couple standing before the minister just before the sermon to take their vows were taking a serious step, one of intense concern, not only for themselves, but also for the church and the republic. That every possible aid to the success of that relationship be theirs, and every eventuality taken care of in case of failure, was the intent of the ordinance. We shall look at several of its features.

The first striking freedom evident in the document was the concern that those who marry do so of their own free will. This is at variance with the picture we usually have of that period when wills, dowries, and inheritances often made marriage such a serious concern, politically and financially, that in many places arranged marriages were the rule. Here, such arrangements are recognized as quite legitimate, but not against the will of the partners. Article 8 reads:

> That no father may force his children into whatever marriage may seem good to him without their good pleasure and consent, but that the son or daughter who may not wish to accept the party which the father may wish to give him, may excuse himself, retaining modesty and reverence always, and the refusal will not entail any punishment by the father; the same will be observed for those under guardianship.[21]

Article 7 underlines this freedom of choice: the dowry must be paid even when a couple marry without parental consent, as long as the couple are of age (20 for men, 18 for women). If the marriage was legally made and contracted without parental consent "because of the negligence or over-rigor of their parents," then the dowry or financial settlement must be "as if they had consented."[22]

The second, and more striking, freedom written into the marriage laws was the freedom of the woman from the onerous double standard which had been practiced in Christendom from time immemorial. The regulation we are concerned with comes under the general heading "Causes for which a marriage may be annulled."

> Although from antiquity the right of the woman has not been equal to that of her husband in case of divorce, since according to the witness of the apostle the obligation is mutual and reciprocal pertaining to the marital bed [*la cohabitation du lict*], and because in that regard the wife is not more subject to her husband than the husband to the wife; if a man is convicted of adultery and the wife demands to be separated from him, it should be granted her as well, unless by good admonitions one is able to reconcile them. Nevertheless, if the wife should fall into adultery by the obvious blame of her husband, or the husband by the wife, so that both are culpable, or if it is verified that some deceit has been committed for the purpose of divorce, in this case they are not allowed to request it.[23]

This is a good illustration of the mutual regard and basic equality which Calvin believed to have been true originally and to be partially reconstituted in Christ. It also illustrates the fact that

Calvin was concerned with legality, not for its own sake, but for the sake of harmonious human relationships, as well as the honor of God. Pure legalism would never have taken into account the blame of the "innocent" party in a marriage disrupted by adultery.

One has the impression that Genevan morality was not exceptionally high despite Calvin's preaching, and that couples were not above that same deceit practiced in England today, where the accusation of adultery is necessary to obtain divorce. This was perhaps why the deceit (*fraude*) clause was written into the ordinance. On 31 October 1548, François Favre, father-in-law of Ami Perrin, came to the Consistory to demand a divorce on the grounds of adultery, but (so Calvin thought) more likely for financial reasons. Since François also confessed adultery, Calvin argued that the divorce might just as well be granted his wife, and warned the pastors that the whole thing might be a case of collusion between the two. The outcome is not discussed, so it is not clear how this was worked out, except it must have been one of the many causes of friction between Calvin and the Favre family.[24]

The concern for the wife's rights went so far as to make sure she was not mistreated by her husband.

> If it be known that a husband treats his wife badly, beating and tormenting her, or that he threatens to outrage her in some manner, or he is known to have an unbridled temper, that he be sent before the Council in order that express prohibitions be made against beating her, under certain punishment.[25]

However, there is no indication that wife-beating was added to adultery and desertion (which seems to have presumed adultery) as grounds for divorce. Adultery was an obvious reason, since biblical; desertion not so obvious to us today perhaps, although a discussion with welfare workers or assistant county attorneys will generally reveal that the problem is still with us to an astonishing degree. The absence of a husband for seven years was sufficient to give a woman grounds for remarriage, evidently on the assumption that he was dead. *Abondonment par debauche-*

ment or some other evil reason in such a way that he could not be reached was also grounds for divorce.

The marriage contract—even before the ceremony—was considered binding if made seriously before two witnesses. This did not mean drinking promises, as is evident from the claim against Jean de la Forest by the daughter of Berthod de Satigny. She claimed before the Consistory that Jean had promised to marry her. He denied it, saying they had been drinking together and that she toasted him in the *nom de mariage*, but he did not respond. The Consistory must have enjoyed their joke of sending the couple to the Council "in order to make them drink a little water," i.e., probably prescribing three days in jail on bread and water. The promise of marriage was declared null.[26] But if the promise was a serious one, breaking it was extremely difficult. We saw earlier that Philibert Berthelier ran afoul of that regulation when he attempted to break a marriage contract between himself and Jeanne Pignon because her fortune was not what he had supposed.[27] This was the beginning of the influential Berthelier's fight with the Consistory and Calvin, which finally led to his exile and the beheading of his brother. The Consistory sent the case to the Council with a negative recommendation, and on 27 August 1548, the Council decreed that the promise of marriage would not be broken.[28] Whether such a decision was to the interest of the two parties is not clear, but that such a contract was binding, thus removing the temptation to easy promises, is evident.

Other actions in the area of sexual morality were about what we would expect. Adulterers were not allowed to marry.[29] A 1547 edict notes that no punishment had been given to "women pregnant by fornication" because they couldn't be sent to jail in that condition, and certainly not after delivery—so something had to be done. The result was that the women had to appear at worship on Sunday at the great sermon (second sermon on Sunday morning) and "cry mercy to God and to justice, so that they repent of their sins."[30] Another problem had to do with those who contracted marriage but fornicated before the ceremony. Calvin and Beza both proposed to the Council that when

such couples came to the church for the ceremoney "the minister make public declaration of their fault which they ought also
to recognize in order to undo the scandal." [31] Four months later
the penalty against fornication was raised from six days on bread
and water to nine days, plus a fine; if they tumbled in a second
time, then besides that penalty they had to appear in church before the sermon and make reparation.[32] It would seem that community pressure was the main censure in this case, a punishment
that depended a great deal on community consensus. No doubt
the spirit of Calvin influenced that consensus a great deal as the
years went on.

Choisy's conclusion on the subject of marriage under Calvin is the best summation I have seen.

> This legislation raises some serious objections today, because it
> consecrates the intrusion of the public powers in private matters,
> the usage of physical constraint in an area that ought to be re-
> moved from that, and finally the complete absence of religious
> liberty. But it is penetrated by a powerful spirit of morality, the
> law is put to the service of the Christian ethic [morale], all the
> prescriptions have for an end the purifying of morals in lifting
> the institution of marriage, in making the importance of holi-
> ness felt, in giving to the family—basic to the social order—a solid
> organization. It is, with the school and the Calvinist diaconate,
> one of the better elements of the theocratic system, one of the
> most happy applications of the principle of the authority of the
> Word of God.[33]

To this I would only object that all societies have considered
marriage something more than simply a private matter, hence
public powers have always intruded, and therefore this legislation surely cannot be regarded as a consecration of this intrusion.
The strict separation of private and public, like spiritual and
temporal, has never been possible. That some attempt to demar-
cate was made is an effort attributable to Calvin's training in both
canon and Roman law. The attempt to enforce ecclesiastical
censure by the temporal sword, however, presents more difficulty. To this we turn.

CHAPTER IX

Church and Society:
The Difficulty
of Sheathing Swords

CALVIN'S GENEVA was a city with all the problems of its age. It had to deal with heretics and confessed spreaders of the plague, but also with chickens that left droppings in church and a cemetery too close and therefore too offensive; [1] with chimneyless and privyless houses, and nurses who endangered the lives of infants by sleeping with them; [2] with serious problems of defense against Savoy, and the constant problems of getting enough wheat to feed the people.

In that city the stature of Calvin grew as the years went on. Nothing seems to have been beneath his notice, and no duty too trivial for the Council to ask his advice. In addition to being chief pastor, lecturer at the college, and ofttimes law codifier, and in addition to his voluminous correspondence, his ecumenical, apologetical, and polemical efforts, and his diplomatic concerns, the little world of Geneva continually called for his best efforts. It was Calvin who complained to the Consistory about the high cost of dying, when the undertakers—following their practice of eating and drinking at the expense of the relatives of the deceased—ate and drank a poor man's supper.[3] At a period when he was involved in renewal of the federation with Berne, but also devastated by the adultery of his sister-in-law with his own servant, he and three members of the Council were appointed a commission to examine a new invention, that was supposed to make stoves, furnaces, ovens, and fireplaces heat at half the expense.[4] From furnace examiner he must needs turn to literary criticism, to decide whether a *cantique* written by young Michel Roset to celebrate the renewal of the alliance was worth presentation. Roset's thrill at being involved in the alliance negotiations at the age of twenty-six must have been immeasurably heightened by hearing his work praised by Calvin, who "found it beautiful and elegant in poetry, sense, substance, and understanding." [5]

But in more serious matters he was also available. As we have seen, it was Calvin whose advice finally proved acceptable to the city when it had to decide how far to help Lyons in defense of Reformation in 1562, when the city of Geneva felt threatened as well. No wonder the Council refused to allow him to travel to France to take part in the Poissy negotiations unless "some notable hostages" were received in return! [6]

As Monter puts it: "In Genevan history, all roads lead eventually to Calvin." [7] His ability to distinguish the spiritual and the temporal was uncommon for his day; his refusal to allow the spiritual be subject to the temporal was uncommon to Protestantism in his day; his ability to suffuse the temporal with the values of the spiritual without robbing the former of its identity is instructive for our day.

But not everything was well in the permeation of Calvin's thought into Genevan politics and society. We shall survey briefly the actual relationship between the Genevan church and the political arm, and then criticize the harshness that too often reflects badly on Calvin's influence at this critical point in his practice of Christian ministry.

The Church in Politics

We have argued elsewhere that the theoretical separation of church and state existed for Calvin more in theory than in practice. By his words Calvin expressed an ideal of separation; by his practice it is quite clear that separation for Calvin did not mean what it does for most Americans today.

> The gospel is not to change the administration [*polices*] of the world, and to make laws which pertain to the temporal state. It is very true that Kings, Princes, and Magistrates ought always to consult the mouth of God and to conform themselves to His

Word; but our Lord has given them liberty to make the laws which they know to be proper and useful by the rule which is committed to them.[8]

We have seen, however, that Calvin fought for the church's right to enforce its discipline on its members in such a way that city officials feared it was usurping the liberty of the magistrates. We would expect the line to be very hard to define and to see Calvin and the other pastors constantly stepping into the political circle both as individuals and as representatives of the church in Geneva.

Nothing illuminates better Calvin's insistence that as individuals the pastors have full political duties and privileges than his argument when the Perrinists denied the pastors their right to vote. All the city's clergy except Calvin were received into the *bourgeoisie* when they were sworn into office, and this carried with it the right to vote in General Council. The Perrinists, as part of their war against overzealous pastors, took from them the right to attend or vote, citing the practice of the priests in Roman Catholic days. But Calvin argued that they were not priests, that unlike them the pastors did not wish to be exempt from temporal judges, and therefore the comparison was faulty.[9] He lost the argument, as we have seen, but his point was clear.

Calvin's own involvement is pointed up in his efforts to maintain the federation with Berne. This alliance was absolutely necessary to Geneva's independence, and in both instances when it was essential that it be renewed despite Berne's dislike of Geneva's internal affairs, Calvin was picked to help in the negotiations. In 1541 the deposed "Artichauds" were the friends of Berne, and Calvin was enemy, therefore, to both. Yet he worked patiently in the political arena and wins praise from the balanced Roget.[10] The second negotiations were even more difficult, for they stretched over a several-year period immediately after the fall of the Perrinists and their flight to the protection of Berne. We have already noted Calvin's efforts then, but have scarcely indicated how dependent upon him the city was. The final renewal agreement had little in it of religious matters, but dealt with the defense of Geneva against aggressors, the inviolability of the two cities from molestation (here the Word of God is named, however, as a cause for which some outsider might attempt such molestation), the adjudication of differences between the cities, imprisonment for debts of citizens of the two, and other matters mainly economic and contractual in nature.[11] How many pastors would involve themselves in such grubby bargaining when there are "spiritual" matters in plenty to take care of? But Calvin subjected himself to the political arm, worked with all the legal knowledge he had learned from his early training, and labored to effect a "perpetual alliance" firm enough to continue long after he was gone. The only extra pay he would accept from the city was the gift of wine.

The real problem here is not to find evidence that the church under Calvin's leadership meddled in the political arena, but to ascertain whether Calvin considered the church to be *over* the magistrate in any way reminiscent of the medieval Pope Boniface's bull *Unam Sanctam*, where "temporal authority [is] subject to spiritual." [12] He did not, of course. This is evident from his concern that kings, princes, and magistrates have the freedom to rule as God has given them liberty to do so. Even Eugene Choisy, as we have seen, who described the Calvinistic regime as a "theocracy," makes clear that this did not mean the domination of the church over the state, or the clergy over the political government.[13] But it did mean for Calvin a vast, all-encompassing concern for the way the government handled its affairs. Calvin was an almost thoroughgoing secularist in the sense that he understood the gospel to be irrevocably concerned with the world. And the magistrate who did not "consult the mouth of God and conform . . . to His Word" would find that the mouth of God (here, Calvin!) was giving advice anyway.

It may be that this concern for the world was overparticular. Berthold Haller, reformer and chief pastor in Berne, wrote in 1554, just when Calvin's trials were hardest: "I do not know any one among us [ministers at Berne] who accuse Calvin of heresy. But the truth is that some of ours love him very little because he seems to be mixed up in too many affairs." [14] But Choisy admitted that much of the concern for morals and decency on the part of the church, i.e., by the Consistory, was commendable:

It intervenes in order to re-establish peace and unity in families, in order to recall individuals to their duty; it takes in hand with a commendable energy reforms favorable to the small and the weak; it sends for and censures the lazy and the idle, the fathers and creditors who are too harsh; it shows itself without mercy for usurers, monopolizers, and speculators, for merchants who defraud their clients. It combats the rudeness of the mores of the time, the brutality of men, the negligence in the care given to the ill. . . . It interdicts the Supper to "scandalous" persons, that is to say, those guilty of lying, fraud, or bad conduct.[15]

The theoretical separation, then, was honored in a sense: the pastors did not try to make laws. But they tried to influence the making and enforcing of good laws—laws of all kinds pertaining to the lives of men—and certainly at times stepped over that hazy boundary between concern and domination that is always difficult to delineate. Too many problems that another age might consider political or economic seemed to Calvin and the other pastors to be religious. And their influence, as we have seen and will see, was brought to bear directly upon the Councils of Geneva.

Peter's Sword in Caesar's Hand

The marks of the true church for Luther were the right preaching of the Word and the administration of the dominical sacraments (Baptism and the Supper). To these marks the radical reformers added a third, that of godly discipline within the redeemed community. This led the radicals, such as Menno Simons, to develop intricate and rather legalistic guidelines and procedures whereby the church could exercise excommunication (or the ban) and thereby keep the church pure. It was a fateful decision when Calvin chose to include this godly discipline as the third mark of the church. The other two major branches of the Reformation—Lutheran and Anglican—did not do so. Had Calvinism been confined to little pockets of godly piety, as with the Anabaptists, then the problems this raised would have been self-contained, producing stability and purpose within the redeemed community. But Calvin understood church and state to be coterminous, the church to be concerned for the whole of life. So the inclusion of godly discipline optimally would be accepted by the total society. This is what is really meant by the term "theocracy."

But if all society is governed by this discipline, as well as by the ordinary legalities that all societies must maintain, then the ecclesiastical sword (discipline) must be wielded by the police arm of the state. This did not mean in Geneva, as it did with Pope Boniface two and a quarter centuries earlier, that the church controlled the state, but only that in certain cases ecclesiastical censure required state punishment. Nor is this entirely strange to modern secular man, for the modern state still punishes adulteries, fornications, desertions, and other "consistorial" matters if they endanger the common good.

But in Geneva the church's call for the use of the secular sword was often quite shrill, not only when seen in retrospect but even by contemporaries. The long process of dismissing de Ecclesia from the ministry is an illustration. The discussion between the Company of Pastors and Council over that sad figure ran on for exactly four years, the pastors wanting to dismiss their wife-beating, heretical, insolent, incorrigible, usurious brother; the Council either unconvinced or unable to fire him. And when it was all over, Pierre Viret, in Lausanne, informed the brethren that, unknown to them, the Council gave de Ecclesia a good recommendation to the burghers of Berne. The secular officials simply refused to wield the sword, and since the church-state entente was such that the church's discipline was merely verbal, ecclesiastical discipline did not happen.[16]

If the church's weakness is exposed in the affair of Pastor Philip, its strength is exhibited in another strange situation. For in the affair of names not to be given children at baptism, church pressure caused the state to exercise its authority in an area clearly removed from its rightful province (although modern secular France continues to make such ludicrous prohibitions). It all began because too many babies were being named after St. Claude, a local saint, and therefore the name of an *jdole*. Calvin came to the Council twice late in August 1546 over this problem, getting nowhere. Then a ruckus broke loose at St. Gervais when one of the pastors refused to baptize a child "Claude" and insisted on naming him Abraham. Finally, after Calvin had wearied the Council to death with the matter, *Messieurs* proclaimed an edict prohibiting the use of certain names: idols, such as Claude and Mama; the three kings (presumably Caspar, Melchior, and Balthazar); names of offices, such as Baptiste, Iuge, Evangeliste; names pertaining to deity, such as Dieu le filz, Espeoir, Emanuel, Saulveur, or Jesus; inept or absurd names, Sepulchre, Croix, Typhaine, Nouel, Pasques, Pentecoste, Toussainctz, Dimenche, Chrestien (because common to all); names with bad sounds, such as Comin, Mermet, Sermet, or Allemande; double names; or corrupted names, such as Tyvan or Tevenot for Estienne, or Monet in place of Simon.[17]

Of course, many of these names might well have been refused by the ministers. To name a child Sepulchre or God-the-Son is to do him no favor. But for *Messieurs* to pass an ordinance prohibiting names—some, like Claude and Balthasar, belonging to Councilmen—strikes us as ridiculous, and evidently struck the Council the same way. Here ecclesiastical influence was exerted in a farcical, if not hurtful, manner.

Human Solidarity and the Rights of the Individual

For the past one hundred years mankind has found itself torn between two unchristian theories of man, Marxist collectivism and radical individualism. Propagandists for both views rival each other in the denatured rationalism of their respective anthropologies. Neither view, whether expressed by a Lenin or a Robert Welch, has room for the obligation to love one's neighbor, which was preached (if often broken) by the church in the Middle Ages and preached (if often broken) by the pastors of Geneva. The partially reconstituted human life of man—in Calvin's theology—must be a life in loving community. In discussing the Supper, Calvin wrote:

> We shall benefit very much from the Sacrament if this thought is impressed and engraved upon our minds: that none of the brethren can be injured, despised, rejected, abused, or in any

way offended by us, without at the same time, injuring, despising, and abusing Christ by the wrongs we do; that we cannot disagree with our brethren without at the same time disagreeing with Christ; that we cannot love Christ without loving him in the brethren; that we ought to take the same care of our brethren's bodies as we take of our own; for they are members of our body; and that, as no part of our body is touched by any feeling of pain which is not spread among all the rest, so we ought not to allow a brother to be affected by any evil, without being touched with compassion for him.[18]

In order to preserve a degree of purity in the church, the Body of Christ, that Body—though bound together by the love of God—must exercise internal discipline. Calvin's discussion of that discipline is really quite moderate. He called for private admonitions for smaller or private sins, public admonitions for notorious sins, and excommunication for "flagitious and enormous crimes." The latter was practiced for three ends: that God be not dishonored by numbering with the Body of Christ such "foul and decaying members"; that the good be not corrupted by constant association with the wicked; and that those censured be led to repentance. The latter end means that the excommunicated brother, though now a stranger to Christ, is still, paradoxically, a brother, else "there is danger lest we soon slide down from discipline to butchery." [19]

So far, so good. We know from Calvin's preaching that he tried to reform Geneva from the pulpit, but we also recognize that private admonitions were his way of dealing with smaller sins. The public admonitions sometimes got out of hand, as when he called the Council a "Council of the devil" from the pulpit— but it is easy to recognize the temptation. Excommunications seem to have been handled pretty much as he said.

The problem arises at this point: for many sinners the way led straight from the ecclesiastical censure of the Consistory (made up, you will recall, of Council members and preachers) to state punishment inflicted by the Council. Often the punishment was written directly into the church ordinances.[20] And this welding of ecclesiastical censure and the temporal sword was part and parcel of Calvin's view of the duty of the magistrate:

Yet civil government has as its appointed end, so long as we live among men, to cherish and protect the outward worship of God, to defend sound doctrine of piety and the position of the church, to adjust our life to the society of men, to form our social behavior to civil righteousness, to reconcile us with one another, and to promote general peace and tranquillity. . . .

Let no man be disturbed that I now commit to civil government the duty of rightly establishing religion, which I seem above to have put outside of human decision. For, when I approve of a civil administration that aims to prevent the true religion which is contained in God's law from being openly and with public sacrilege violated and defiled with impunity, I do not here, any more than before, allow men to make laws according to their own decision concerning religion and the worship of God.[21]

What often happened in practice was that the human solidarity which men have in Christ, and which is expressed in the church, was defended and pursued in such a manner that the rights of the individual in Geneva were ignored. Throughout the last three chapters, we have argued that generally the church's pursuit of the common weal was beneficial. Here we shall argue that sometimes privacy was violated, the weak were browbeaten and at times physically beaten, and brutality was promoted and condoned in the name of religious and civil harmony. The tension between society and the individual is always likely to tip; in Geneva it sometimes tipped over and distributed horror on the individual.

It is one thing to admonish in private for private sins. It is another to play peeping tom to catch persons in private peccadilloes. We can sympathize with one Jean Guidon who, on 10 May 1553, was brought before the Consistory for swearing by the Body of God and making a ruckus in his home. M. Jean declared ". . . that it was neither fair nor honest to go along the rooftops in order to see what people are doing, and that if he had had a crossbow or a blowtube [*sarbacane*] he would have dislodged those so well informed about what goes on in his house." [22]

This amusing practice proved quite deadly in the affair of Jaques Gruet. On 28 June 1547, someone had attached a note to the pulpit at St. Pierre's. Aimed primarily at Pastor Abel Poupin, who had been particularly vitriolic in Consistory hearings with the Favre family, it was addressed to "fat belly and your companions." The note warned them to leave the city, referred to them as "fucking renegade priests," and threatened them with the fate of an ecclesiastic who was killed in the riots preceding independence.[23] The author of the note was thought to be Jaques Gruet, *bon vivant* and freethinker. He was arrested, and confessed under threat of torture that he had composed the document, though it was not in his handwriting. Then his quarters were searched, and books and papers showing his heretical views came to light. Among other items to anger Calvin and/or the Council: he spoke well of the pope, but referred to Calvin as *abuseur, ambitieux, fier, glorieux, pertinax;* he wrote, concerning Moses, "That horned one says much and proves nothing," and "all laws, both divine and human have been made by the caprice of men"; he objected to officers of justice investigating the private lives of individuals; and worst, from the magistrates' point of view, was a letter in which he advised a Frenchman to write to Francis I (*du grand Turc*) to come to close the mouth of Calvin. The latter was treason, or close to it, but Gruet argued that it was not meant seriously, and it had not been sent, anyway. Imprisoned the day the note was found, he was tried before the Council daily from 2 July for three weeks. It is interesting that the Consistory had nothing to do with this trial, though part of the charge was heresy. Less than a month after his incarceration he was sentenced to death for blasphemy and rebellion, "in the name of the Father, of the Son, and of the Holy Spirit. Amen." [24]

The public, then, was protected, but not the individual. His house was searched. Every confession he made was extracted either by torture or by the threat of torture. The verdict was already in, and he had only to confess his crimes and to be put away. Thus the solidarity of the human community required the blood of the one who threatened that community. It is difficult, of course, to abstain from imposing modern ideas upon the Reformer and the magistrates of Geneva. They did, after all, live in the sixteenth century. And they did develop a siege mentality, not surprisingly. But there was nothing in the arrest, trial, and beheading of Jaques Gruet to give us reason to think that any regard whatsoever was had for his rights as a man.

It could be argued that a deplorable lack of private morality in that day justified some of the extreme measures taken. Extracts from the *Registres du Conseil* prior to the Reformation indicate that the priests and monks of Catholic days were constantly getting into trouble because of prostitutes and lewd women.[25] Some of the early Protestant pastors fared no better, Simon Moreaux being deposed in 1545, the next year two losing their posts together for attending the baths "nud a nud" with one Huguenne and her sister, and Jean Fabri being removed for suspicion as late as 1556.[26] The absence of public disapproval is well illustrated by the case of the *lieutenant de justice*, Jean Ami Curtet, who was tried and imprisoned for fornication, degraded from office, and compelled to seek pardon from the Two Hundred in 1536. Six months later he was elected first syndic, the highest post in Geneva! [27]

But there was more to the defense of public solidarity than simply chaotic moral conditions. One could, I think, say that the authorities went out of their way to search for dissenters. A case in point was that of the card-manufacturer Pierre Ameaux in 1545. Ameaux was a member of the Small Council who complained to a private gathering in his home that Calvin was an evil man, only a Picard, and had preached false doctrine.[28] The Council duly examined the evidence—brought in by an informer at the private gathering—and decided Ameaux should pay a fine and, with bared head and torch in hand, kneel to the ground and confess his sins. But this did not placate Calvin, who wanted a harsher sentence imposed upon one who could call his ministry into question. Before the whole quarrel was over, the Council was split into two factions; the original prosecutor, Claude Roset (Michel's father), resigned his task in disgust at the overzealousness; the Consistory made protracted statements in favor of Calvin; a riot took place in St. Gervais; pastor Henri de la Mare was cashiered for friendship with Ameaux; and the unlucky card-manufacturer spent more than two months in prison, lost his office, and had to make a complete tour around in the city in a shirt, with head bared, carrying a lighted torch, and then kneel to the ground confessing to libel. He also had to pay the expenses of the trial.[29] Christian love simply departed in this sad affair as Calvin pressed rigorously for civic solidarity, which could only be guaranteed if dissent was put down severely. One reads the account even today with shame and sorrow.

There is evidence that the Consistory did not always perform its task with moderation. In the drawn-out affair between the Favre family and the Consistory, the Council had to counsel both sides to have more care for their language. Pastor Abel Poupin was picked out pointedly and warned not "to use what he uses against those who are called to the Consistory." [30] Since he had called François Favre a dog, it is no surprise that Favre's daughter referred to Poupin as a "fat loin of a French pig" and nearly rode him down with her horse when he was fleeing to the family estates in Bernese-controlled territory to avoid prison. The next day the Council made a special resolution to the effect that people should be treated more graciously in Consistory meetings. Thus suspicion arises that in practice Calvin's views concerning private and public admonition really amounted to something only a few steps removed from an inquisition. However, it must be admitted that in the case of the Favres, they probably got everything they were asking for.

Calvin's instincts were for the good of the public, but too often the good of the individual—which must be protected if in the long run the public is to benefit—was not protected. If anything, Calvin himself was harder on the wrongdoer than others in the Genevan community. An example of this occurred in 1563 when Jacques de St. Mortier was arrested for embezzlement and theft and would not confess. The Council gave the case to five judges, one of them Calvin, whose office does not make clear how he came to be involved in this bit of judiciary or magistracy. The other four judges concluded that the offender should be whipped, but Calvin that he should be put to death! The Council, still perplexed, sent him to the crane (*grue*) and then released him after this torture, although he never confessed.

Calvin was sure of his guilt despite lack of proof and would have sacrificed the individual for the sake of community.[31]

However, in at least two instances Calvin tried to intervene to secure better conditions for prisoners and easier death for the condemned. In the Servetus case, as everyone knows, Calvin wished for death, then burning. Nine years earlier, on 9 March 1545, Calvin had come to the Council pleading for better treatment for prisoners convicted of spreading the plague by smearing excretion from infected bodies upon doorposts. The whole story sounds like witchcraft trials where people actually believed they had sold their own souls to the Devil. Anyway, the executioner was asked to make sure those being burned were already dead. A small thing, perhaps, but of some consequence at a time of fear and horror at the plague and those convicted of spreading it (*empoysonneurs*) from house to house.[32]

Sixteenth-century Geneva was probably not made a more merciful state because of the influence of Calvin. In some ways, it does not seem to have been the aim to treat prisoners badly. Jailing was common, many councillors having seen the inside of L'Evêché themselves, and generally the treatment there must have been pretty good by medieval standards. The Council kept strict surveillance over the man and woman in charge. But the common method of third-degree interrogation was torture, pure and simple, and there is no hint that Calvin ever tried to protect the individual from this trial. Punishments often were rude and cruel also. In addition to public whippings, tongues were pierced and ears trimmed, people were branded with the mark of the *Seigneurie*, and at times burning was done in effigy.[33]

All of the items mentioned in this section are part of the material taught in humanities classes or reviewed without understanding by a Stefan Zweig. They are dished up as if Calvin contributed nothing to Protestantism, but simply brought the Inquisition into the Reformation. This, as we have argued, is simply not so. These conditions had long existed everywhere. But they do show the Reformer in a bad light precisely because his theory was weighted toward love and justice. They serve, perhaps, as warnings (if we need any) that even the common good must be protected with discretion, that evildoers must be tried justly and punished mercifully, that the public weal does not demand individual woe. Or, as C. S. Lewis has said somewhere: It takes a saint to make an inquisitor. That is, you have to care more about good and evil than most of us do to want to take extreme measures against evil.

Calvin's Political Blinders

Before we leave the subject of the church and the sword of the magistrate, we should say a word about the one instance when Calvin's religious convictions caused political blindness and outright injustice. It should be said at first, however, that such was not always the case. As he looked afar, Calvin could see quite clearly the earthen vessels God had raised up to foster and protect the Reformation. He had no delusions about the strength or morals of the Prince de Condé, for example, nor about King Anthony of Navarre (father of Henry of Navarre, Henry IV), who for a time espoused the Huguenot cause. One simply cannot imagine Calvin allowing a Philip of Hesse to con him into permitting bigamy.

We have recounted in Chapter II some of the events surrounding the defeat of the Perrinists. There is no need to rehash them here, except to recall that the evening of 16 May 1555 a riot broke out in the streets of Geneva, which was interpreted by the majority of the Council to have been an attempted coup d'etat. There was almost no evidence for that charge, and in the surrounding cantons opposition to the executions and the flight of the more fortunate almost amounted to a storm. Haller wrote to Bullinger that "Calvin is blamed now by those who, up till now, were always his supporters." Later, he wrote that one could hardly find one person in a hundred to speak well of Calvin. François Hotman wrote from Basel that "Calvin isn't spoken of here any better than in Paris." And Musculus from the same city lamented: "The hatred around here for our well-loved brother Calvin increases every day." [34]

Calvin's response to these calumnies, contained in a long

letter to Bullinger (to whom the other letters were addressed), is certainly disappointing. He avers he was not present at the tortures, which he describes as quite light, and defends this barbarity by saying:

> But it was quite natural to do this; without that they would have denied everything, being encouraged by their adherents. The judges were not able to allow that they deny the plot, since it was evident.[35]

Here, as later with the embezzler, Calvin presumed the guilt of the accused. The trial was quite unnecessary under such a judiciary. That there was a plot at all is denied by more balanced scholars such as Roget and Williston Walker. As the latter says,

> . . . the facts speak too clearly against the existence of any well-planned conspiracy to overturn the Genevan government to make that interpretation tenable.

Of Calvin's assurance that it was a plot to overthrow the magistrates, he writes,

> There is no reason to doubt that Calvin and most of his sympathisers sincerely believed that the affair was a deep-laid plot. He thought no good of Perrin, and Vandel. Their work was, and had long been, in his judgment one hostile to God. But it was a very convenient belief, also, in the existing political situation.[36]

Indeed it was a convenient belief. The usually perspicacious Calvin, who cared not for the appearances put up by men, was in this case certain that Perrin had troops waiting to attack. Despite the fact that only one man received a stone on the ear, the whole city was presumed to have narrowly escaped assault. Dislike for the silly, comical, pugnacious, infuriating *comique Caesar* and his friends turned Calvin's judgment to nonsense in this affair. The common weal, the solidarity of the community, had to be protected.

Conclusion: The Saint and the State

If the attempt to impose a godly discipline for the sake of the common good sometimes resulted in evil for the individual rather than good, this does not mean that the Calvinist understanding of the dynamic relationship between church and state was in the long run bad. There is something very positive to be said about the way Genevan politics became saturated with moral considerations. To understand public office as a charge, to view politics as a conscientious and continuous labor, is far from bad doctrine.[37] Historians with a penchant for the medieval have long regarded the ability of Calvinists to overturn such social traditions as the divine right of Stuart kings and to dispense with other traditional social structures as an evil which has denatured modern social existence. Revolutionaries know better. Medieval society was largely one where common men were nonparticipants. "Calvinism taught previously passive men the styles and methods of political activity and enabled them successfully to claim the right of participation in that on-going system of political action that is the modern state."[38] Rising nations and tribes everywhere today are claiming precisely this right to participate politically which Calvinist concern for the total community taught Genevans in the middle of the sixteenth century.

Franklin H. Littell, whose sympathies in the Reformation period lie with the radicals, not the Calvinists, argues that in Germany under Hitler the active resistance to Nazism was largely Calvinist because the Reformed tradition of lay initiative was better equipped to cope with persecution than the "pyramided church structures" of German Lutheranism.[39] Here again is evident a responsibility for society fostered by the Calvinist insistence that the will of God must extend to the total community.

These short paragraphs are not meant in any way to mitigate the evils we saw earlier in this chapter. Instead, they are meant to show that the Calvinist position inculcated an involvement in the political order, for better and for worse. It was in no sense pacifist or withdrawn from the total society. Calvinists were instead active and aggressive, and participated in that revolutionary ferment—so little understood by many who lived in the midst of it—which was even in the sixteenth century changing the physiognomy and psychology of northern and western Europe.

But the evils sometimes perpetrated in the name of human love and justice must also be examined in terms of the thought of Calvin himself. To this subject we now turn.

CHAPTER X

Success and Failure:
A Critique of the Permeation
of Calvin's Thought

ONE HAS only to glance at the preceding chapters to see that the author counts the positive results of Calvin's views and actions on Geneva's community of saints far more important than the failures. However, we must attempt to answer the problem raised in the preceding chapter about Calvin's failures. The success, the positive results of his views, will not be neglected, but are not so puzzling. If the Christian gospel, which proclaims the love of God to be inextricably bound up with Jesus Christ, whose compassion for humankind took him even to the Cross, if this good news will not have a beneficial effect on men in society when once it grips a man of Calvin's stature—then it is of dubious value. That it did, for the most part, have this salutary effect is a main thesis of this study. But the gospel at times became a club, an excuse for foolishness and insensitivity, for torture, even death. What went wrong?

In the following pages, we shall briefly examine two ways of interpreting our data, and from these will turn to the crux of the problem, Calvin's doctrine of Christ.

A Socio-Economic Critique

Economists speak of three ways of evaluating an economic model: its conformity with the economic facts of life, its acceptance by contemporary policy-makers, and its inner consistency. We shall examine Calvin's socio-economic views under these three headings.

First, how did Calvin's views conform with the facts of life in his age? Economically considered, we can see some problems. Calvin was neither by profession nor by interest a scientific student of economy. Nor was anyone else in his period. He had a high view of the value of commerce for his day, particularly when compared to the evaluation of other theologians. In this respect he was in tune with the direction of European progress, where the growth of larger economic units through the emergence of the great nation-states, plus the discoveries of huge amounts of precious metal in the New World and the complete exploitation of the silver mines of Germany, all contributed to the tremendous burst of commercial traffic which Geneva was already party to. His views on usury tended to be realistic in principle, but probably were repressive in practice.

Calvin's ideal society—and one he helped mold in Geneva —was very protectionist or paternalistic. Again, we can say this was in general conformity to his time, and was an expression for Calvin of the common good which the biblical message makes clear to be God's plan for the life of men.

We have already examined hit-and-miss the second criterion: the acceptance of his views by the city's policy-makers. Like Adam Smith and John Maynard Keynes but unlike the French Physiocrats, Calvin's views made a strong impact upon the civil leadership of his day. The Council was responsive to the pastors, and particularly to the head of that venerable company. After the defeat of the Perrinists, the influence of Calvin loomed over Geneva like the Salève mountain at her back. He was consulted about almost everything—literature and laws, troops and taverns, finances and furnaces; name it, and Calvin was involved. After his death that influence was extended (though not quite so persuasively so) in the person of Theodore Beza, who remembered not only the name but also the concerns of Calvin as he and the other pastors aimed their "cannon balls of Christian Socialism" at *Messieurs* when they stepped out of line.

The third criterion, inner consistency, reveals the flaw in Calvin's generally benevolent social creed. How bound together in common humanity and by Christian compassion is worldly

society, how interdependent and compassionate is human existence! But Calvin's influence promoted woe as well as weal. In
Geneva the tie that binds often turned out to be a noose; Christian discipline degenerated into pettiness, foolishness, and even
cruelty for the sake of the faithful, and in the name of the Father
and of the Son and of the Holy Spirit. There was more here than
the problem which every society faces of balancing society's
rights and the individual's. In Geneva the balance was not maintained. Contemporaries of lesser acumen than Calvin in neighboring cities were perplexed by this rigor that, had St. Paul applied
it (Haller said), would have excommunicated every person in
Corinth.

So this critique leaves us where we began. By every standard Calvin rates pretty high. Geneva was a much better city for
Calvin's presence. But the dark splotches are exposed, not explained, from this vantage point.

A Political Critique: Church and State

We have returned time and again in this
account to take another look at Calvin's view of the relationship
of the church to the secular state. We have seen that Calvin had
a high regard for the honor of the state and its rightful leaders,
and that his regard for the secular was so great that he did not
propose to place the church over it. Yet he saw the church as
independent in its sphere, in no way subservient to the realm,
the great fault he thought he detected in Germany and England,
as well as in the Catholic countries. The two were to exist side
by side, serving and ruling the same people with mutual respect
and aid. The church did not attempt to prescribe civil laws, nor
the state to usurp spiritual discipline. But the church preserved
its right to speak *as a church* to the state, not just through the
influence it exerted on individual Christians who might be magistrates. It is this last insistence that has called forth the term
"theocratic."

I would defend this as a constructive approach on the part
of Calvin, one that we see arising wherever his influence was

felt, though one sometimes perverted, as any other approach in this area has been perverted. This surely is part of the reason for the terrific ferment Calvin's influence had in nation after nation: overthrow of government in the Low Countries, in Scotland, and —after nearly a century—in England; revolution and war in France; and independence from Spain for the Low Countries. The theocratic stance may be seen in Knox and his arguments with Mary, Queen of Scots; in the ministers at the Westminster Assembly haranguing the members of the Long Parliament; in the theocracy of New England, where the unfortunate attempt to weld an inclusive society to an exclusive, non-Calvinist ecclesiology produced finally so much bitterness and loss. Milton Powell has shown that in the Methodist Episcopal Church in the twenty years prior to our Civil War it was the avowedly activist New England leaders who rejected the conservative approach to slavery—the attempt to evangelize the souls of men who controlled a sinful institution—and consciously adopted a *theocratic stance* over against an evil legal and political institution. Men like Gilbert Haven chose the New England Congregational and Calvinistic approach to the political realm, convinced that it was wrong to think Christian responsibility could be exercised only by individuals in their private capacity as citizens.[1] One of the few bright spots in the German church's response to Nazism was the Barmen Declaration of 1934, where Lutheran, Reformed, and United Churches spoke formally *as the church* against the government's racial and ecclesiastical position.

Even today that theocratic stance is responsible for forcing Presbyterian churches in this country to make public statements of policy in the political and social arena, not just for the sake of its members, but also for the eyes and ears of the world. That Presbyterians often dislike such directives and write articles attempting to show that Calvin ". . . believed that the church should not become involved in outside affairs" is not strange.[2] But it would be strange if Calvin's troop ceased such activity because someone didn't like it or considered such unspiritual activity to be outside the province of Christ's church.

But critics, and critical adherents to Calvin's view of the role of the church vis-à-vis the state, point out that the approach has often been accompanied by a spirit not of Christ at all—a spirit which wants the church not to minister but to be ministered unto. In Geneva one is constantly aware that the church must be protected, her purity must be ensured by the state, her status must be recognized, and her ministers protected from harsh criticism and searching opposition. The student of medieval history does not find this surprising, but the student of the New Testament finds nothing in Christ that justifies his Body to ask and demand such coddling and ornamentation. One may call this a "medieval barnacle" if one wishes, but Calvin had turned back to the sources, back to the New Testament and to the early church, which had no status, few defenders, and precious little protection—nor demanded anything but freedom to preach and teach in defiance of all that state or society could do. In a nutshell: the New Testament advocates for Christians a positive approach to the state, praying for authorities and even railing against them; but one searches in vain for any hint that the church can expect the privileges that Calvin demanded. Why did the barnacles remain?

A Theological Critique: Calvin's Christology

One could approach this problem from several directions. Perhaps the rigorous surveillance of private life in Geneva was merely a "siege syndrome"—perfectly understandable in the light of the political and military vulnerability of the Protestant Rome. Or if Calvin merely clung to medieval theories, then how did the church before Calvin come to demand the position expressed in *Unam Sanctam*? What was Calvin carrying over that threw his views out of shape and contributed to the problems we have raised? But our approach is a different one: we shall try to see if there was in Calvin's theology anything that might have allowed the perversions we have noted, or at least have kept Christian love from wider application. If we can ascribe the benefits of the Calvinist regime to a theology grounded in God's justice and love, then it may be possible to find the defects have their roots in theology as well.

I have chosen, for this purpose, to study Calvin's Christology, his understanding of God's supreme Word to man, the Incarnation of God, the divine humanization. Christology is central in Christian theology. Here, after all, is the primary revelation of God, who may have spoken to man in many and various ways, but spoke finally in his Son. It is in Christ that Christians believe they see normatively what God is like, what he intends, and in Christ's resurrection, hints of the fulfillment of his promises to man. The whole New Testament is the primary witness to God in Christ reconciling the world, and Christian theology has generally understood the Old Testament to be fulfilled in him, its savageries corrected and Yahweh's Word to the prophets now become human.

Not to overstate a hypothesis, let us say that *there is in Calvin's Christology a lack of divine involvement in the sin and despair of humanity which is curiously like the lack of rapport with sinful man seen in Calvin's Geneva.* Let us examine his understanding of the Person of Christ more closely.

Following rather carefully the decree of the Council of Chalcedon (A.D. 451), Calvin's understanding of Christ expresses clearly both his divine and human natures:

> . . . God's natural Son fashioned for himself a body from our body, flesh from our flesh, bones from our bones, that he might be one with us. Ungrudgingly he took our nature upon himself to impart to us what was his, and to become both Son of God and Son of man in common with us.[3]

The picture of the atonement Calvin offers is Anselmic, with the twin ideas of substitution and satisfaction clearly affirmed. He represents Christ as presenting

> our flesh as the price of satisfaction to God's righteous judgment, and, in the same flesh, to pay the penalty that we had deserved.[4]

Like Luther, Calvin was apparently convinced that the only true knowledge of God was the knowledge of God in Christ *for us.* Witness the following epistemological statements:

> [In Scripture] he is shown to us not as he is in himself, but as he is toward us.[5]
> In this ruin of mankind no one now experiences God either as

Father or as Author of salvation, or favorable in any way, until
Christ the Mediator comes forward to reconcile him to us.[6]
For it is not so much our concern to know who he is in himself,
as what he wills to be toward us.[7]

But, strangely enough, Calvin *seemed* to know a great deal about
God apart from Christ; or, at least, the outline of the *Institutes*
is such that he can write for some four hundred pages before he
deals with this central issue in theology. Paul van Buren notes the
same problem:

> Calvin begins his treatment of the doctrine of Reconciliation
> with the problem of fallen man. It is not self-evident, however,
> that this should have been his starting place. Calvin has estab-
> lished in Book I of his *Institutes* that the knowledge of God must
> precede the knowledge of man, and it is precisely this knowl-
> edge of God that has been lost to man, and which now can be
> recovered only by means of God's Word, faithfully heard. *In*
> Christ, that is, we learn what we were *out of* Christ. Would it not
> have been better, therefore, to begin with the solution rather
> than with the problem? [8]

This minor criticism takes on larger proportions when it is
seen in the light of Calvin's treatment of the two natures of
Christ. Calvin's insistence on the complete humanity of Christ
is thoroughgoing. Not only did Christ suffer physically, but the
union of the two natures was such that he could suffer torments
of the soul, he could know fear and loss and sorrow.

> Certainly those who imagine that the Son of God was exempt
> from human passions do not truly and sincerely acknowledge
> him to be a man.[9]
> If Christ had died only a bodily death, it would have been inef-
> fectual. No—it was expedient at the same time for him to un-
> dergo the severity of God's vengeance, to appease his wrath and
> satisfy his just judgment. . . . No wonder, then, if he is said to
> have descended into hell, for he suffered the death that God in
> his wrath had inflicted upon the wicked! . . . in order that we
> might know not only that Christ's body was given as the price
> of our redemption, but that he paid a greater and more excel-
> lent price in suffering in his soul the terrible torments of a con-
> demned and forsaken man.[10]

Calvin goes even further and says that Christ not only feared
death, but his agony can only be explained by asserting that he

also feared the curse and wrath of God. Calvin's concern to assert the complete and true humanity of Christ goes further than most orthodox preachers would dare from the pulpit.

But the problem arises when we ask what share God had in this suffering, this fear and horror of death. We find that at these low points when Christ is most human, closest to the depths of human experience, that the divine nature is *retired* or *reposed*. Commenting on the verse in the Fourth Gospel in which Jesus speaks of his soul being troubled, Calvin writes:

> Nor was it absurd that the Son of God should be troubled like this. *For his divinity was hidden* [*occulta*], *did not put forth its power and, in a sense rested*, that an opportunity might be given for making expiation. . . . He feared, not because he was forced to, but because of his own accord he had subjected himself to fear. Yet we must believe it was not in pretense but in truth that he feared.[11]

When he writes of Jesus' denial of omniscience—the litmus test for examining a man's Christology—Calvin again asserts the true humanity of Christ, but in such a way as to pull back his divinity:

> We must endeavor to find some other meaning which is more suitable [than the Arian claim that Christ did not know the last day]. . . . We know that in Christ the two natures were united into one person in such a manner that each retained its own properties; and more especially *the Divine nature was in a state of repose, and did not at all exert itself*, whenever it was necessary that the human nature should act separately, according to what was peculiar to itself, in discharging the office of mediator. . . . If Christ, as man, did not know the last day, that does not any more derogate from his Divine nature than to have been mortal.[12]

To speak of the divine nature as "hidden," "resting," "in a state of repose," evidences a leaning toward Nestorianism, an oversharp distinction between the two natures of Christ. Van Buren rightly observes that Calvin here again seeks to assert what God must be like by some other criterion than his supreme revelation of himself in Christ.

> Is it not to His own glory that God incarnate, precisely as God, seeks not His own glory? . . . What is the source of Calvin's idea

of glory, yes, and of his idea of divinity, which permits him to
say that they were hidden in God's revelation of Himself in Jesus
Christ? Has God truly revealed Himself in Jesus or not? . . .
What other source does he have for the true nature of the Son of
God, and therefore of God himself? . . . Clearly there is a serious
problem at the very heart of Calvin's theology, a failure to
carry through consequentially his statement that 'they who
imagine God in His naked majesty apart from Christ have an
idol in place of God'.[13]

And commenting on Calvin's approval of Irenaeus' belief that the
divine nature was quiescent when Christ suffered, van Buren
continues his attack:

What is the source of Calvin's knowledge, and of that of Irenaeus before him, of human nature and of divinity that allows
him to measure Christ and assign part of His work to this nature
and part of it to that? Is not the humiliation of Christ the humiliation of God Himself? [14]

Our concern is not so much with Calvin's epistemology as
with the consequences which flow from it. What it means in
practical terms is that God has only hesitantly entered into the
place of sinful man; he is only *somewhat* involved with the human process, with human presumption, pride, anger, stupidity,
and ignorance—all of what received such short sympathy in Calvin's Geneva! Calvin tended to see God abstractly, apart from
Christ, or, conversely, to interpret the concrete self-disclosure
of God in Christ by some abstract standard of what God is in
himself; Calvin was thus able to force into his theology a non-
human rigor which is absent in the Garden of Gethsemane or at
the Cross. Because Calvin saw God as withdrawn from man at
man's worst moments, Calvin could also be withdrawn, unsympa-
thetic at the sight of men in "the stink of filthy flesh" failing in
their response to the love of God in Jesus Christ.

Karl Barth, the greatest theologian to follow in Calvin's path,
once lamented Calvin's exclusion of true and thoroughgoing
humanity from the deity of Christ. Had Calvin pushed on,
Barth says ruefully, "His Geneva would then not have become
such a gloomy affair. His letters would not then have contained
so much bitterness." [15]

The author is aware that this analysis of Calvin's Christology has raised more snakes than we can kill. Was Calvin's Christology orthodox or truly Nestorian? Had he departed from the medieval tradition or from the Chalcedonian formulation? If he did not, then perhaps the heresy lies with the present writer, not with Calvin? All these and many other questions present themselves to us. My own reflection is that Calvin was true to Chalcedon, that he followed scholastic theology, and that the difficulty lies with the impossible task which Chalcedon presents to the biblical theologian.[16] A passage such as "My God, my God, why hast thou forsaken me?" or Jesus' denial of omniscience invites the scholar to be Nestorian or Monophysite in his approach, and of the two, Nestorianism has the virtue of preserving intact the humanity of Jesus Christ. To argue, as some theologians did, that Christ was equivocating, that the human nature, hypostatically united with the divine, knew everything —such a solution swallows the human by the divine nature and leaves one nature, hence Monophysitism.[17] It has the further disadvantage of directly flying in the face of the New Testament witness.

We may test our hypothesis on Calvin's most "inhuman" doctrine. Calvin's well-known doctrine of double predestination, which even he called the "horrible decree," arises out of the same confusion: Calvin knows in some prior way that it is true, and even Scripture cannot shake this most biblical of theologians. If one turns to the New Testament passages that speak of Christ being offered to all or God wishing all to be saved, we find Calvin backing off from the clear meaning of the passages (as Augustine before him). For example, in discussing 1 John 2:2—"he is the expiation for our sins, and not for ours only but also for the sins of the whole world"—Calvin, after scotching "the dreams of fanatics" who make it extend salvation even to the reprobate, writes of the word *all:*

> For John's purpose was only to make this blessing common to the whole church. Therefore, under the word "all" he does not include the reprobate, but refers to all who would believe and those who were scattered through various regions of the earth.[18]

And 1 Timothy 2:3–4—". . . God our Savior, who desires all
men to be saved and to come to the knowledge of the truth"—
gets short shrift as well:

> Hence we see the childish hallucination of those who represent
> this passage to be opposed to predestination. . . . They might
> have some grounds for this if Paul were speaking here about in-
> dividual men. . . . But I say nothing on that subject because it has
> nothing to do with this passage; for the Apostle simply means
> that there is no people and no rank in the world that is excluded
> from salvation; because God wishes that the gospel should be
> proclaimed to all without exception.[19]

So the first "all" means all the church, the second means people
from all ranks. Calvin already knows about predestination,
hence need not wrestle seriously with these passages. Just as
he already knew what was divine and what was human in Christ,
and hence could exclude God from human anguish in Christ.[20]

We have tried not to overstate our case and make a clear
cause-and-effect relationship between Calvin's Christology and
the failure of consistency in his social action. They, at least,
mix well together. For in both failures the same theme is present
—an unwillingness to come completely to grips with the world.
God does not quite wrestle with the depths of human experience
in Christ, but is resting or in hiding. Calvin's Consistory does not
quite take into account the humanness of people—arrogant, ignorant, or foolish—but beats, exiles, and humiliates them. Calvin's
church stands bravely against the state on many occasions, but
sometimes hides behind the government's skirts, demanding protection and insurance from the civic officials, as it asks the state
to coerce and threaten the obstinate and weak. It turns from min-
istering and demands to be ministered unto.

We admit that these same observations could be made
twenty times over in the history of the church. But Calvin rejected so much of what obtained in other centuries and other
lands on the basis of the Word of God. He had in *so many ways
begun to live in the fresh air of a new world*. Is it not possible
that the failure to agonize fully with weak and willful men is
rooted in his semi-failure to understand God's involvement in
human life in Jesus Christ?

This error of Calvin's was not a minor one. The relationship between God and man expressed by the doctrine of double predestination is complete subservience on the part of man. He may acquiesce; he may rebel; but he can hardly assume the mastership over nature, politics, and history which Calvin himself preached in his sermons to the *habitants* of Geneva. This unresolved tension helped create a great number of spiritual heroes—witness the bravery of Pilgrims and Puritans, the realism of a Cromwell. They knew themselves predestined to give man a new beginning. But when the heroics were over and it was time to get with the task of shaping the future, the Calvinist found himself confronted by a tyrant God, not a heavenly Father. If he could not be free spiritually, how could he be free to create human community? It is probably no accident that the theological consequences for Calvinist-influenced cultures have been disastrous. When Lutheranism went modern, God went underground (Hegel, Schleiermacher, Tillich); but Calvinism—more forthrightly—has produced deists and atheists (Hume, Franklin, Paine, van Buren), whose God is either dead or sufficiently removed from ordinary human pursuits to allow man freedom to seize life by himself.

In Geneva "all roads eventually lead to Calvin." [21] In his own person and, for this study, in his city's social and economic policies, we see the impact of a monumental attempt to understand and appropriate the Word of God for human activity. Despite some dark spots, we would not apologize for the impact this man and his city have had on the world during the past four centuries. Perhaps as those churches which call themselves Reformed bring their insights into today's movement for church unity, a total concern for man in the world will profit the whole church of Christ.

PART **III**

Postmortem: The Influence of Calvin

CHAPTER XI

Calvinism and Capitalism: The Weber Thesis in the Light of Calvin's Thought and Practice

AMONG the many arguments that historians have indulged themselves in, perhaps none has been as loud and as tangled as that over the relationship between Protestantism and laissez-faire capitalism as developed by the great German sociologist Max Weber, and supplemented by the religious historian Ernst Troeltsch and the English economic historian R. H. Tawney.[1] I shall begin the chapter with a brief description of Weber's argument linking Calvinism and capitalism, proceed to outline some of the weaknesses, oversimplifications, and objections raised against Weber's study, and conclude by trying to show that despite these problems Weber was insisting on an inescapable element in the relationship between Calvinism and the development of modern Western society.

Weber was struck by the qualitative difference between medieval men of commerce who pursued profit in order to enjoy the benefits of wealth, and those entrepreneurs who emerged about the time of the Reformation, who pursued profit in business as if it were a healthy end in itself. He saw that in comparison with the traditional businessman of the Middle Ages the new enterpreneur had a code of economic conduct which was strikingly different. What would make men, he asked, pursue profit without regard for their own physical welfare, the traditional standards of society, or the good of the community? What could induce Christian men to work unremittingly for money which, when gotten, was not used for wine, women, or song, but was used solely to make more money? What inner drive created a human urge to accumulate capital and then to turn it into more goods or trade? Why did men defy ancient traditions about the evils of gain? Whence came the new traditions of unremitting toil and investment far beyond the modicum necessary to meet the needs of the flesh? What new needs of the spirit had been created which modern economic man took for granted and spent his life in feeding?

He begins his analysis by quoting the thrifty, rationalistic, moralistic advice of Benjamin Franklin, who insisted that time was money and, like money, goods, and credit, had to be used with extreme care that it be turned into profit. This, Weber observes, was capitalism, "the pursuit of profit, and forever renewed profit, by means of continuous, rational, capitalistic enterprise." But what made the spirit of capitalism for Weber was that in Franklin and others this profit-making had become an ethos, a way of life, where unremitting gain is pursued for purposes other than enjoyment. The new man is temperate, reliable, honest, and completely devoted to business. In short, he is a disciplined worldling, or in Weber's terms, a "worldly ascetic."

Weber then notes that this worldly asceticism is much more observable among Protestants than Catholics, and he lays this partly to Luther's belief that a person's worldly labor is his vocation, his calling (*Beruf*). Thus the Christian does God's will in his work, whether he be pastor, farmer, or businessman. But Weber finds that Calvinism, and the various sects he connects with Calvinism (Anabaptists, Quakers, Methodists), produced this worldly asceticism more abundantly than Lutheranism. Why? Weber argues that the impetus for this change came unwittingly from Calvin, and that impetus was the doctrine of predestination, with its twin decrees of election (heaven) and reprobation (hell). The Calvinist had no priest to stand between him and God or to give him the sacraments that would ensure his salvation. He stood before God alone. He was either saved or damned by an arbitrary divine decree. He could, like Calvin, assume that he was predestined to glory and battle subsequent doubts to the contrary. Or, says Weber, he could look for evidences of God's blessing in his worldly calling to prove that

God's attitude toward him was gracious. The result was a human being who strove unremittingly to glorify God in his daily toil (which made good workers as well as good managers!), one whose success would not be used for dissipation or self-aggrandizement, but soberly as befits God's worldly Protestant monk. Weber's description of asceticism released from solitary monasticism for labor in the world via Calvinistic disquiet is powerful:

> Christian asceticism, at first fleeing from the world into solitude, had already ruled the world which it had renounced from the monastery and through the Church. But it had, on the whole, left the naturally spontaneous character of daily life in the world untouched. Now it strode into the market-place of life, slammed the door of the monastery behind it, and undertook to penetrate just that daily routine of life with its methodicalness, to fashion it into a life in the world, but neither of nor for this world.[2]

So we now have an ascetic human being, his fleshly appetites tamed by the rigors of Calvinistic morality, anxiously watching his worldly success to observe whether God is blessing him or not, and determined in that daily work to glorify his Master. Weber uses a famous English Puritan divine, Richard Baxter, to show how this movement toward the world for the sake of one's soul and God's glory became—almost unnoticed—toil for maximum profit. Baxter inveighed against waste of time as the deadliest of sins, passionately approved of hard work, and counseled against all the temptations occasioned by sloth. Weber's concluding quote from Baxter's *Christian Directory* is the clincher:

> If God show you a way in which you may lawfully get more than in another way (without wrong to your soul or to any other), if you refuse this, and choose the less gainful way, you cross one of the ends of your calling, and you refuse to be God's steward, and to accept His gifts and use them for Him when He requireth it: you may labour to be rich for God, though not for the flesh and sin.[3]

But, of course, if one is still glorifying God by his toil—even if realizing maximum profits from that work—he will use much of his increase in supporting good causes, giving to the poor, and other charities. But, Weber concludes, the mere fact of acquisition itself has a deleterious effect on the Christian man. It causes him to lose his piety while yet remaining an avid pursuer of profit who has lost the Christian graces necessary to hinder any longer the uses to which money is put. Here he quotes John Wesley in the eighteenth century, who observed that as his own converts grew diligent and frugal, they grew rich, and as they grew rich, there set in the decay of true religion.

In sum, Calvinism, via the psychological effect of its general Protestant doctrine of calling and the specifically Calvinist doctrine of election, created a new spiritual type—the entrepreneur—who only needed then to lose his religious zeal to become simply and unashamedly a rationalistic, remorseless pursuer of profit for its own sake.

It is my conviction that many of Weber's arguments in *The Protestant Ethic and the Spirit of Capitalism* are wrong or badly need modification. We shall look at some of them. But, in a larger sense, Weber was right: Calvinism had something very definite to do with that larger rationalizing of human activity—of which the development of capitalism is an important part—which revolutionized Western society in the eighteenth and nineteenth centuries and has produced our present technopolitan world. Let us look at some problems with Weber's thesis first.

To begin with, it is obvious that Weber's capitalist is an ideal figure, artificially constructed to appear only in Western society and among the Protestants in that society. Critics of Weber have pointed out how he systematically ignores such perfectly good rationalistic, utilitarian, but non-Protestant capitalists as the Medici family of Florence, the German Fuggers who dominated European banking through the Reformation period, the Renaissance writer Alberti, and many others. It is difficult to understand why Jacob Fugger, banker to popes and emperors, who refused to retire even when old and wealthy, should not be an example of the spirit of capitalism, when Franklin, who quit the unrelenting pursuit of money when still a relatively young man in order to serve his country, is a perfect example of that *Geist*.

And more than one writer has pointed out that the French Catholic Jacques Savary, in his many-editioned *Le parfait négociant* (1675), makes just as good rational, frugal, religious, capitalistic sense as Franklin did a century later. In his monograph Weber finds capitalists only where he wanted to find them—among the Protestants.

Again, Weber has a maddening way of confusing Calvinists—whose theology drove them into unremitting toil in their calling—with men of differing theologies whom he exhibits as representatives of the nascent capitalistic spirit. Only Richard Baxter was a real Calvinist. John Wesley was consciously and overtly anti-Calvinist in theology and yet showed awareness of the capitalistic *esprit* among his followers. And Franklin, the secularizing son of a non-Calvinistic Quaker, may have come by his capitalistic leanings honestly, but any Calvinistic influences must have been pretty well buried in his ancestral past.[4] In other words, his thesis seems to place an emphasis on an ideal Calvinist as well as an ideal capitalist. It is perhaps not hard to find each, but only with Richard Baxter do they inhabit the same skin.

The use of Baxter has also been challenged. The church historian Winthrop Hudson argues that the quotation which Weber leans so heavily upon is in its context surrounded by so many qualifications that it is almost useless for Weber's purpose. Before worrying about how much money the calling will bring in, Baxter's Christian must first think of service to God and the public good, then whether a calling will be good for his soul, next whether it will promote physical and mental health. Then, after all this soul-searching, if one finds two vocations otherwise equal, opined Baxter, he should choose the more profitable. Baxter, says Hudson, agreed with most of the Puritans that "very few rich men escape the snare and come to heaven." [5]

Finally, the theological-psychological cornerstone for Weber's thesis will bear very little weight. There is no evidence whatsoever that concern over one's election in the mysterious councils of God acted to turn a Calvinist toward his worldly calling in order to find there evidence of the working of God's grace. For the most part Calvin's predestinarianism comforted rather than terrified his own listeners (except perhaps those who were excommunicated!), and this seems to be typical even in English Puritanism. It is noteworthy that Oliver Cromwell did not get overly concerned about whether he was "in grace" until he lay on his deathbed, at which time his chaplain assured him that once he had it, he could never lose it. Furthermore, of all the doctrines of Calvinism, the first to go was generally predestination, which is perhaps the reason it was defended the most frantically by true believers. Its long-range effect on merchants becoming gradually secularized under the anti-Puritan reigns of Charles II and William and Mary, or laboring beside a very few complete saints under New England's famous Half-Way Covenant, must have been very slight. More than likely the few places where one can find a Calvinist ascribing success in business to God's election indicate not an inner inquietude but rather an untroubled good conscience. Herbert Lüthy is surely accurate when he says that that part of Weber's thesis which describes the movement from the terrors of the solitary soul to finding one's salvation in work is "the part best known, the most fascinating, and the most fragile." [6]

However, despite these and other weaknesses in Weber's thesis, the reader who knows very little of social or economic history will still recognize that certain facts continue to support his central argument: that there must be some connection between Protestantism and capitalism. After all, was it not the newly Protestant countries which began to lead the world in commerce and then in industry? Why did France, with the great wealth of the Bourbon monarchy, dissipate its resources and energies instead of becoming a major commercial and industrial power? Was it not something in the Protestant "mix" which had an influence? How else does one explain the great advances made by Dutch and Anglo-Saxons after the Reformation, as against the relative stagnation of one Catholic country, Spain, which in the sixteenth century had its fingers on all the gold of Central and South America, as well as great trading opportunities elsewhere about the globe? Surely there is something correct in the suspicion with which Weber began his research, that societies impregnated by the Calvinistic spirit have been the best prepared for the rigors of the capitalistic organization of the economy. Was it not these Protestant, and especially the Calvinist-influenced, countries which, in contrast to the Catholic, honored work and blamed inactivity, and were best able to cut the yoke of religious traditions, as well as those traditions which adhered to land and title? Despite the strong criticisms which can be made against Weber's specific arguments, we must grant him the right of further hearing and perhaps more complete understanding of what he was saying.

I think what we must understand in order to evaluate the thesis of Weber aright is that, despite his concentration on capitalism, what he was really after was a clue to the total rationalization of human life in the West after the Protestant Reformation. Capitalism is but one illustration of this. The entrance of common men into the political arena in order to determine their own future is another. The ability to disregard traditional interpretations of the physical universe and to begin to probe and discover its secrets is another. The intent to manipulate the universe for the good of man is another, in contrast to the more primitive acceptance of the world as a nearly unyielding cocoon to which man must conform. This is what Weber was after, I am convinced, when he began his projected study. He was convinced that Protestantism was at least part of the reason that Western Protestant society, in contrast to Catholic Europe and to the Orient, was dynamic, tradition-denying, forward-looking, inventive. In short, he wanted to explain the emergence from traditional society of a new breed of mankind which tried to rationalize life and thus seize control over its total existence.

Once seen in this light, the influence of Calvin on producing such a breed of humans can be evaluated more adequately. Most of the pointers to capitalism per se run counter to Calvin's thought and practice. He stood squarely against a free market and for strong state regulation. He was more concerned for the common weal than for the rights of the individual when the latter's presumed rights ran counter to society's benefit. He was keenly aware that riches were usually wrested from the life of the poor. Calvin's thought helped produce a small welfare state in middle Europe in the sixteenth century. In Tawney's phrase, it was Christian socialism.

But in other respects Calvin was very much at the forefront of the newly-born, world-affirming, rational approach to human existence. Tradition, for him, was good only insofar as it contributed to human betterment. It was not good in itself, and Calvin lived in a city which had destroyed its traditional feudal ties to its bishop. He was also pastor in a church which had dealt violence to the traditions of the past. The stress on education for everyone would inevitably raise reason above enthusiasm in Calvinist circles. Politically, his concern that public office be a trust led to new traditions of involvement and concern in public life, which historians have noted to be one of the major outgrowths of the Puritan upheaval in England, and contributed mightily to doctrines of self-rule and self-determination in the new world. Seen from this vantage point, and not from the fragile psychology of the legendary Calvinist anxiously proving his election from his job, then the influence of the Reformers *in toto* and Calvin specifically had a great deal to do with the new dynamic activism which the Protestant West entered into about the time of the Reformation.

Perhaps Weber's thesis would have been less vulnerable to his critics had he concentrated upon new developments in science and technology as evidence of Protestant penetration, rather than the more dubious area of economics.[7] One historian of technology has asserted that an important factor in the intensification of research into nature during the second half of the seventeenth century and the attempt to gain control over nature by technical means was the practical ethics of Calvinism with its clear concern for the world around man.[8] Indeed, there was in Calvin this utilitarian approach to education, vocation, politics, and all the other facets of human activity which understood them all to be subsumed to the benefit of the common good. And while Calvin himself seems to have had but little curiosity about the physical sciences, this worldly concern often led his followers to praise inventions as gifts of God's grace. Writes

Richard Baxter: "What delight had the inventors of the sea-chart and magnetic attraction, and of printing, and of guns, in their inventions! [He had read his Bacon!] What pleasure had Galileo in his telescopes, in finding out the inequalities and shady parts of the moon, the Medicean planets, the 62 adjuncts of Saturn, the changes of Venus, the stars of the Milky Way." [9]

Robert Merton's study of the Puritan influence in English and Scottish scientific developments makes much of the close connection between religious virtuosity and scientific curiosity. Among the list of original members of the Royal Society of London (dedicated to experimental science) were a large group of Puritans, and the nuclear group was made up of divines and religious men of Puritan persuasion. This is not the place for a summary of the studies made on this question, but suffice it to say that whether one is searching for adherents to the new spirit of scientific inquiry on the continent or in England, or determining the *esprit* behind the utilitarian and empirical philosophy of John Locke, or examining the move toward a new realistic method of education oriented toward exploring nature—to whichever field one turns, he finds the persuasive influence of the Protestant and, more exactly, the Calvinist. Indeed, contemporaries recognized the Calvinism of many scientists so clearly that opponents of the Royal Society during the days of the later Stuart kings argued that its methods were subversive of the (non-Calvinist) Church of England. [10]

Weber's narrowing of the focus of his study to capitalism, and the further narrowing made by his Platonic definition of capitalism—which sets up an ideal type that is definitely post-Reformation—has helped obscure a truth known to every student who has surveyed Western history: namely, that the rationalization of life began in that rather strange blend of Greek thought and Roman Christian practicality known as scholasticism. [11] Medieval theology, the possibilities inherent in Roman (Christian) law, the methodical work-prayer regimen of the monasteries— all of these point to significant areas of rationalization while the rest of medieval life was still slumbering in its feudal traditions. Luther did not add much to this except his willingness to pierce deeply into the sacred Scriptures, relying on their "plain" sense rather than on various levels of presumed meaning, and perhaps in his determination to understand his own inner turmoil, which involved him in an agony of self-appraisal that was perhaps not duplicated until Sigmund Freud.[12] These were significant advances, of course, but advances on a line already marked out by humanist literary scholars such as Erasmus, or solitary explorers of the soul whom the church had generally approved with posthumous canonization.

Nor did Calvin really add much to the increasing rationalization of occidental life. He was not himself a scientist, economist, or political scientist. What he did was stand more surely than any other thinker of his time within this new world. As we have seen, he approved of the city and its activities. He was not instinctively disgusted with business and trade, as were medieval churchmen and Brother Martin. And he had the sure instinct to perceive the place of religion within this new age, and to curb the worse instincts of the age by the Word of God and godly discipline. No one who has studied the foregoing chapters and has heard Calvin thundering against avarice from the pulpit of St. Pierre's can suppose that he subsumed the religious under this new secularity. Neither Calvin, nor Huguenot, nor Puritan of old or new England thought for a moment that riches were good or business holy. But they had decided to live in this world, and did their utmost to leash it to the Word of God.

Herbert Lüthy is right: the seed of capitalism began in Catholic circles, and the real problem is not the causal relationship between capitalism and Calvinism. The heart of the problem lies with the sudden rejection of the nascent world by the Catholic Counter-Reformation. Both capitalism and the mentality of the planner flourished among the bourgeoisie of free cities all over Catholic Europe, and it is simply not helpful to exempt—as Weber does—families like the Medicis or the Fuggers from the capitalist label. It was a fully Catholic, pre-Reformation phenomenon. Then came several checks to the development of industry and commerce in all of Europe: the Italian Wars, the Wars of Religion in France, and the Thirty Years' War in Germany. After these checks the Protestant countries picked up the same thread again and went on. The Catholic world, on the other hand, retired into the past and became politically, economically, and intellectually dormant.

So the new element is not really Protestantism, but the Counter-Reformation. The Roman Catholic Church tried to refeudalize and clericalize Europe, and only France, which for the most part rejected the conclusions of the Council of Trent (1545–1563), moved ahead intellectually. We must remember that the Catholic countries had all that was necessary for this new, dangerous adventure of the human spirit. They had capital, wealth, a high degree of development in the arts and professions, knowledge of navigation, distant colonies, the gold and silver of Incas and Aztecs, control of major printing centers in Paris, Lyons, and Belgium. They had all of India and parts of Africa and South and Central America to milk. But a century later all that they had was sclerotic or dead. "The most fantastic error of this long discussion concerning the historic role of Protestantism . . . has been simply to forget its counterpart, the historic role of the Counter-Reformation. . . . For the rupture of the ascending line poses a problem more grave than its continuation [in Protestantism]." [13]

After all, Protestantism has not always led to successful capitalism nor to the rationalization of human effort. No area on the globe is more Protestant than the "Bible Belt" of the American South. But capitalism did not fare well there. Certainly those eighteenth-century Scotch-Irish settlers were capitalists, expecting to make a return on their capital. Perhaps they were less sophisticated than their Yankee relatives. Perhaps they came expecting to receive wealth without sharing community responsibility. Perhaps the use of the slave as a tool was an inefficient way for the Scotch-Irish of the southern Piedmont to make his exploitative thrust into the modern world. At any rate, he was not able to make a Calvinist out of the slave, who steadfastly refused to believe that he was laboring for the glory of God. [14] The result seems to have been that while the Catholic of Spain was channeling and drying up his psychic energies in feudal defensiveness, conquest, and inquisition, the Southern white Calvinist filled the vacuum in his soul, not with planned toil, but with the kindling of religious enthusiasm. This absence of the modern spirit among Protestants can be duplicated elsewhere. A recent study shows the Chilean Pentecostal also turning away from the world in order to affirm his moral regeneration.[15] In neither the Protestant South nor among the Latin Pentecostals has Protestantism allied itself with the rational character of the modern age. This gives weight to our thesis that Calvinism or Protestantism itself is not determinative for this bold new step, but that other factors must be given weight.

It is precisely at this point that Marshall McLuhan, in many ways a prophet for our era, leads us so hopelessly astray when he tries to interpret history according to his famous contention that "the medium is the message." McLuhan contends that the introduction of printing in the late fifteenth and sixteenth centuries was a significant step in the rationalizing of Western man, substituting for the "magical world of the ear" the "neutral visual world" of the linear page.[16] Consequently, the printed page *itself* suffices to explain the popularity of new ways of thinking and organizing life which fitted Protestantism so well, or to which Protestantism was a religious response. But of course his argument falls flat when one remembers that the Catholic countries were just as avid for the printed page as were the Protestant. He is willing, for example, to grant that printing in the vernacular helped cement Spanish nationalism in that unsteady period after the deaths of Ferdinand and Isabella. Spain did not again fall back into the feudal regionalism of Castile and Aragon. But he has no convincing answer as to why Spain turned its back on the other products of printing—leveling and homogenizing peoples (i.e., democratizing), planning, concern for time, and all that I have subsumed under the rubric "rationalization." The plain reason is, of course, that here the medium was not the message. The message was the message, and Spain missed it. The message of Protestantism, democracy, freedom from fear of men, activism, anti-traditionalism, simply did not get through to the Spanish because of strict censorship and judicious use of the Inquisition.[17]

Calvin was a religious revolutionary. We can now see that he was a secular revolutionary as well, although the second revolution was for him a by-product of the first. Calvin did not begin the movement, but he certainly took a leading part in it. He is to be praised or blamed not only for the advent of capitalism, but also for democracy, science, technology, and all the other world-affirming and exploitative ways in which modern man has tried to control his own future by rational methods.

But as for laissez-faire capitalism, it no longer exists. It ruled a good share of the West from 1832[18] until 1933, this "utopian world of the self-regulating market." It broke down after World War I, as the Great Depression and the subsequent rise of fascism, communism, and the New Deal in this country all testify. Today we have government regulations over hours, wages, prices, markets, and standards of workmanship. None of these are left anymore to the "invisible hand" of the unregulated market. We are, in a sense, back in Calvin's Geneva, with its open, calculated, and necessary governmental interference. We have collective bargaining, oligopolies (e.g., the triopoly in the American auto industry), government health and work-safety standards, consumer research, better business bureaus, and a hundred-and-one other indications that the sheer determination of economic liberalism is dead.

Today our freedoms of choice are broader. Despite our Calvinistic love of work, we have freedom of time and are trying desperately to learn to deal with leisure before it leaps upon us too savagely. The middle classes today have more freedom with all our regulations than anyone had under the freedom of the self-regulating market system where only the rich were free. Today, as Karl Polanyi has observed, we have rediscovered society by freeing it (and thus ourselves) from the stranglehold of the individual. This was the direction Calvin's own world-affirmation should have led and did lead until smothered under individualistic rationalisms which denied the total community. This still must be the larger Christian concern. For Christianity can't do much intentionally about the salvation of the individual soul—a greater than Calvin made that clear.[19] But a world-affirming Christianity can continue to keep human needs uppermost in a confident society which still believes that rational man can mark out his own future.

CHAPTER XII

Calvin
and the Agonies
of Modern Secularity

MODERN MAN'S decision to rationalize his life was also the decision to secularize it, although this was certainly not clear to the Puritan shopkeeper who was faithful about his business, his prayers, and his attendance at divine worship. And while it may be too strong to say with Gabriel Vahanian that Calvin "was the founder of a new civilization," [1] it was the religious revolutionaries of whom Calvin became the leader who first affirmed the world, then began to dominate it, and have in our day apparently terminated man's need for God.

Whether this was inevitable or not is not the question. The point is that it happened and it happened in precisely those areas of the globe where rational Western man, with Calvinism as midwife, gave birth amid terrible and bloody travail to men both confident and free. With so much psychic effort expended in ferreting out the secrets of the earth and in manipulating the globe to man's profit, it is not strange that guidance "from above" should finally be regarded as questionable and perhaps meaningless. And even those today who question the wisdom of their fathers, who would like to turn nostalgically from the secular city's asphalt and electronics to some medieval guild economy or a conglomeration of hippie monasteries—even these modern romanticists who have nearly given up on man in civilization no longer turn to God. They have bought more of this world than they like to be reminded of.

There is no question but that man's mastery of the cosmos

has gone awry. He has not always dominated wisely the garden he was given to till and keep, but has savagely exploited it. He has explored its secrets, only to turn those secrets upon himself, so that the physical world really does groan and travail with yet-to-be-redeemed man, and indeed threatens to extinguish him. He has used his freedom to carve his own future, but the very tools he has used have turned upon him as if to scorn him as a robot among automatons. He looks into his noblest creation, the city, that great symbol of man's freedom to build a universe, and there he sees misery and an unfreedom terrible to contemplate and even more terrible to live. He stands in the heart of that secular city and cries for a universe with a heart. He peeps fearfully from his suburban paradise caught up in guilt and fear, lest some of those dark objects of his exploitation march out against the people with power and dig up their lawns. He awkwardly attempts to retain control by doling out support to the unfree and succeeds only in spawning a new profession which has become fat on poverty and dedicated to its maintenance. Even the noble university is trapped in the professionalism of the white ghetto, sallying forth into the real world only when absolutely necessary, tied by traditions it has only begun to examine. Western man seized the world from God in order to make the future, and that future has receding horizons which no longer promise a good hope.

Furthermore, the West has exported its rational dream of world domination and self-determination to the rest of the world, so that the whole noosphere is pulsating with energy and frustration. Rationality, punctuality, zeal for the future, the end of traditionalism—these have been given to Latin America, the East, and Africa by missionaries, educators, and Marxists alike. But the surprising result has been a narrowly interpreted demand for self-determination, by national, tribal, or language groups, many of whom see revolution as the shortcut to local prosperity and thus are locked in a xenophobia which threatens to make an end to the world. Nor is this true only of Asia or Africa. Anyone sensitive to the resentments of the Flemish in Belgium or the French in Quebec knows better. And so the peoples of the world, compressed ever more closely together by man's new electronic nervous system, at the same time move away from solidarity and perhaps closer to an Armageddon of chosen people. Furthermore, this world secularity is uprooting the non-Christian gods in many lands and is substituting worldly, demonic deities even more fanatically followed than their predecessors. What we have are Utopian, nationalistic, or Marxist-futuristic fanaticisms replacing the gods of earth and sky.

The Birth and Development of Secularization

Religious historians have agreed that the movement toward world affirmation and world domination has been a Western product, and more specifically a Hebrew-Christian product. Primitive man lived in a universe regarded as generally unfriendly, and he constantly gathered at sacred times in sacred places where he could experience and participate in the work of the primeval gods to re-create and thus re-sacralize the world, to make it friendly and comfortable for himself. He had little sense of history, for he lived in harmony with the ceaseless round of nature and looked forward as a people only to the reenactment of the sacred past which had in "that time" brought the world into order from chaos.[2] He did not dominate the world but instead participated in ceremonies through which he could guarantee that the world would continue to produce enough grain, lambs, and children to perpetuate the race.

It was the Hebrew who came as a dynamic mutation to this static, closed-in understanding of man in the world. He came from captivity and the desert with a nomad's understanding of God. For these fierce men Yahweh was not the one who created and participates in the life-death-life cycle of nature, but one who travels before, who makes promises which are kept, and whose will is not reenactment of the past, but justice in the present. Of course, when the Hebrew settled down to an agricultural existence, he adopted many of the ceremonies of those he settled with. But he did not submit to nature deities because the prophetic element in Israel's faith consistently interpreted national disaster as the judgment of Yahweh against injustice and social disregard, not as the result of neglected sacral ceremonies. Indeed, attendance at the ceremonies was regarded as proof that Israel had turned from Yahweh to the nature-religion of Baal (whoring after other gods!) and thus incurred Yahweh's judgment. Amos, Hosea, Isaiah, and Jeremiah consistently portrayed Yahweh as God of justice, rewarder of good, destroyer of social evil.

In addition, they all (with the possible exception of Amos) looked ahead for the fulfillment of God's good promises to Israel. Consequently Israel's faith at any given time was in tension between the past, when Yahweh covenanted with the people, and the future, when Israel would fulfill its part of the covenant or when God would cut a new covenant with his people. God was not perceived through the round of nature, but through history, and that history was not the mythic primordial past, but the historical past which led straight through the present into a future fulfillment. Thus, while it is too strong to say that the prophets *invented* history, it is proper to say that they were the first to find history meaningful because they understood God and man as being in motion forward. They did not want to re-create the past or make sacred the present, but to try to understand present ills as disobedience to be overcome through tomorrow's promise. They eliminated the "eternal return" of the holy past of primitive religion by visions of a society with a future under Yahweh. This meant that the world was regarded as part of history, important but not in need of constant re-sacralization. The Israelite affirmed history and thus affirmed the world.

Christianity's major addition to the faith of Israel was to universalize it. Of course Deutero-Isaiah understood Israel to be a light to the nations, and the story of Jonah is one of missionary outreach, however obscured by arguments about the possibility of a man-swallowing fish. But early Christians understood that the church's explicit mission was to all men, that Yahweh had a plan for the fullness of time to unite all things in Christ.

The conflicts of St. Paul with the Judaizers was really over the methodology and degree of particularity to be retained in this worldwide mission: whether one needed to become physically a Jew in order to respond adequately to God.

But later Christian thought and practice, mixed with many pagan elements, tended to re-sacralize the world. It is quite clear that in many ways Catholic Europe had abandoned the tough-minded secularity of the Hebrew roots of the Christian faith. When the city fathers in Geneva forbade citizens from making pilgrimages to a spring named for a St. Claude and even forbade naming babies after that *jdole*, they were saying, in effect, that the Reformation had cut itself off from the medieval sacralization of certain spots, the aura of which carried over into the rest of life. The Reformers rejected the medieval church's passion for sacred relics, sacred places, sacred men, the Sacred Host. The next crusade would not be one to wrest the sacred lands from the infidel, but one to cast aside the whole medieval understanding of sacred polities, sacred economics, sacred people, and allow common people to take life into their own hands. It was not accidental that a Calvinist farmer-turned-politician ordered the death of Charles I, the last king by "divine right."

They were not alone in this rejection, of course. Erasmus, the humanist, had heaped biting satire upon holy men, relics, and pilgrimages in his *Praise of Folly*, and Rabelais was to try with a buffoonery born of rationality to retain the good in monastic life while de-sacralizing that life completely in his *Gargantua* and *Pantagruel*. Both humanist and Reformer rejected medieval Christendom's inauthentic attempt to return to a religion of sacrality. And both taught men to turn the eyes of faith resolutely forward. While it is true that this affirmation of the future was accomplished by going back *ad fontes*, to the primitive Christian witness or to classical models, even here the Hebraic pattern was picked up again: one secures the future by looking backward to the faithful action and promises of God.

Some of the doctrinal differences among Reformers which make minimal sense to modern men are better understood as squabbles over the degree to which ideas of sacred time and place were to be discarded. We understand these arguments better within the context of world affirmation, of the growing determination to seize time, in other words, of an often unconscious attitude of secularity. An example is the quarrel between Calvin and the followers of Luther over the presence of Christ in the Supper. The latter wanted with Brother Martin to affirm that Christ is physically present "in, with, and under" the bread and wine, that Christ's risen body shares his divine attributes and consequently has ubiquity, the character of omnipresence. The disciples of Zwingli and Calvin were inclined to regard this interpretation of Christ's risen body as destroying the humanity of the Lord and reducing his physicalness to some sort of ghostly phantasm. Or else they accused Luther of advocating something approaching cannibalism. Each side produced numerous volumes of literature in which they spelled out clearly the heresies of the other, quoted the ancient fathers and the Scriptures in support of their own position, and engaged in a theological name-calling as tasteless as it was unedifying.

Several things are clear about the argument about the Table from our modern point of view. First, Luther was more closely tied to the traditional past and wanted to retain the Mass without having to hang on to what he considered the philosophical absurdities of transubstantiation. Calvin was a town-dweller, a bourgeois, much less upset about making necessary changes so that God would be honored. Luther was also more in tune with the idea of "sacred place," which is evident not only in the greater beauty of Lutheran worship, but in his attempt to re-present (but not re-offer or re-sacrifice) the divine at each hour of worship. Calvin, on the other hand, was too much a rationalist to care so deeply about sacred place: it was enough that God was present to the believer; he need not be locatable. Luther tended to bring Christ down to make his dwelling place with men for their comfort and hope. Calvin was content to leave Christ in heaven with God in order that men might attend his Word and not cleave to re-sacralized elements of the world.

I am not arguing here who was right, or more nearly right. (The notion of "transignification" developed by some modern

Catholic theologians is essentially the Calvinist theory.) It is a question of the way they "felt" the presence of God. Luther leaned toward the medieval idea of God present at holy times in holy places. He understood history to be nearing its end, and waited in anticipation for the imminent divine disclosure. Calvin pointed toward the future and had little need for holy times or places. His God was dynamic, futuristic, concerned for human obedience in the present. It is no wonder that Lutheranism tended toward quiescence in the economic and political realms, Calvinism toward activism and seizure of the reins of power, whether political or technological. One need only walk the main shopping street in modern Geneva to see clearly the hidden Calvinistic distaste for holy places. There, appropriately enough at the busiest market area, the city in the early 1700's built a temple. It may not be the ugliest church in Christendom, but it will do until some Wesleyan chapel wins that laurel. It is drab, plain, gaunt, ugly—words cannot really paint the uncluttered, non-sacred character of the Church of St. Pierre de la Fusterie. Why? Because in Calvinism—at least as interpreted by the city fathers a century and a half after Calvin's death—what made a place sacred was that *men* came there to worship. Men could come anywhere and accomplish the same end because they bore within themselves all that God needs to break open his Word to them. Calvin, of course, would not have put it quite this way. But it was not by accident that his descendants arrived at that architectural decision so ugly it has a charm denied to the merely beautiful. No wonder the Calvinist understanding of the sacrament has so emphasized the faith of the men who come to it—not the sacrality of the elements themselves—that it has often been accused of receptionism. There is this real tendency in Calvinism to take charge of everything—even of one's own salvation—despite strong and explicit theological doctrine to the contrary.

In respect to de-sacralization of the world and a historicity which fashions the future, Marxism is fully within the Hebrew-Christian movement we have been surveying. World history is seen by Marxist philosophy as the history of men who are at last able to comprehend and thus seize power over hitherto obscure economic and social forces. Gone are all the puddles of world sacrality which Protestant and Enlightenment thought had overlooked. Marxism believes itself to be a future-oriented revolutionary movement dedicated to the smashing of all the unhealthy traditions of the past, establishing complete social justice, marshaling and channeling human resources into the technological revolution, and consciously substituting human knowledge in place of God. (Did not the French revolutionaries crown Reason queen and worship her?) In exalting the society far above the individual, Marxism flies in the face of most Western revolutionary thinking since the Reformation. But both Calvin and Rousseau expressed clearly enough this same tendency for us to see how this too could have been a possible direction for their revolution to have gone. But individual free man won out over the social order, so that in the Christian West, affirmation of the world by the individual tended to negate social concern; in the Marxist East, on the other hand, social concern has tended to obliterate the individual. These are two sides of the same coin, dug from the same ore.

The Role of the Church in a Secular World

How shall we regard this secular society? There are many answers to that. Ordinarily, Christian thinkers have not been happy with it. A few, like Karl Barth, have rejoiced that it tolls the death knell for "religion" and leaves the field open for the Christian faith, which Barth has argued is basically irreligious. ("Religion" is a human invention by which man elevates a false sacrality into a God.) But most thinkers, like Paul Tillich, have mourned the passing of "depth," the absence of the sense of divine presence, the mystical *a priori* which impels men to all religion and to the Christian faith. The one theologian who regards the secular as an almost unqualified good, Harvey Cox, has thereby won for himself a momentary fame or notoriety almost unparalleled among contemporary Protestant theologians. Cox, like Barth, understands the Christian faith not to be threatened in its essentials by the death of the sacred character of the earth and the meaninglessness of old rites and rituals tied to that sacrality. For him the slow march of Western intellectual history has been in the revolutionary paths hacked out by Moses and Calvin. He is not concerned with a God to whom men resort because they do not like cities, freeways, and telephones, but with the God who gives man the earth and tells him to get with the job of tilling, keeping, filling, dominating, subduing, and city-building. Cox informs us that God must be thought of primarily as apart from man—or beckoning from the future for man to catch up.[3]

Other writers remind us that secularity is a neutral term, that there is a good secularization which tries to deal with this world in such a way as to make it more fit for humans, and a bad secularism which affirms the world simply in order to exploit it.[4]

Certainly the role of the church in this society has scarcely been more difficult, for the church is by its gospel committed to social justice and human concern, and yet it cannot help but be bewildered by the roles thrust upon it by a world which no longer believes in God. So the church is given the private task of preserving the human, personal elements in a technical, impersonal society.[5] Since the objective world outside man is in his grasp and control, there remains only his subjectivity to be dealt with, and this task the church has tackled with gusto. One need only consider the wide range of action and the varied philosophies and psychologies which churchmen have embraced to understand how eagerly the church rushes to do the world's bidding. Methods and philosophies vary. For many preachers the essence of the church's proclamation is the message of heroic self-affirmation, of liberating man from premature inauthentic attempts to answer the question of his own being. Elsewhere on the spectrum we find Norman Vincent Peale preaching the power imparted by the assurance of God's inner-direction for the faithful man. The first message knows that the world can never liberate men from bondage. The second seeks success and happiness through the world. The first is dangerously near to world denial, a high-minded but nevertheless self-serving mys-

ticism, more lately termed existentialism. The second is dangerously near to an uncritical affirmation of the world and one's
place in it. Either may effectively negate social criticism and
revolutionary change. Regardless of the message preached and
the advice offered, the church has responded affirmatively to
the task of providing islands of personal meaning in an impersonal, disenchanted world.

The church has also been given the task by society of helping provide one of the many small communities in which men
find warmth in a cold world. Indeed, one of the humorous aspects on the ecumenical scene is to hear enlightened Protestants
speak bitterly of the warm "togetherness" of many Protestant
congregations which keeps them from welcoming the stranger,
the poor, those of another race. Whereas in the Catholic avant-
garde men unmindful of the pitfalls of ecclesiastical neighbor-
liness blithely speak of a church of the future where all congregations will be small face-to-face societies.

Calvin had a different understanding of the church, one
which is critical of the philosophies adopted by many modern
churchmen seeking to understand how to be the church of
Christ in a secular world. The church is that community where
the original solidarity of men is restored. It is not a group of
like-minded neighbors—indeed, its true nature is best seen when
its membership is as diverse as possible. But, more important than
that, the church has the task of pointing to the provisory character of human inequality, of publicly promoting justice among
men, of exposing for the world those instances and situations
where man's lack of love has expressed itself by corrupting the
social order.[6] The Calvinist church does not do what society tells
it to do, nor assume the tasks that society is ashamed of. Its business is with the Word of God—to understand that Word, to proclaim it, to labor actively for its penetration into the world of
men. For the Calvinist there was no separation of the sacred and
secular as there was for the Anabaptist, or as there is for the
modern Christian who finds the church a refuge from the world.
Is it not ironic that it is precisely those Christians who are most
successful in the entrepreneurship of modern society who are

often most adamant in their insistence that the church not speak to this secularity? But it is those Christians and honest pagans who see the underbelly of human society—the horror of the cities, the aimlessness of poverty, the hopelessness of welfare living—who ask the church to reassert its prophetic ministry and challenge those evils which modern society handles so awkwardly.

The great blasphemy of the church since the Reformation has been its uncritical adaptation to the revolutionary new world it helped bring into being. Calvinism especially helped produce the new age of world affirmation and world domination, and at its best knew how to build out of this a human community. Mumford has shown how the New England town plan expressed a sense of community unexcelled in all of Europe. But eventually the Protestant ideal of a community of believers was perverted from a priesthood of *all* believers into a priesthood of *each* believer. Stark individualism and self-seeking righteousness took the place of rather stern compassion and concern for the total community's economic, social, and political structures. Community builders were replaced by spiritual loners, inner-directed men adequate to subdue a continent by diligence and force, or to invent and make practical a new method of production. But these hard, brave men were poor planners of a good society, poor guardians of the commonweal.

What a contrast between crowded little Geneva, trying its best to remain human when flooded with needy refugees, and the new city of the Victorian period. In the latter, industrialization coupled with laissez-faire capitalistic attitudes toward society—egged on by the Darwinian, deterministic *esprit* of nineteenth-century man—produced a "new species of town, a blasted, de-natured man-heap adapted, not to the needs of life, but to the . . . 'struggle for existence.'" Mumford is right—these builders of inhuman cities did not have to plan, for chaos needs no planning.[7] It is not enough to object that these malefactors were not generally Presbyterians. What must be observed is that they were products of all those movements toward the rationalization of life which the Calvinist part of the Reformation helped so vitally. Who can say whether these solipsistic economic barons would have arisen with their crass, greedy individualism if the followers of Calvin had been as careful over love for the neighbor and the good of the community as they were over the doctrine of election?

Indeed, one of the great mysteries of church history is the almost complete acceptance by the descendants of Calvin of two 'anti-evangelical secular philosophies which helped produce and excuse the brutality which marked the onset of the modern industrial society. Laissez-faire capitalism was accepted in the nineteenth century even though it was understood to be the baptism of individual selfishness and greed. Men were persuaded that so much evil would cancel itself out and somehow produce the common good. The Darwinian concept of natural selection and survival of the fittest, translated from biological evolution to the marketplace, merely reinforced the already inhuman quality of social thought accepted by many thinking people in western Europe. In both concepts the indiviual is everything, society nothing. Self-seeking struggle is rewarded, compassion neglected. How our fathers could have swallowed such crude doctrines which made so little of even fundamental human decency is almost beyond belief, particularly since many of them refused to believe Darwin in his proper field. This economic "liberalism" (as it was called then), like its opposite reaction, Marxist socialism, are both secular religions nourished on Christian affirmation of the world, but stripped of any true regard for man-in-community. Why any Christian should feel bound to accept either uncritically is pause for wonder.

The great defection occurred within American evangelicalism. From the founding of the Republic (1789) until the Civil War, this movement tried to transform men into Christians and society into the Kingdom of God. The same men who were active in saving souls sounded the trumpet against slavery, and bravely (if not always circumspectly) attacked other social evils of the early nineteenth century. But after the war the evangelical movement was tamed. Success in abolishing slavery turned into scorn and contempt for former slaveholders and, indeed, all Southerners. In the South the evangelical turned his attention to the lonely soul and allowed social concerns to dribble away into minor titillating gossip about drink and sex. In the North dispute over evolution divided the movement. But those who accepted Darwin's thesis tended also to accept an individualistic biological doctrine whose effects on social concern were disastrous. Whereas those evangelicals who rejected evolution also turned from society, in contrast to their Calvinist fathers they retreated into the monastery of soul-saving and Bible defense and slammed the door shut behind them. Today within the church that polarization has left us with many theologically concerned Christians who have never had a serious thought about transforming the world, and a goodly number who want to transform the world, but—disenchanted with traditionalism and fundamentalism—know no theology.

The task of the church in this society is not to turn from the world in order to affirm another. But neither is it called to baptize the world as it is or to run to do the world's bidding— to make a warm spot for troubled souls. Its task is to proclaim the total gospel message which affirms the world in order to transform it,[8] which cooperates with but is not identical with secular programs and institutions because Christians seek "another city"—one which is only attained, however, through the effort to build the earthly *civitas*. When men deny the individual for the sake of society, then the Christian must proclaim the rights of each man. But, as has happened in industrial societies in the West, when individualism runs rampant over the common good, then the church must point out by deed and voice the message of human solidarity. It cannot expect other institutions to do this. Mr. Galbraith's "intellectual elite"—the faculties of the universities—have too deeply drunk from the individual cups of educational entrepreneurship to take the lead. Faculty members are too fascinated by the "academic marketplace" with its explicit connection to some of the least humane features of economic enterprise for them to be leaders in community-building in any large-scale way.

Of all of our modern institutions only the despised church

carries within itself enough moral belief and dynamism to initiate reform. The Black Power movement has recognized this by threatening and, in the same breath, calling the churches to begin the indemnity and reparations payments white America owes the black. Significantly, the attack was not made on affluent business, government, or university. But on the church, which is possessed by the gospel with its clear teaching about love for the brother and all the brethren. But, further, the church is not confined to the present, and therefore it is free to criticize and move the world. For its orientation is backward to Yahweh's actions for Israel and his power in the raising of Christ, and then forward to the promise of universal salvation. "For he has made known to us . . . the mystery of his will . . . a plan for the fulness of time, to unite all things in him, things in heaven and things on earth" (Eph. 1:9–10). The church has, therefore, a built-in denial of despair. Besides, through the Protestant Reformation, the church of Christ helped bring the world to maturity and secularity. Therefore it has an obligation to the world to proclaim that true secularity is love for mankind.

Notes

Note: Unless otherwise indicated, all translations are by the author.

CHAPTER I
THE FIRST GENEVAN REVOLUTIONARY

1. The definitive and very readable account of the training and dispatching of these pastors to the French underground church is by Robert M. Kingdon, *Geneva and the Coming of the Wars of Religion in France, 1555–1563* (Geneva: Droz, 1956).

2. After 1549 Calvin's sermons were written down verbatim by Denis Raguener, a French refugee, on wages paid by an association of French refugees. Of these sermons preached four times weekly until early 1564 there must have been about 2,300, of which about 1,000 were lost when sold injudiciously by the city library during the Napoleonic occupation after 1798. See Bernard Gagnebin, *L'Incroyable histoire des sermons de Calvin* (Geneva, 1956).

3. For a Catholic analysis of the plight of medieval Christology, see Robert E. McNally, S.J., *The Unreformed Church* (New York: Sheed and Ward, 1965).

4. The contrast between humanists and Reformers is often striking, although ostensibly they had the same end—to reform church and society. I am indebted to Alain Dufour here. See his *Histoire politique et psychologie historique* (Geneva: Droz, 1966), the essay "Humanisme et Reformation."

5. Although McLuhan's fascinating theses are spelled most fully (not to say clearly!) in *Understanding Media*, it is in *The Gutenberg Galaxy* (Toronto: University of Toronto Press, 1962), pp. 218–227, that he argues the transforming, revolutionary power of the visual-linear medium on western Europe. He is not able to explain the lack of revolutionary ferment in lands such as Spain, although a vague reference to Moorish influence is brought in as a possible explanation. He is guilty of the pioneer's need to use hyperbole, and here his thesis fails badly.

6. A good analysis of the failure of Calvinist leadership in France contrasted with the success of that leadership in England may be found in *The Revolution of the Saints: A Study in the Origins of Radical Politics*, by Michael Walzer (Cambridge, Mass.: Harvard University Press, 1965), pp. 66–74.

7. *Ibid.*, p. 47. Since I am only an amateur student of Rousseau, it seems best to refer the reader who wants to check these parallels to several excellent monographs on Rousseau. Especially penetrating is that by Ernst Cassirer, *The Question of Jean-Jacques Rousseau*, trans. Peter Gay (New York: Columbia University Press, 1954); a recent biography is that by F. C. Green, *Jean-Jacques Rousseau: A Critical Study of His Life and Writings* (New York: Cambridge University Press, 1955). The parallels with Calvin, however, I have drawn.

8. Alexandre Ganoczy, *Le jeune Calvin: Genèse et évolution de sa vocation réformatrice* (Wiesbaden: Franz Steiner Verlag, 1966), p. 367.

9. The youngster who says that "nothing will be changed until everything is changed" is not making a revolutionary statement. He is protecting himself from the necessity of really doing anything to modify the national life in the direction of freedom and humanness. But when students or ex-students attack a specific target—such as the draft—then their protest is pointed and packs within itself the possibility of succeeding. Unfortunately, one hears more of that great enemy the Establishment than of specific evils to be fought. The student's parents are apt to regard international Communism in much the same way. It is the looming evil which keeps them from recognizing more specific, attackable evils about them and within them. No wonder they resist anyone who tells them that they must readjust their thinking about monolithic Communism in the light of recent history.

10. See, for example, Robert Heilbroner's predictions in *The Future as History* (New York: Grove Press, 1961).

11. Louis Blondel, *Le développement urbain de Genève à travers les siècles* (Geneva, 1946).

CHAPTER II
GENEVA—CALVIN'S CITY

1. *Les Sources du droit du Canton de Genève*, ed. Émile Rivoire and Victor van Berchem (Aarau: H. R. Sauerländer, 1933), Vol. III, edicts 976, 979, 984, 985, and 992. In the Council's edicts we are given some insight into the commercial, private, and sporting life of Geneva.

2. *Calvini opera quae supersunt omnia*, ed. G. Baum, E. Cunitz, and E. Reuss (59 vols.; Brunswick, 1863–1900), vol. 21, col. 204. From the *Registres du Conseil*, vol. 29, fol. 51. 5 September 1536. "Mag. Guil. Farellus exponit sicuti sit necessaria illa lectura qualem initiavit ille Gallus in S. Petro." Volume 21 contains helpful excerpts from Council records and a few other sources which help illumine Calvin's life and work.

From this point on the volume and column number in the *Opera* will be designated thus: *Opera*, 21, 204. Similarly the *Registres du Conseil* will be abbreviated, for example, R.C., vol. 29, fol. 51.

3. *Eidgenot* was the term used to describe those who wanted to be confederates with the German Swiss; it comes from the German *Eidgenossen*, "confederates," and was used to describe the members of the Swiss Confederation. Geneva would not officially belong until the eighteenth century. It is likely that the term *Huguenot* is a perversion of *Eidgenot*, though this is disputed.

4. The author has consulted several works on Genevan history during this period. *Histoire de Genève des origines à 1798* (Geneva: La Société d'Histoire et d'Archéologie de Genève, 1951) contains separate chapters written by students of the various phases of this period. Henri Naef, *Les origines de la réforme à Genève* (Geneva: Droz, 1936), is complete.

5. Froment's own account: *Les Actes et gestes merveilleux de la Cité de Genève*, ed. Gustave Revilliod (Geneva: J.-G. Fick, 1864), pp. 12 f. Froment's work waited three hundred years to be published, the city Council refusing publication in 1551.

6. Herbert D. Foster, "Geneva before Calvin," *Collected Papers of Herbert D. Foster* (privately printed, 1929), p. 7.

7. *Opera*, 21, 201 f.

8. Foster, p. 26.

9. Amédée Roget, *Histoire du peuple de Genève* (7 vols.; Geneva: J. Jullien, 1870–1883), Vol. I, pp. 15–20. Roget's seven volumes are the outstanding record for the Calvinist period. He intended to carry his history to 1602, the time of the defeat of Savoy in its last attempt to subdue the city, but death interrupted his account several years after Calvin's death in 1564.

10. *Opera*, 21, 219. R.C., vol. 31, fol. 146. For indications of concern that the Confession was being ignored, see 1537, 29 July, 30 October, 12 November, 15 November, 26 November, 14 December.

11. *Opera*, 21, 222. Roget adds that they were told to preach the gospel as God has commanded them. Roget, I, 80.

12. Roget, I, 86–94, taken directly from the *Registres du Conseil*, gives an exceptionally clear account of the circumstances leading up to the exile of Farel and Calvin.

13. *Opera*, 21, 226. R.C., vol. 32, fol. 35. 23 April 1538.

14. *Opera*, 21, 267, for this particular reference. 19 October 1540.

15. *Opera*, 21, 400. 21 March 1547. R.C., vol. 42, fol. 63.

16. *Opera*, 21, 400–401. 25 March 1547. R.C., vol. 42, fol. 68.

17. *Opera*, 21, 400–401. 29 March.

18. *Opera*, 21, 426. 21 May 1548. R.C., vol. 43, fol. 94.

19. A brief résumé of the peccadilloes of the Calvin women can be found in Williston Walker, *John Calvin* (New York: G. P. Putnam's Sons, 1906), pp. 357–358.
20. *Opera*, 21, 432. 23 August 1548. *Registre du Consistoire*. 24 August. R.C., vol. 43, fol. 174.
21. *Opera*, 21, 442. R.C., vol. 43, fol. 265.
22. *Opera*, 21, 457. 24 and 28 October 1549. R.C., vol. 44, fol. 247. We're not sure how long the preachers usually preached, although once Abel Poupin insisted he had held forth only thirty minutes at a service. I think it extremely unlikely that the protracted preaching of the Puritans had its origin at Geneva.
23. *Opera*, 21, 494. 3 December 1551. R.C., vol. 46, fol. 106. The Strasbourg editors of the *Calvini opera* call Bourgeois *l'imprimeur*, "the printer," but Jacques Bourgeois, the printer, is not known prior to 1556. Roget, III, 210, more correctly says "chantre." Bourgeois was one of the first professional Calvinist church musicians.
24. *Opera*, 21, 476. *Reg. du Consistoire*. The affair is dealt with at some length by Roget, III, 144–151.
25. *Registres de la Compagnie des Pasteurs de Genève au temps de Calvin*, ed. Robert M. Kingdon and Jean François Bergier (2 vols.; Geneva: Droz, 1962 and 1964), II, 54–55. An English translation in one volume, with somewhat different notation, has been done by Philip E. Hughes, *The Register of the Company of Pastors of Geneva in the Time of Calvin* (Grand Rapids: Wm. B. Eerdmans Publishing Co., 1966).
26. *Opera*, 21, 554. 18 September 1553. R.C., vol. 47, fol. 155.
27. Roget, IV, 72.
28. *Opera*, 21, 536–538. Roget, III, 280. Michel Roset, *Chroniques de Genève*, ed. Henri Fazy (Geneva: Georg, 1894), p. 350. Roset's *Chroniques* were finished by 1562, but existed only in manuscript form till Fazy's editorial job in 1894. Next to the *Registres du Conseil*, *Registre du Consistoire* (as yet unedited), and *Registres de la Compagnie des Pasteurs de Genève au temps de Calvin*, Roset's is the most valuable firsthand account of the period.
29. *Opera*, 21, 547. 24 July 1553. R.C., vol. 47, fol. 116.
30. Paul F. Geisendorf, ed., *Livre des habitants de Genève* (2 vols.; Geneva: Droz, 1957–1963), Vol. I, p. ix. Geisendorf has listed in Volume I the names of all those who came from 1549 till the first book was closed in 1560. New persecutions in France caused the book to be opened twice again, and these names Geisendorf has covered in Volume II. Eight days after St. Bartholomew's Day 1572, with its terrible massacre, a new flood of Huguenots caused the first reopening of the *Book of Habitants*.

31. Alfred D. Covelle, *Le Livre des Bourgeois* (Geneva: J. Jullien, 1897), pp. 227–235.
32. Roset, 362–363.
33. Cited in Roget, III, 285, 286n.
34. Covelle, pp. 241–242.
35. The whole story can be read in Roget, IV, 245–336.
36. Bolsec got his revenge by publishing after Calvin's death a scurrilous biography of the Genevan Reformer, *Histoire de la vie, moeurs, actes, constance, et mort de Jean Calvin*. According to Walker (p. 117), Bolsec asserted that Calvin in his early life had been convicted of moral turpitude and in punishment had had the fleur-de-lis branded on his shoulder with a red-hot iron. So, while Bolsec may have been more agreeable to a modern age theologically, his literary prevarications seriously compromised his integrity.
37. Walker, p. 343. The most adequate work on the subject is certainly by Roland H. Bainton, *Hunted Heretic: The Life and Death of Michael Servetus* (Boston: Beacon Press, 1953).
38. The whole process is found in *Opera*, vol. 8. Here, col. 829, Bainton's translation, from *Hunted Heretic*, p. 209.
39. Bainton, p. 215.
40. *Reg. Comp. Pasteurs*, II, 59.
41. *Opera*, 21, 654. 15 November 1556.
42. Kingdon, *Geneva and the Coming of the Wars of Religion in France*.
43. *Opera*, 21, 754–756. 18 July 1561. R.C., vol. 56, fol. 217.
44. Roget, VI, 79–80. This is taken from R.C. for 28 March 1562.

CHAPTER III
CALVIN'S CRITIQUE OF HUMAN SOCIETY

1. Roget, IV, 156n.
2. *Opera*, 45, 613.
3. *Opera*, 23, 28. *Commentarius in Genesin*, Gen. 1:28. Translations throughout from the Commentaries basically follow the 1840 editions.
4. *Opera*, 27, 639. Sermon CXIX on Deut. 20:16–20.
5. *Opera*, 21, 432. 23 August 1548, *Reg. du Consistoire*, and the next day from *Registres du Conseil*, vol. 43, fol. 174.
6. *Opera*, 27, 350. Sermon XCVI on Deut. 15:16–23.
7. See, for example, the comments of Calvin on I Cor. 11:3.
8. *Opera*, 51, 231–232. *Commentarius in Epistolam Pauli ad Ephesios*, Eph. 6:9.
9. *Opera*, 5, 437. From *Petit Traicté de la Saincte Cène*.
10. *Calvin: Institutes of the Christian Religion*. Trans. Ford Lewis

Battles; ed. John T. McNeill. Vols. XX and XXI of the Library of Christian Classics, ed. John Baillie, John T. McNeill, and Henry P. Van Dusen (Philadelphia: The Westminster Press, 1960), Book IV, chapter xvii, section 38.

11. *Opera*, 21, 222, from R.C., vol. 32, fol. 4. 12 March 1537. Roget adds that they were ordered to preach the gospel as God had commanded them. Roget, I, 80. How modern that sounds to the present-day churchman who dares to be a prophet!

12. *Opera*, 21, 457. R.C., vol. 44, fol. 247. 24 and 28 October 1549. I am not clear what the magistrates wanted to do with the commandments—perhaps to substitute Jesus' summary of the law for the recital of the Ten Commandments.

13. *Opera*, 52, 267. *Commentarius in Epistolem ad Timotheum I*, I Tim. 2:2.

14. *Institutes*, IV, xx, 31, is the *locus classicus* for his discussion of the remote possibility that a legitimate rebellion could be led by such lesser magistrates.

15. *Opera*, 38, 769, 770. *Commentarii in Librum Psalmorum*, Ps. 82:3.

16. *Institutes*, IV, xx, 9.

17. Eugène Choisy, *La Théocratie à Genève au temps de Calvin* (Geneva: J.-G. Fick, 1897), p. 6. The italics are his.

18. *Opera*, 43, 145 f. *Duodecim Prophetas Minores*, Amos 8:4.

19. H. Richard Niebuhr, *Christ and Culture* (New York: Harper & Brothers, 1951), chapter 6. He distinguishes five different stances of Christians toward society: Christ against culture, Christ of culture, Christ over culture (the medieval theories of Innocent III and Boniface VIII), Christ in tension with culture (Luther), and Christ transforming culture (Calvin, F. D. Maurice).

20. Thomas G. Sanders, *Protestant Concepts of Church and State* (New York: Holt, Rinehart and Winston, 1964), Chapter V.

CHAPTER IV
WEALTH AND POVERTY

1. *Sources du droit*, III, no. 905. 12 May 1553, "Ordonnances sur l'Hôpital."

2. *Opera*, 45, 199. *Com. Harm. Evang.*, Matt. 6:11.

3. *Opera*, 31, 418. *Com. Psalmorum*, Ps. 41:1.

4. *Opera*, 27, 337 f. Sermon XCV on Deut. 15:11–15.

5. *Opera*, 46, 406. *Com. Harm. Evang.*, Luke 16:14.

6. *Opera*, 46, 549. Sermon XLIV on the Harmony of the Gospels. Matt. 3:3–10. Italics mine.

7. *Opera*, 50, 101–102. *Commentarius in Epistolum Secundam ad Corinthios*, II Cor. 8:15.

8. *Opera*, 50, 98. So far as I can find, Calvin nowhere enjoins tithing

on the Christian. Whether this Hebraic charitable calculation was made incumbent on the serious Christian by the Puritans or whether it is strictly an American invention is unclear to me.

9. *Opera*, 27, 338. Sermon XCV on Deut. 15:11–15.
10. *Opera*, 55, 340–341. *Com. in Johannis Apostoli Epistolam*, I John 3:17.
11. *Opera*, 45, 205. *Com. Harm. Evang.*, Matt. 6:20.
12. *Opera*, 28, 181. Sermon CXXXIX on Deut. 24:10–13.
13. *Opera*, 53, 639 f. Sermon LIII on I Tim. 6:17–19.
14. André Biéler, *La pensée économique et sociale de Calvin* (Geneva: Georg, 1959), pp. 336 f.
15. *Opera*, 50, 101. *Com. Sec. Cor.*, II Cor. 8:13.
16. *Opera*, 43, 145 f. *Duodecim Prophetas Minores*, Amos 8:6.
17. *Opera*, 46, 552. Sermon XLIV on the Harmony of the Gospels. Matt. 3:9–10.
18. *Opera*, 55, 424. *Com. Iac. Ep.*, James 5:4.
19. *Opera*, 48, 59. *Com. Acta Apost.*, Acts 2:44.
20. *Institutes*, IV, xx, 3.
21. *Opera*, 27, 567. Sermon CXIV on Deut. 19:14–15.
22. *Institutes*, IV, xx, 13.
23. Biéler, pp. 389 f.

CHAPTER V
Economic Activities

1. *Opera*, 45, 569. *Com. Harm. Evang.*, Matt. 25:20.
2. John W. Baldwin, *The Medieval Theories of the Just Price* (Philadelphia: The American Philosophical Society, 1959), pp. 38, 39, 67.
3. Martin Luther, *An Open Letter to the Christian Nobility of the German Nation*, in *Three Treatises*, trans. C. M. Jacobs (Philadelphia: Fortress Press, 1947), pp. 106, 108.
4. *The Church and the Exploding Metropolis*, ed. Robert Lee (Richmond: John Knox Press, 1965), pp. 24–25.
5. *Opera*, 45, 209. *Com. Harm. Evang.*, Matt. 6:25.
6. *Opera*, 23, 73. *Com. Genesin*, Gen. 3:17.
7. *Opera*, 46, 554. Sermon XLIV on the Harmony of the Gospels, Matt. 3:11–12.
8. *Opera*, 51, 639. Sermon XXXI on the Epistle to the Ephesians, 4:26–28.
9. *Opera*, 45, 540. *Com. Harm. Evang.*, Mark 10:21.
10. A free translation from *Opera*, 28, 188. Sermon CXL on Deut. 24:14–18.
11. *Opera*, 28, 161 f. Sermon CXXXVII on Deut. 24:1–6.
12. *Opera*, 24, 677. Com. on Deut. 24:6.

13. *Opera*, 45, 570. *Com. Harm. Evang.*, Matt. 25:24.
14. *Opera*, 52, 316. *Com. Epis. Tim. I*, I Tim. 5:18.
15. *Opera*, 28, 222 f. Sermon CXLII on Deut. 25:1–4.
16. *Opera*, 27, 345 f. Sermon XCV on Deut. 15:11–15.
17. *Opera*, 38, 383. *Praelectiones in Ieremiam*, Jer. 22:13.
18. *Opera*, 27, 357. Sermon XCVI on Deut. 15:16–23.
19. *Opera*, 27, 347. Sermon XCV on Deut. 15:11–15.
20. *Opera*, 28, 189. Sermon CXL on Deut. 24:14–18.
21. *Opera*, 28, 11. Sermon CXXV on Deut. 22:1–4.
22. *Opera*, 23, 401 f. *Com. Genesin*, Gen. 29:14.
23. This struggle with Pastor Philip can best be followed in *Reg. Comp. Pasteurs*, I, 47, 56–57, 76, 132–148. Beginning in 1549, he hung on until 1553, when he was deposed and Nicholas Collodon took his place. Whether the Council simply wanted to thwart Calvin, or was friendly to de Ecclesia, or knew it could not get another pastor at the low salary paid is difficult to know.
24. For example, James W. Thompson, *Economic and Social History of the Later Middle Ages, 1300–1530* (New York: Frederick Ungar, 1960), pp. 439 f., lists three methods of evading the accusation of usury. First, the sale of rent charges, whereby a landlord who needed money would sell land on which he received rent to a usurer. The latter would give him back his land with the stipulation that henceforth and for a specified time the rent would be paid to the lender, the sum being fixed at a usurious rate above the sale of the land. (Today this would be a land mortgage.) Partnerships or companies, *commenda*, gave easy means of investing money and receiving back more. A third means was to lend money without interest till the expiration date, then—both parties having agreed beforehand—the lender sued for his money and damages for the breaking of the contract, the damages, of course, amounting to a tidy profit, known as *damnum emergens* (damages arising from lending) or *lucrum cessans* (gain lost because the money was not available to the lender). Noonan shows (see note 27) that partnership—*commenda*, *societas*, or *foena nauticum*—was early allowed, there being a presumption of shared risk, though the scholastics do not make clear why risk must be the criterion, nor why money can fructify here but not in a regular loan (pp. 151 f.). "In the Middle Ages, the *societas* make risk-sharing investment a substantial form of capital-rewarding enterprise" (p. 153). Of the type of investment Thompson calls rent-contract, but Noonan *census* (probably the root of the German *Zins*), the latter writes: "The *census* theory tends to the adoption of an analysis, which, if not contradictory to the usury theory, at least offers an alternative to it which would

make the usury theory dead in practice" (p. 154). So, all other arguments and practices aside, the guaranteed triple-contract (*infra*) and guaranteed *census* cut the ground from the argument that riskless profit is wrong (p. 358).

25. R. H. Tawney, *Religion and the Rise of Capitalism* (New York: Mentor Books, 1961), pp. 45, 46.

26. Raymond de Roover, *The Rise and Decline of the Medici Bank, 1397-1494* (Cambridge, Mass.: Harvard University Press, 1963), p. 1. He also observes, "there were unnumerable ways of circumventing the usury prohibition and, it must be said, they were encouraged by the quibbles of the Doctors and theologians. . . . The latter, unwittingly, gave the merchants a chance to make the most of technicalities" (p. 11).

27. John T. Noonan, Jr., *The Scholastic Analysis of Usury* (Cambridge, Mass.: Harvard University Press, 1957), p. 192. The two most exhaustive accounts of *usura* in the Middle Ages are Noonan's work and Benjamin Nelson, *The Idea of Usury* (Princeton: Princeton University Press, 1949).

28. Nelson, pp. 19-22. Noonan, pp. 294-310, discusses the *Montes Pietatis* at some length. Though attacked by a theologian like Cardinal Cajetan, they were approved in 1516 by the Fifth Lateran Council, when that Council accepted Pope Leo's bull *Inter multiplices*. (It should be noted that Leo was a Medici.) Though the little Franciscan lending agencies were at first financed by donations, they soon accepted the deposits of anyone who wanted to invest, paying 5 percent on such loans and charging from 8 to 10 percent in Italy and 15 percent in Belgium. Taking the place of Jews and Lombards (Italian moneylenders), they are hard to distinguish from a modern savings and loan institution.

29. Noonan, pp. 208-210.

30. *Zinskauf* was a species of rent charges. See note 24. The letter may be found in *Luther's Correspondence and Other Contemporary Letters*, ed. Preserved Smith and Charles M. Jacobs (2 vols.; Philadelphia: Lutheran Publication Society, 1918), II, 237. The new *Luther's Works* edition will supercede this edition when it is off the press.

31. Nelson, p. 52, says Luther's position abounds in "hesitations and contradictions." For Luther's best-stated position, read *Usury and Trade* (1524), in *Luther's Works*, vol. 45, trans. Charles M. Jacobs (Philadelphia: Fortress Press, 1962), p. 308.

32. Noonan, p. 365.

33. We assume Sachinus was the friend to whom he wrote, since the undated letter from "Iehan Calvin a quelquun de ses amys" fits the question asked by Sachinus, 7 November 1545. Sachinus' letter

is found in *Opera*, 12, 210; the reply in 10a, 245–249. I am using the Georgia Harkness translation from her *John Calvin: The Man and His Ethics* (Nashville: Abingdon Press, 1931), pp. 204–206. I have added certain words from the original in brackets.

34. *Opera*, 24, 679 f., contains his analysis of the Deuteronomic prohibition. His commentary on Ezekiel 18:5–9 absolutely condemns moneylending as a profession; the usurer (*foenerator*) is not to be tolerated, but is to be expelled from communion with his fellowmen. *Opera*, 40, 431.

CHAPTER VI
Geneva's Struggle for a Decent Life

1. *Opera*, 21, 216. R.C., 30 October 1537. Perhaps this is a good place to transcribe the whole citation from the *Registres du Conseil*, so that the modern reader who handles the French may have occasion to see how it was written in Geneva in the sixteenth century. It should be borne in mind that most Genevans then spoke a patois that has disappeared completely, leaving only one or two faint literary traces. "Calvinus a propose que question se porroit engendrer entre les citoyes a cause que aulcungs hont iure le mode de vivre les aultres non. Item des enfans quil sont aux escolles a la papisterie et de savoir la doctrine des enfangs. Item de l'Hospital quest tresmal moble don les paovres soffrent." R.C., vol. 31, fol. 81.

2. *Opera*, 31, 30.

3. Gaston Zeller, *Les institutions de la France au XVIᵉ siècle* (Paris: Presses Universitaires de France, 1948), p. 384.

4. *Ibid.*, p. 386.

5. *Ibid.*

6. The French text may be found in *Reg. Comp. Pasteurs*, I, 1 ff. The translation here used is that of J. K. S. Reid, Vol. XXII of the Library of Christian Classics, *Calvin: Theological Treatises* (Philadelphia: The Westminster Press, 1954), pp. 64–66. Unlike Reid, who uses footnotes, I have added the few important additions made by the Council in brackets. I have also used the original French word *procureurs*, rather than his latinization, *procurators*.

7. From the accounts of Treasurer Amblard Corne, given in E. William Monter, *Studies in Genevan Government, 1536–1605* (Geneva: Droz, 1964), p. 18. According to Monter, only quit-rents and interest paid at Basel (fl. 6,213½), purchases for public domain (fl. 2,706½), the wages of seventeen ministers (fl. 3,995), and embassies and messengers, chiefly in France (fl. 3,698½), cost more.

8. *Reg. Comp. Pasteurs*, I, 19. ". . . le tiers aux procureurs des

parroisses, le tiers au chastelain et curial, et l'aultre tiers aux paouvres de la parroisse et lieu." As we have seen, three of the deacons were called *procureurs*. The other ran the hospital.

9. *Opera*, 21, pp. 404–405. 24 May 1547. R.C., vol. 42, fol. 116.

10. *Opera*, 21, 752. R.C., vol. 55, fol. 210.

11. Paul Chaix, *Recherches sur l'imprimerie à Genève de 1550 à 1564* (Geneva: Droz, 1954), p. 77.

12. Zeller, pp. 381–383.

13. Natalie A. Z. Davis, "Protestantism and the Printing Workers of Lyons: A Study in the Problem of Religion and Social Class During the Reformation" (unpublished Ph.D. dissertation, Department of History, University of Michigan, 1959), p. 68.

14. *Reg. Comp. Pasteurs*, II, 77, for January 1557. See also p. 70, where a new schoolmaster was appointed for the hospital, and when he was ordained to the ministry a replacement was made.

15. *Sources du droit*, III, no. 905. 12 May 1553, "Ordonnances sur l'Hôpital."

16. *Opera*, 21, p. 343.

17. Roget, II, 150. Roget points out that Calvin did not bring the industry single-handedly to the hospital, as is sometimes thought.

18. Cited by Léon Gautier, *La médicine à Genève jusqu'a la fin du dix-huitième siècle* (Geneva: Georg, 1906), p. 177. Later, on 14 March 1570, the Council assigned the doctors their places during a plague. Two were given charge of the stricken, one to care for the ill "only at a distance" (p. 45). Dr. Philippe Rustici—who was responsible for the first Protestant translation of the Bible into Italian—complained of the wages the city was paying him. Throughout all November 1570, he argued about his pay, finally getting two or three sols per visit, instead of the six he had wanted. Later, that same doctor at the hospital (he has hired at 120 florins per year plus lodging) was convicted of adultery, thrown in prison, released, then re-incarcerated for hitting another doctor. He was exiled from the city, returned, and was the editor of several almanacs, which were printed, after being examined by Beza, "on condition that he strike out the prognostications" (pp. 46–49). Doctors often had a difficult and rather short life in sixteenth-century Geneva—witness doctors Bolsec and Servetus.

19. *Sources du droit*, III, no. 905. 12 May 1553, "Ordonnances sur l'Hôpital."

20. *Histoire de Genève*, p. 227. There were 1,031 *maisons* listed in 1537. The problem, of course, is to figure just how many people, on the average, shared a house. Louis Blondel estimates ten, but others like Doumergue and Williston Walker estimate thirteen per house, and arrive at a population of about 13,300. This figure

is also accepted by Georgia Harkness, p. 8. Cf. Émile Doumergue, *Jean Calvin: Les hommes et les choses de son temps* (7
vols.; Lausanne: G. Bridel, 1899–1927), III, 73n., 74. Walker, p.
161.

21. Roset, p. 297.
22. Paul F. Geisendorf, "Métiers et conditions sociales du premier
refuge à Genève, 1549–1587," *Mélanges . . . Antony Babel*, II,
240–241.
23. Doumergue, III, 74.
24. Roget, IV, 183.
25. *Opera*, 21, p. 720. 7 August 1559. R.C., vol. 55, fol. 78. So in addition to Magdalen, St. Pierre, and St. Gervais, where there had
been regular services since at least the fall of 1541, there were
added services at St. Germain and Notre Dame the New, with
the possibility of restoring the Rive monastery chapel. This
probably did not mean weekday services, but only on Wednesday morning, the day of prayer, and Sunday morning at the
"accustomed hour" (8 or 9 A.M.—Choisy, p. 233), and perhaps at
daybreak on Sunday as well. St. Germain, after a curious non-
ecclesiastical gap post-Reformation when it served as a butcher
shop, among other things, became Roman Catholic again during
the period Napoleon's troops were in town, and is now used by
the Old Catholics. Notre Dame the New, formerly the bishop's
private chapel, is now the place where one may hear Dutch,
Italian, Spanish, but mostly Scottish, sermons. It stands beside the
Cathedral of St. Peter.
26. Lewis Mumford, *The City in History* (New York: Harcourt,
Brace & World, 1961), p. 132.
27. Antony Babel, *Histoire corporative de l'horlogerie, de l'orfèvrerie
et des industries annexés* (Geneva: Georg, 1916), pp. 35–36, writes
that the refugees made a radical economic transformation in
Geneva, arriving without resources but with a profession to practice which brought life to Genevan industry and economy.
28. Davis, p. 35.
29. Geisendorf, "Métiers et conditions sociales du premier refuge à
Genève, 1549–1587," *Mélanges . . . Anthony Babel*, II, 246. In the
second refugee period, 1572–1574, the liberal professions—jurists,
medical men, scholars, and schoolmasters, with some booksellers,
printers, and ministers—made up a much higher percentage. But
in the third book, 1585–1587, the list is much like the first. The
French Huguenot constituency was quite average, neither noble
predominantly nor bourgeois. However, its leadership, as noted
in the first chapter, was found in the lesser nobility.
30. *Opera*, 21, 353. 4 May 1545. R.C., vol. 40, fol. 102.

31. *Opera*, 21, 353. 16 May 1545. R.C., vol. 40, fol. 118.
32. Roget, II, 168. In 1548, one Iehan Beguyn, a cloth-maker, was admitted to the *bourgeoisie* gratis because "he has set up a cloth-making trade in this city by means of which many poor people live." Covelle, p. 235.
33. Roset, pp. 309, 362 f.
34. Monter, p. 24. I would think Bergier's language too strong when he writes of "vast movements of capital following the Huguenot flight." However, he may have in mind refugees of the next century. Jean François Bergier, *Genève et l'économie européenne de la Renaissance* (Paris: S.E.V.P.E.N., 1963), p. 83.
35. Roget, III, 211–212.
36. Roget, II, 80. The percentages are mine, so no mathematical mistake should be blamed on Roget.
37. Roset, p. 399. According to Bergier (p. 110), a *coupe* held 79.365 liters, or on our scale, 2.25 bushels.
38. Monter, p. 126. I have extracted these from the "Table of Net Revenues of Geneva Treasuries." The return on customs duties shows a similar rise—856 florins in 1540, 1,802 in 1550, and 3,154 in 1555; similarly, the tax on meat—1,716 for 1541, 2,620 for 1550, and 3,640 for 1555. In each case, note that the receipts rose quite sharply in the last, five-year period.
39. *Opera*, 21, 705. 27 September 1558. R.C., vol. 54, fol. 295.
40. *Sources du droit*, III, no. 974. 11 October 1558.
41. *Sources du droit*, III, no. 1015, 6 April 1562, prohibits anyone's playing at a game in the streets or public places on the days the *Cène* is celebrated, in order "that each may employ himself that day to meditate the graces of God toward us." *Sources du droit*, II, no. 850, 2 August 1548, indicates that the day for the shooting tournament was the third Sunday after Easter. This was a high, festive occasion for Geneva.
42. Monter, p. 68.
43. Zeller, p. 21.
44. Roget, II, 233–234.
45. *Sources du droit*, II, no. 860. 17 December 1549.
46. See Roget, II, 228. Earlier laws prohibiting dancing were passed in 1487 and 1517, as well as 1539. The text of the 1550 ordinance makes it clear that the situation was simply not being dealt with. *Opera*, 21, 460. 20 January 1550. "The ordinances concerning dancing should not be lessened [i.e., the fines], but that they no longer be allowed. [This is the report of Calvin and Pastor Poupin to the Council.] Concerning which it is decided that proclamations should be made at the sound of the trumpet that no one should dance in any fashion at all: the penalty being three days in

prison on bread and water, and sixty sous for each time, half for the hospital and the other half for the court." The last division is important, I think; it was meant to encourage the *lieutenant de justice*, at that time Jean A. Curtet, to do his duty in enforcing an unpopular edict. R.C., vol. 44, fol. 306 v.

47. *Sources du droit*, III, no. 1050. 8 June 1564. Particular mention was made of hats in this regard.

48. *Opera*, 17, 464.

49. For example, *Opera*, 21, p. 308. 5 March 1543. "Ordained that the men ought not to go to bathe with the women, nor the women with the men, and also that each man and woman should be separate unless they be joined in marriage and therefore able to sleep together, but not to bathe, and to make commandment to the *estuviers*." So even husband and wife could not bathe together, though the awkward wording makes one wonder if the secretary didn't start to write one thing and end up writing another. Mixed bathing was regarded as "a scandalous thing among the faithful." R.C., vol. 36, fol. 26. We read later complaints that two of the pastors went "nud a nud" to the baths with one Huguenne and her sister. They were later deposed. *Opera*, 21, 367. 11 January 1546. R.C., vol. 40, fol. 345. In England the word for public bathhouses, "stew" (*estuve* has the same meaning), became synonymous with whorehouse.

50. See Max Weber's use of this in his *The Protestant Ethic and the Spirit of Capitalism*, trans. Talcott Parsons (New York: Charles Scribner's Sons, 1930), p. 175. There we have his famous misquotation of Wesley: "we must exhort all Christians to gain all they can, and to save all they can; that is, in effect, to grow rich," leaving out "give all they can" till the next page.

51. Mumford, p. 453. See below, pp. 212–213.

CHAPTER VII
BUSINESS AND FINANCE

1. Herbert Lüthy, *Le passé présent: Combats d'idées de Calvin à Rousseau* (Monaco: Éditions du Rocher, 1965), p. 79.

2. Paul E. Martin, "Calvin et le prêt à intérèt à Genève," *Mélanges . . . Antony Babel*, II, 252.

3. *Ibid.*, p. 253. "De ceux qui trepassent sans faire de testament.— Item que se aulcun clerc, citoyen, juré ou habitant de la dite cité meurt sans testament, ou soit usurier public ou non, bastart ou aultre, quelqu'il soit ou de quelle condition, les enfants qu'il aura soient ses heritiers."

4. *Ibid.*, p. 254.

5. *Ibid. Sources du droit*, II, nos. 343, 344.

6. Martin, p. 256. R.C., vol. 38, fol. 10.

7. *Sources du droit*, II, no. 612. "Ordonné que tous reneves, tan ble que vin et aultres choses, soyent reduyctes a cinq pour cent." That is, the cash equivalent must not exceed 5 percent.

8. *Sources du droit*, III, no. 816. 19 February 1544.

9. Martin, p. 257.

10. *Sources du droit*, II, no. 841.

11. See above, p. 91.

12. Martin, p. 258. Some of this information is in *Opera*, 21, 668, but Martin has dug deeper into the unpublished *Registres du Conseil* than the Strasbourg editors.

13. Monter has done the definitive work so far on the little-known *Chambre des Comptes*. It was set up soon after independence in 1536 and was presided over by one of the four syndics. It acted as a clearinghouse for all fiscal transactions of the city, signed the *mandements* with which Geneva's public debts were paid, and surveyed the books of the treasurer, the granary superintendent, and others on public works. "It centralized Geneva's finances in an age when such centralization was still uncommon" (pp. 15–16).

14. Martin, p. 258, quoting from R.C., vol. 53, fol. 338.

15. *Sources du droit*, III, no. 953, "Conditions des prêts à intérêts." *Pour quinze*, one-fifteenth, was the new ceiling, i.e., 6⅔ percent.

16. Martin, p. 260.

17. *Sources du droit*, p. 49. ". . . en tous contractz de prest d'argent à cense ou profict y aura serment expres de la somme vrayement receue." Translation: ". . . in all contracts of lending money for rent income or profit there will be a precise declaration of the true amount received." *Cense*, I believe, is equivalent to *Zinskauf* (see above, p. 90).

18. It should be noted here that Martin does not agree that this reflects Calvin's influence, because "in the present case there is only record that the advice of men of affairs in the stream of commerce and the circulation of money be sought, the opinion of Calvin or the ministers not being cited" (p. 260). It seems to me that since the committee to study the matter was to include ministers (which meant Calvin, above all) and there is no indication that the edict published a month and a half later met with their disapproval, then we must conclude that they accepted the necessity for new regulations without murmur. Had Calvin complained, we would surely know of it!

19. *Sources du droit*, III, nos. 953, 957. The former reads: "Item ne sera permis bailler et prester argent soubz colleur et conventions d'achepter bled ou vin estant encores pendant en herbe, ou soit en fonds et possessions et à recuillir, synon à la charge d'y mettre

le prix selon que le bled ou vin vauldra au temps de la cueille d'iceulx; et que les achaptz des fruictz et prises et les ypothecques se feront à priz raisonnables; et s'il y a excès notable, comme du tiers plus, seront reduictes à la raison du dict profict d'argent, comme dessus dict est."

20. Monter, p. 82. The statement about taxation, while not my concern here, is apropos to a discussion of the way the city republic treated its rural holdings. Paternalistic, yes, but fair.

21. Martin, p. 261.

22. *Ibid.*, p. 262. R.C., vol. 60, fol. 127. 10 December 1565.

23. Monter, pp. 22–23.

24. *Ibid.*, p. 29; André E. Sayous, "La Banque à Genève pendant les XVIe, XVIIe et XVIIIe siècles," *Revue Économique Internationale* (September 1934), p. 443.

25. Monter, pp. 30–32.

26. *Ibid.*, p. 32.

27. *Ibid.*, pp. 32–37; Sayous, p. 445.

28. Bergier, p. 84.

29. Sayous, p. 442.

30. Tawney, p. 94.

31. Robert M. Kingdon, "The Economic Behavior of Ministers in Geneva in the Middle of the Sixteenth Century," *Archiv für Reformationsgeschichte*, 50 (1959), p. 39.

32. Sylvia Porter, *Detroit Free Press, et loc. al.*, 30 December 1964.

33. *Supra*, pp. 73–74, 55–56, 82–83, 86–87, 61–62.

34. Luther wrote: "All festivals should be abolished, and Sunday alone retained. If it were desired, however, to retain the festivals of Our Lady and of the greater saints, they should be transferred to Sunday, or observed only by a morning mass, after which all the rest of the day should be a working-day. The reason is this: the feast-days are now abused by drinking, gaming, idleness, and all manner of sins, so that on the holy days we anger God more than on other days, and have altogether turned things around; the holy days are not holy and the working days are holy, and not only is no service done to God and His saints by the many holy days, but rather great dishonor." *An Open Letter to the Christian Nobility*, in *Three Treatises*, p. 73.

35. *Opera*, 21, 211. R.C., vol. 30, fol. 248.

36. *Sources du droit*, II, no. 824. 4 September 1545.

37. Henri Sée and Armand Rébillon, *Le XVIe Siècle* (Paris: Presses Universitaires de France, 1950), pp. 25–26.

38. *Sources du droit*, III, no. 980. 23 March 1559.

39. Cited by Roget, VI, 193. Not in *Sources du droit*.

40. Roget, VI, 193.

41. *Opera*, 21, 382. 11 June 1546. R.C., vol. 41, fol. 112.

42. *Opera*, 21, 680. 22 November 1557. "Des enfans de feu M. Abel Popin ministre a este mis en avant quilz sont deias grans allans vacabondans. Arreste quon remecte ce a la charge de M. le Sindicque Chicquand et aux procureurs dlhospital de y pourvoir." R.C., vol. 53, fol. 421.

43. Now the site of Geneva's gold-spired Russian Orthodox Church.

44. *Opera*, 21, 683.

45. *Opera*, 21, 685.

46. *Reg. Comp. Pasteurs*, II, 81–83, follows several changes before the the definitive one. *Opera*, 21, 709, for 6 December 1558, where the replacement of money for wheat was seen to accord with the pastors' wishes because the wheat was not good (*beau*). Roget, V, 175.

47. Roget, V, 220. As with the other men, free lodging was also his.

48. Roget, VI, 289.

49. Roget, VI, 290. *Reg. Comp. Pasteurs*, II, 99.

50. Bergier's discussion of wheat policy (pp. 100–109), together with his appendices on the prices of wheat (pp. 110–113) and wine (pp. 117–120), are interesting but not particularly helpful. After 1536 most of the records seem to be for times of particular crisis, and thus are emergency prices.

51. Abbott Payson Usher, *History of Mechanical Inventions* (Boston: Beacon Press, 1959), p. 238.

52. Bacon finished his *Novum Organum* in 1620, sixty years after Geneva's Council passed its printing ordinance. This citation is from the First Book, aphorism 129.

53. Chaix, pp. 8–11.

54. *Opera*, 21, 248. R.C., vol. 33, fol. 115. Chaix, pp. 15–16.

55. Germaine Martin, *Histoire économique et financière* (Paris: Plon, 1927), p. 187.

56. Sée, pp. 35, 236.

57. *Ibid.*, p. 236.

58. Germaine Martin, p. 187.

59. *Opera*, 21, 672. 9 August 1557. After speaking of violations in usury, Calvin denounced ". . . les superstitions et dissolutions des mestiers quand quelquun y passe maistre." R.C., vol. 53, fol. 265.

60. *Sources du droit*, III, nos. 949, 950.

61. Taken from R.C., vol. 55, fol. 87. Chaix, p. 19.

62. See Chaix, pp. 20–25, for the text.

63. *Ibid.*, p. 26.

64. *Ibid.*, p. 35.

65. Davis, p. 404.

66. Chaix, pp. 27–29, for details of a very hot squabble which took

place in the summer of 1561. The workers were accused of monopoly and forcible measures against their fellow workers; a
species of automation was looked into—"an invention to make two
sheets for one"; and the journeymen argued they needed the
second Wednesday in order to hear the Word of God!
67. *Ibid.*, p. 21.
68. Roget, VI, 192–193. *Opera*, 21, 772. 12 January 1562. R.C., vol.
56, fol. 292 v. The R.C. say "Jehan," but the Anastaise brothers
were often confused.
69. *Opera*, 21, 739. 12 December 1560. R.C., vol. 56, fol. 114. This order, the same year the ordinance on printing was issued, denied
licenses to Anastaise and two others "who do not understand their
job."
70. *Opera*, 21, 773. R.C., vol. 56, fol. 300.
71. This list is reproduced in Chaix, p. 32.
72. *Ibid.*, p. 141. Chaix gives us a short repertory of Genevan printers in which he says that Anastaise was married to a daughter of
Robert Estienne, one of the two greatest printers of Geneva—the
other being Crespin—but "this illustrious alliance does not seem
to have influenced his work . . . which remained perfectly medi-
ocre."
73. Babel, pp. 9–14.
74. *Sources du droit*, III, no. 981. "Item que nul laboureur ny aultres ouvriers n'ayent à faire complot ensemble pour divertir le
cours desd. cries et ordonnances, sus peine d'estre chastié jouxte
l'exigence du cas." 23 March 1559.
75. Chaix, pp. 39, 40. One worker so accused was said to debauch
others by attempting to get others to join.
76. Davis, pp. 431–446.
77. *Ibid.*, pp. 473–485.
78. *Ibid.*, pp. 376, 390, 402.

CHAPTER VIII
THE COMMON LIFE

1. *Opera*, 21, 202. R.C., vol. 29, fol. 112.
2. *Reg. Comp. Pasteurs*, I, 1.
3. *Histoire de Genève*, p. 225.
4. Monter, p. 20. I disagree, however, with Monter in his criticism
of the city's spending habits prior to 1559. From his own figures
for 1544, I note 7,006 florins received from traditional ecclesiastical sources and 6,195 paid out, a difference of only 3 percent of
the budget, and this does not count pensions to six priests totaling
at least 600 florins, which would be counted as charity.
5. *Sources du droit*, III, no. 905. 12 May 1553.

6. Roget, VI, 188–189, has the whole account.

7. *Opera*, 21, 480. 11 May 1551. R.C., vol. 44, fol. 270.

8. *Opera*, 21, 708. R.C., vol. 54, fol. 336. The whole affair is discussed by Roget, V, 207–223.

9. Roget, V, 232. Among these were the famous printer Robert Estienne, Parisian refugee, usually given credit for versifying the Bible. The best work on the college is Charles Borgeaud, *Histoire de l'Université de Genève*, Vol. I, *L'Académie de Calvin, 1559–1798* (Geneva: Georg, 1900), pp. 34 f. During the first fifty years, the college received more than 500 bequests.

10. Roget, V, 233.

11. Monter, p. 25.

12. Roget, V, 244n.

13. Quirinius Breen, *John Calvin: A Study in French Humanism* (Grand Rapids: Wm. B. Eerdmans Publishing Co., 1931).

14. *Sources du droit*, III, no. 983. The writings to be covered are found in the rules for the seven classes of the *Schola privata*, the first of two major divisions, pp. 94 and 95. The concern for the manner of teaching the ancients, in "The Order for the Regents of the College," p. 91. The second major division, the advanced *schola publica*, was very unregimented, somewhat like European universities today. Borgeaud, pp. 43–45.

15. *Sources du droit*, III, no. 983.

16. Roget, VII, p. 69. It began with 600 students (Borgeaud, p. 1). Borgeaud, p. 51, cites the disgruntled Haller at Berne, who said the school would be for Geneva alone, since hard times and the uncertainty of their political situation made it unlikely that others would go. But almost all the 300 in the higher school were outsiders.

17. *Calvin: Theological Treatises*, p. 67. Since we cannot imagine Calvin denying this was a spiritual matter, we must assume this was one of the changes the pastors were not allowed to see before the *Ordonnances* were passed.

18. *Reg. Comp. Pasteurs*, I, 30 f., contains an undated *Ordonnance* which was probably adopted in 1546 or 1547—though proof for this is lacking. The 1545 project is found in *Opera*, 10a, 33–44. The differences between the two are very small.

19. *Opera*, Xa, 44.

20. *Supra*, pp. 57–58.

21. *Reg. Comp. Pasteurs*, I, 30. "Que nul pere n'ait à contraindre ses enfans a tel mariage que bon luy semblera sinon de leur bon gré et consentement, mais que celluy ou celle qui ne vouldroit accepter la partie que son pere luy vouldroit donner s'en puisse excuser gardant tousjours modestie et reverence sans que pour

tel refuz le pere luy en face aucune punition; le semblable sera
observé en ceulz qui sont en curatelle."

22. *Ibid.*
23. *Ibid.*, I, 35.
24. *Ibid.*, I, 41.
25. *Opera*, Xa, 40.
26. *Opera*, 21, 780. *Reg. du Consistoire.*
27. *Supra*, pp. 56–57.
28. *Opera*, 21, 432–433. R.C., vol. 43, fol. 177.
29. *Opera*, 10a, p. 38. The 1545 Project.
30. *Sources du droit*, II, no. 845. "Punition des femmes grosses par
    paillardise," 19 September 1547.
31. *Ibid.*, III, no. 1042. 22 November 1563.
32. *Ibid.*, III, no. 1946. 23 March 1564.
33. Choisy, pp. 249–250.

CHAPTER IX
CHURCH AND SOCIETY

1. *Opera*, 21, 648. 10 September 1556: "Raymond Chauvet, minister,
   warns the *Seigneurie* that the dead are interred so close to the
   houses that there is a great stench, and that one named Mouroz
   has a chicken coop of which the chickens make ordures in
   church." R.C., vol. 52, fol. 302.
2. Roget, V, 56 f.
3. *Opera*, 21, 781. 18 June 1562. *Reg. du Consistoire.*
4. Roget, V, 58. "The common measure of humanity was decidedly
   not made for this exceptional person."
5. *Opera*, 21, 682. 28 December 1557. R.C., vol. 54, fol. 25. Also
   Roget, V, 90, 91.
6. *Opera*, 21, 754–755. *Supra*, pp. 52–53. Although there is little likeli-
   hood that the Queen Mother wanted Calvin in France.
7. Monter, p. 118.
8. *Opera*, 51, 797. Sermon on I Sam. 42.
9. *Opera*, 21, 536–537. 28 February 1553. R.C., vol. 47, fol. 29. Priests
   were subject only to the ecclesiastical courts.
10. Roget, II, 109.
11. *Sources du droit*, III, 64–73.
12. *Documents of the Christian Church*, ed. Henry Bettenson (Lon-
    don: Oxford University Press, 1963), p. 160. Writes Boniface
    VIII in 1302: "And we learn from the words of the Gospel that
    in this Church and in her power are two swords, the spiritual and
    the temporal. For when the apostles said, 'Behold, here' (that is, in
    the Church, since it was the apostles who spoke) 'are two swords'
    —the Lord did not reply, 'It is too much,' but 'It is enough.' Truly

he who denies that the temporal sword is in the power of Peter, misunderstands the words of the Lord, 'Put up thy sword into the sheath.' Both are in the power of the Church, the spiritual sword and the material. But the latter is to be used for the Church, the former by her; the former by the priest, the latter by kings and captains but at the will and by the permission of the priest. The one sword, then, should be under the other, and temporal authority subject to spiritual. For when the apostle says 'there is no power but of God, and the powers that be are ordained of God' they would not be so ordained were not one sword made subject to the other. . . ."

13. *Supra*, p. 63.
14. Quoted by Roget, IV, 181n.
15. Choisy, pp. 244–245.
16. Roget, II, 258, 259n. The affair is discussed above in our usury section. See *Opera*, 21, 448–450, 509, 535, 540–541; also *Reg. Comp. Pasteurs*, I, 47, 56–57, 76, 132, 144, 148, 160.
17. *Opera*, Xa, 48, "Projet D'ordonnance sur les Noms de Baptême."
18. *Institutes*, IV, xvii, 38. This whole subject is discussed above in Chapter II.
19. *Ibid.*, IV, xii, 1–13.
20. Not the 1541 Ecclesiastical Ordinances for the city, but the "Ordinances for the Supervision of Churches in the Country" specify the fines for missing worship, midwives who baptize, persons who "spin wildly round in the dance," and other sins. *Theological Treatises*, pp. 76–82.
21. *Institutes*, IV, xx, 2, 3.
22. Roget, III, 282, digs this one from the still-unpublished *Reg. du Consistoire*.
23. French translation of the patois placard is found in Roget, II, 290.
24. Roget, II, 289–312, discusses the trial at some length, as well as the letters written by Calvin which refer to it. Gruet seems to have been a freethinker in a frivolous way, immoral and resentful of authority, but not deep enough to have been called a heretic or dangerous enough to be convicted of lèse majesté.
25. Froment, *Actes et gestes*, "Extracts," c–cv.
26. For Moreaux, *Opera*, 21, 350–354; for Champereaux and Megret, *ibid.*, 367; for Fabri, *Reg. Comp. Pasteurs*, II, 66.
27. Foster, "Geneva before Calvin," p. 19. Roget appends to the end of each of his seven volumes the names of councillors and pastors, and we see that Curtet served on the Small Council every year but one from 1537 to the end of Roget's work in 1567. He was first syndic again in 1541, 1545, 1552, 1556 (the first election after the Perrinist defeat), 1561, and 1565.

28. *Opera*, 21, 368. 27 January 1546. "Lon a revelle que Ameaulx a diest que M. Calvin estoyt meschant homme et nestoyt que un picard et preschoyt faulce doctrine." R.C., vol. 40, fol. 359.

29. The Annals are full of this trial, *Opera*, 21, 368–377. Roget, II, 207–223, gives a good account and tells us something of Ameaux's later citations before the Consistory, which give some evidence that Ameaux neglected public worship but conducted services in his own home.

30. *Opera*, 21, 499. 21 March 1547. R.C., vol. 42, fol. 63.

31. Roget, VII, 42. Roget gives a résumé of a number of instances in 1563 where cases tried before the Council, probably first tried in Consistory, had penalties affixed after consultation with Calvin. Most likely the reason was not his position as pastor, but his legal knowledge. Examples: two arsonists were burned in effigy, whipped, and imprisoned four years; upon the advice of Calvin a woman oft tried for *impudicité* was given two hours in the stocks in addition to six days in jail; upon the advice of Calvin a man who pushed his mother-in-law against a door was put to the *collier;* a bigamous woman was whipped publicly; on the other hand, it was due to Calvin's advice that a young scholar who stole from his father was released because the father had not initiated a complaint. Roget adds: "Could not Calvin, hampered by illness and overworked, have transferred to others these magisterial concerns in criminal matters, quite sterile and having little connection with tasks of a minister of the gospel?" pp. 43, 44.

32. *Opera*, 21, 348. 9 March 1545. R.C., vol. 40, fol. 42v.

33. See, for example, Roget, VI, 194–195. The hot pincers used on the *empoysonneurs* in 1545 seem not to have been used again.

34. Roget, IV, 321–322.

35. Roget, IV, 323. From *Opera*, 15, 830

36. Walker, pp. 352–353.

37. See, for example, Walzer's discussion, p. 2 *et passim*.

38. *Ibid.*, p. 18.

39. Compare Littell's *The Anabaptist View of the Church* (Boston: Starr King Press, 1952, 1958) and his monograph on American church history, *From State Church to Pluralism* (Garden City, N.Y.: Doubleday Anchor Books, 1962), to see his Free Church sympathies. As far as the German situation is concerned, see Littell's *The German Phoenix* (Garden City, N.Y.: Doubleday and Co., 1960), pp. 10 f. Although he substantiates his position that the Lutheran resistance to Hitler was largely passive, the Reformed active, we should be careful not to overstate this, when men like the Niemoellers, Hans Asmussen, and Dietrich Bonhoeffer represented the Lutheran side.

CHAPTER X
SUCCESS AND FAILURE

1. Milton Powell, "The Abolitionist Controversy in the Methodist Episcopal Church, 1840–1864" (unpublished Ph.D. dissertation, Department of History, State University of Iowa, 1963). See especially Chapter VII, "The Theocratic Challenge," pp. 170–195. This dissertation is in process of publication.

2. J. Howard Pew, "Our Reformation Heritage," *Christian Economics*, Vol. XVI (October 20, 1964), p. 1. Mr. Pew suggests that the two reasons our nation is losing its precious Reformation heritage are that "the Church no longer strongly believes the Bible to be the very Word of God, and too, because she has left her proper spiritual sphere to meddle with social, economic, and political matters." How a Presbyterian layman who sponsors Genevan Reformation research ever dug this out of the facts will remain one of the mysteries of our time, though certainly a minor one.

3. *Institutes*, II, xii, 2.

4. *Ibid.*, II, xii, 3.

5. *Ibid.*, I, x, 2.

6. *Ibid.*, I, ii, 1.

7. *Ibid.*, III, ii, 6.

8. Paul van Buren, *Christ in Our Place: The Substitutionary Character of Calvin's Doctrine of Reconciliation* (Grand Rapids: Wm. B. Eerdmans Publishing Co., 1957), pp. 3–4. Van Buren shares Barth's (to me) exaggerated fear of natural theology which makes this statement too strong. Why does one have to tremor at the mere idea of knowledge of God outside Christ? Is it not enough to assert that God's prime revelation in Christ *corrects*, or is the norm for, any other knowledge we may have or think we have? But the criticism of the order of the *Institutes* is still well taken, I think, since Calvin's following the Apostles' Creed did not force him to deal with "God the Father Almighty" apart from "Jesus Christ His only Son our Lord."

9. *Opera*, 45, 719. *Com. Harm. Evang.*, Matt. 26:37.

10. *Institutes*, II, xvi, 10.

11. *Opera*, 47, 291. *Commentarius in Evangelium Iohannis*, John 12:27. Italics mine.

12. *Opera*, 45, 672. *Com. Harm. Evang.*, Matt. 24:36; Mark 13:32. Italics mine.

13. Van Buren, p. 13. I think, however, that van Buren overstates his case, if he means by God *truly* revealing himself in Christ that God has *fully* revealed himself in Christ. Perhaps it was van

Buren's hyper-Christism which led him later to posit not a "God
. . . apart from Christ" but a Christ apart from God in his celebrated *Secular Meaning of the Gospel.*

14. Van Buren, p. 22.

15. Karl Barth, *The Humanity of God* (Richmond: John Knox Press,
1960), p. 49.

16. According to Yves Congar, medieval theology did not wrestle
seriously with the problems present in the decree of Chalcedon
because it was "crypto-Monophysite" in understanding the union
of the divine and human in Christ. See Geddes MacGregor, "The
Kenosis," *Anglican Theological Review*, XLV, no. 1 (January
1963), 75. Perhaps if this were a study of theology proper we
would need to ask if the idea of God held by the bishops of the
fifth century admits of a solution which can be correlated with
the New Testament witness to the God of Israel and the Father
of Jesus Christ. Can God—unchangeable, immutable, impassible
—relate seriously to time-fettered humanity or bring any new
thing to pass? Is the God of Chalcedon and Calvin recognizable in
the Bible?

17. This was the argument used by the Jesuit John Gerard in 1597
when he argued with his English captors that his method of
equivocation had the blessing of being practiced by Jesus. His
captors asked him, "When did Our Lord use equivocation?" His
answer: "When He told His Apostles that no one knew the day
of judgment, not even the Son of Man; and again when He said
He was not going up to Jerusalem for the feast, and then went.
He knew He was going when He said He was not." His prosecutor then said: "Christ was ignorant of the day of judgment as
Son of Man." "The word ignorant," Gerard said, "cannot be used
of the Incarnate Word of God; His human nature was hypostatically united to the divine. He was constituted Judge by God the
Father, and would therefore know all that touched His office.
Moreover, He was infinite wisdom and knew all that concerned
Himself." John Gerard, *The Autobiography of a Hunted Priest*,
trans. Philip Caraman, S.J. (New York: Doubleday Image Books,
1960), p. 155.

18. *Opera*, 55, 310. *Com. Ioh. Epis.*, I John 2:2.

19. *Opera*, 52, 268. *Com. Epist. Tim. I*, I Tim. 2:4. H. Jackson Forstman observes that Calvin was tormented by a need for certitude
which forced him to such interpretations, that the Scriptures
which spoke of divine election and reprobation (Romans 9) might
be harmonized with the rest of the New Testament. Cf. Forstman,
Word and Spirit: Calvin's Doctrine of Biblical Authority (Stanford: Stanford University Press, 1962), pp. 60, 112.

20. The argument that Calvin knew double predestination from Romans 9:18—". . . he has mercy upon whomever he wills, and he hardens the heart of whomever he wills"—is valid. But even here Calvin allowed the text to deny the context. In Paul's discussion of the "hardening" of Israel for the sake of the Gentiles, the conclusion is that "all Israel will be saved" (11:26), and "God has consigned all men to disobedience, that he may have mercy upon all" (11:32). But again Calvin must interpret "all" to mean "the whole church," and "Israel" to mean the church, even though Paul's problem was not the church, but the real, literal, Jewish Israel!

21. Monter, p. 118.

CHAPTER XI
CALVINISM AND CAPITALISM

1. Max Weber, *The Protestant Ethic and the Spirit of Capitalism*, trans. Talcott Parsons, foreword by R. H. Tawney (New York: Charles Scribner's Sons, 1939). *Die Protestantische Ethik und der Geist des Kapitalismus* first appeared in the *Archiv für Sozialwissenschaft und Sozialpolitik*, Vols. XX and XXI, for 1904–1905. It was reprinted by Weber with changes and more extensively footnoted in his *Gesammelte Aufsätze zur Religionssoziologie* in 1920, the year of his death. For Troeltsch, read *The Social Teachings of the Christian Churches*, trans. Olive Wyon (2 vols.; New York: The Macmillan Co., 1950). For R. H. Tawney, *Religion and the Rise of Capitalism* (New York: Harcourt, Brace and Company, 1926).

2. Weber, p. 154.

3. Quoted by Weber, p. 162.

4. Biéler assumes Weber's reliability here and refers to Franklin as a Puritan!

5. Winthrop S. Hudson, "Puritanism and the Spirit of Capitalism," *Church History*, Vol. XVIII (March 1949), pp. 3–16.

6. Lüthy, p. 21. Most Puritans found evidence of God's blessing not in their daily work—important as that was—but in the conversion experience which turned them to Christ.

7. Remember also that Walzer holds that the Calvinist influence was shown in politics before it ever made an impact upon economic development and subsequent theory. See above, p. 172.

8. Friedrich Klemm, *A History of Western Technology*, trans. Dorothea Waley Singer (London: Allen and Unwin, 1959), p. 171.

9. From Baxter's *Christian Directory*, Vol. V, p. 535. Quoted by Robert K. Merton, "Science, Technology and Society in 17th Century England," *Osiris*, vol. 4, part 2 (1938), p. 435.

10. See, for example, A. R. Hall, *The Scientific Revolution* (Boston: Beacon Press, 1954), p. 106. Also, Merton (p. 474) says that enemies of Cromwell's Puritan Commonwealth and supporters of the Stuart restoration were so conscious of the Puritan cast of the Royal Society that it is hard to know why later scholars missed the obvious connection.

11. For example, read Alfred North Whitehead's *Science and the Modern World* (New York: Mentor Books, 1948), chapter 1, where he shows how necessary the medieval appreciation of Greek thought was for the possibility of the rise of modern science.

12. Erik Erikson, *Young Man Luther* (New York: W. W. Norton, 1958), especially chapter 1.

13. Lüthy, p. 42.

14. Or so writes James McBride Dabbs, *Who Speaks for the South?* (New York: Funk & Wagnalls, 1964), pp. 62–63. See also David Bertelson, *The Lazy South* (New York: Oxford University Press, 1967), who argues convincingly that the Puritan and the Quaker of the North founded societies based on communities of consent sharing common goals, but the settlers in the South rejected community because they were attracted from the British Isles by the allurement of personal gain.

15. Christian Lalive d'Epinay, *Haven of the Masses: A Study of the Pentecostal Movement in Chile,* trans. Marjorie Sandle (London: Lutterworth Press, 1969).

16. McLuhan, *The Gutenberg Galaxy,* p. 18.

17. McLuhan tries to get out of his corner by saying that the "Spaniards had been immunized against typography by their age-old quarrel with the Moors." But since he argues that Spanish nationalism is a product of printing, it is difficult to see how he can sustain both sides of this. It is much easier to suppose what one would naturally suppose if not hypnotized by McLuhanese, that it was the *content* of the message, not the medium, which made the decisive difference.

18. I borrow without apology this *terminus a quo,* the repeal in England of the Speenhamland Law, from Karl Polanyi, *The Great Transformation* (Boston: Beacon Press, 1957). That law prevented the development of a labor market—indispensable for a free market—by a system of payments to unemployed men and by making up differences between wages and a living wage. Thus men did not have to work to eat until 1832, employers got used to paying very low wages since the parish would make up the difference, and the man who really wanted to work had the ground cut from under him psychologically.

19. "Not by might, nor by power, but by my Spirit, says the Lord."

"Son of man, can these bones live? . . . O Lord God, thou knowest." "God has consigned all men to disobedience, that he may have mercy upon all." "For as in Adam all die, so also in Christ shall all be made alive." The initiative for salvation is always with God, hence Calvin was correct in allowing God's election to take care of Heaven, thus freeing men to take over Earth.

CHAPTER XII
CALVIN AND THE AGONIES OF MODERN SECULARITY

1. Gabriel Vahanian, *No Other God* (New York: George Braziller, 1966), Chapter V, "Calvin: Theology and the Death of God."
2. Those who have read Mircea Eliade, *The Sacred and the Profane* and *Cosmos and History*, will recognize that I am borrowing heavily from this great religious historian. I find his longing for a re-sacralization of the world premature, however.
3. Harvey Cox, *The Secular City* (New York: The Macmillan Co., 1965). Of course, Cox is not quite this one-sided in his appreciation of the secular, but his hyperbole has made it possible to oversimplify his thought in this direction without being accused of willful misinterpretation.
4. For example, Gayraud Wilmore, *The Secular Relevance of the Church* (Philadelphia: The Westminster Press, 1962).
5. This and the next point about the church's role in industrial society are borrowed from Jürgen Moltmann, *Theology of Hope*, trans. James W. Leitch (New York: Harper & Row, 1967), pp. 311 ff.
6. Above, Chapter VI.
7. Mumford, p. 453. (See above, Chapter VI.)
8. "God sent not his Son . . . to condemn the world; but that the world through him might be saved" (John 3:17, K.J.V.). Salvation in the Fourth Gospel is a matter both of eternal life with God and of present life, life abundant.

Bibliography

BOOKS

Ashley, William J. *An Introduction to English Economic History and Theory.* 4th ed., 2 vols. London: Longmans, Green and Company, 1925.

Babel, Antony. *Histoire corporative de l'horlogerie, de l'orfèvrerie et des industries annexés.* Geneva: Georg, 1916.

Bainton, Roland H. *Hunted Heretic: The Life and Death of Michael Servetus.* Boston: Beacon Press, 1953.

Baldwin, John W. *The Medieval Theories of the Just Price: Romanists, Canonists and Theologians in the Twelfth and Thirteenth Centuries.* Philadelphia: The American Philosophical Society, 1959.

Barth, Karl. *The Humanity of God.* Richmond: John Knox Press, 1960.

Bergier, Jean François. *Genève et l'économie européenne de la Renaissance.* Paris: S.E.V.P.E.N., 1963.

Bertelson, David. *The Lazy South.* New York: Oxford University Press, 1967.

Bettenson, Henry, ed. *Documents of the Christian Church.* 2nd ed. London: Oxford University Press, 1963.

Biéler, André. *La pensée économique et sociale de Calvin.* Geneva: Georg, 1959.

———. *The Social Humanism of Calvin.* Translated by Paul T. Fuhrmann. Richmond: John Knox Press, 1964.

———. *Calvin, prophète de l'ère industrielle. Fondement et méthode de l'étheque calvinienne de la société.* Geneva: Labor et Fides, 1964.

Blondel, Louis. *Le développement urbain de Genève à travers les siècles.* Geneva, 1946.

Borgeaud, Charles. *Histoire de l'Université de Genève.* Vol. I, *L'Académie de Calvin, 1559–1798.* Geneva: Georg, 1900.

Breen, Quirinius. *John Calvin: A Study in French Humanism.* Grand Rapids: Wm. B. Eerdmans Publishing Co., 1931.

Calvin, John. *Opera quae supersunt omnia.* Edited by Guillâume Baum, Eduard Cunitz, and Eduard Reuss. 59 vols. Brunswick, 1863–1900. Of these volumes, I have consulted especially 5, 7, 10, 21, 23, 26, 27, 28, 43, 45, 46, 51, 53, and 54. Footnotes refer to other volumes on occasion.

———. *Calvin: Commentaries.* Edited by Joseph Haroutunian with Louise P. Smith. Vol. XXIII of the Library of Christian Classics.

Edited by John Baillie, John T. McNeill, and Henry P. Van Dusen. Philadelphia: The Westminster Press, 1958.

——. *Calvin: Institutes of the Christian Religion.* Translated by Ford Lewis Battles. Edited by John T. McNeill. Vols. XX and XXI of the Library of Christian Classics. Edited by John Baillie, John T. McNeill, and Henry P. Van Dusen. Philadelphia: The Westminster Press, 1960.

——. *Calvin: Theological Treatises.* Translated and edited by J. K. S. Reid. Vol. XXII of the Library of Christian Classics. Philadelphia: The Westminster Press, 1954.

Cassirer, Ernst. *The Question of Jean-Jacques Rousseau.* Translated by Peter Gay. New York: Columbia University Press, 1954.

Chaix, Paul. *Recherches sur l'imprimerie à Genève de 1550 à 1564.* Geneva: Droz, 1954.

Choisy, Eugène. *La Théocratie à Genève au temps de Calvin.* Geneva: J.-G. Fick, 1897.

Covelle, Alfred D. *Le Livre des Bourgeois de l'ancienne République de Genève.* Geneva: J. Jullien, 1897.

Cox, Harvey. *The Secular City.* New York: The Macmillan Co., 1965.

Dabbs, James McBride. *Who Speaks for the South?* New York: Funk & Wagnalls, 1964.

de Roover, Raymond. *The Rise and Decline of the Medici Bank, 1397-1494.* Cambridge, Mass.: Harvard University Press, 1963.

Doumergue, Émile. *Jean Calvin: Les hommes et les choses de son temps.* 7 vols. Lausanne: G. Bridel, 1899-1927.

Dufour, Alain. *Histoire politique et psychologie historique.* Geneva: Droz, 1966.

Ehrenberg, Richard. *Capital and Finance in the Age of the Renaissance.* Translated by H. M. Lucas. New York: Harcourt, Brace & Co., 1930.

Eliade, Mircea. *The Sacred and the Profane: The Nature of Religion.* Translated from the French by Willard R. Trask. New York: Harper & Row, 1961.

——. *Cosmos and History: The Myth of the Eternal Return.* Translated from the French by Willard R. Trask. New York: Harper & Row, 1959.

Ellul, Jacques. *Violence.* Trans. Cecelia Gaul Kings. New York: Seabury Press, 1969.

Erikson, Erik. *Young Man Luther: A Study in Psycho-Analysis and History.* New York: W. W. Norton, 1958.

Forell, George W. *Faith Active in Love: An Investigation of the Principles Underlying Luther's Social Ethics.* Minneapolis: Augsburg Publishing House, 1954.

Forstman, H. Jackson. *Word and Spirit: Calvin's Doctrine of Biblical Authority.* Stanford: Stanford University Press, 1962.

Froment, Antoine. *Les Actes et gestes merveilleux de la Cité de Genève*. Edited by Gustave Revilliod. Geneva: J.-G. Fick, 1864. A firsthand account of the Genevan Reformation by its first preacher, who later became a notary. Finished by 1554, it was not printed for three centuries.

Gagnebin, Bernard. *L'Incroyable histoire des sermons de Calvin*. Geneva, 1956.

Galiffe, J. B. G. *Genève, historique et archéologique*. Geneva: Georg, 1869.

Ganoczy, Alexandre. *Le jeune Calvin: Genèse et évolution de sa vocation réformatrice*. Wiesbaden: Franz Steiner Verlag, 1966.

Gautier, Léon. *La médicine à Genève jusqu'a la fin du dix-huitième siècle*. Geneva: Georg, 1906.

Gerard, John. *The Autobiography of a Hunted Priest*. Translated by Philip Caraman, S.J. Garden City, New York: Doubleday Image Books, 1960.

Green, F. C. *Jean-Jacques Rousseau: A Critical Study of His Life and Writings*. New York: Cambridge University Press, 1955.

Green, Thomas F. *Work, Leisure, and the American Schools*. New York: Random House, 1968.

Grimm, Harold J. *The Reformation Era, 1500–1650*. New York: The Macmillan Co., 1954.

Hall, A. R. *The Scientific Revolution*. Boston: Beacon Press, 1954.

Harkness, Georgia. *John Calvin: The Man and His Ethics*. Nashville: Abingdon Press, 1931.

Haskins, Caryl. *The Scientific Revolution and World Politics*. New York: Harper & Row, 1963, 1964.

Heilbroner, Robert. *The Future as History*. New York: Grove Press, 1961.

Histoire de Genève des origines à 1798. Edited and published by La Société d'Histoire et d'Archéologie de Genève. Geneva, 1951.

Jacobs, Jane. *The Death and Life of Great American Cities*. New York: Random House, 1961.

James, William. *Varieties of Religious Experience*. New York: Mentor Books, 1958. (First published in 1902.)

Jansen, John F. *Calvin's Doctrine of the Work of Christ*. London: James Clarke, 1956.

Jussie, Jean de. *Le Levain du calvinisme, ou commencement de l'hérésie de Genève*. Edited, with a bibliographical notice, by Albert Rilliet. Geneva: J. Jullien, 1866. Written by an exiled sister at the convent of St. Claire; probably first printed in 1611, approximately half a century after its writing.

Kingdon, Robert M. *Geneva and the Coming of the Wars of Religion in France, 1555–1563*. Geneva: Droz, 1956.

————. *Geneva and the Consolidation of the French Protestant Movement, 1564–1572*. Geneva: Droz, 1967.

Klassen, Peter James. *The Economics of Anabaptism*. The Hague: Mouton and Co., 1964.

Klemm, Friedrich. *A History of Western Technology*. Translated by Dorothea Waley Singer. London: Allen and Unwin, 1959.

Lee, Robert, ed. *The Church and the Exploding Metropolis*. Richmond: John Knox Press, 1965.

Littell, Franklin H. *The Anabaptist View of the Church*. Boston: Starr King Press, 1952, 1958.

————. *The German Phoenix: Men and Movements in the Church in Germany*. Garden City, New York: Doubleday & Co., 1960.

Little, David. *Religion, Order and Law: A Study in Pre-Revolutionary England*. New York: Harper Torchbooks, 1969.

Livre des habitants de Genève. Edited by Paul F. Geisendorf. Vol. I, 1549–1560. Geneva: Droz, 1957.

Luther's Correspondence and Other Contemporary Letters. Translated and edited by H. Preserved Smith and Charles M. Jacobs. 2 vols. Philadelphia: Lutheran Publication Society, 1918.

Luther, Martin. *An Open Letter to the Christian Nobility of the German Nation*. In *Three Treatises*. Translated by Charles M. Jacobs. Philadelphia: Fortress Press, 1947.

————. *Ordinance of a Common Chest*. Translated by Albert T. W. Stinhaeuser. Edited by Walther I. Brandt. In vol. 45 of *Luther's Works*. Philadelphia: Fortress Press, 1962.

————. *Usury and Trade*. Translated by Charles M. Jacobs. Edited by Walther I. Brandt. In vol. 45 of *Luther's Works*. Philadelphia: Fortress Press, 1962.

Lüthy, Herbert. *Le passé présent: Combats d'idées de Calvin à Rousseau*. Monaco: Éditions du Rocher, 1965.

McLuhan, Marshall. *The Gutenberg Galaxy*. Toronto: University of Toronto Press, 1962.

————. *Understanding Media*. New York: McGraw-Hill Book Co., 1964.

McNally, Robert E., S.J. *The Unreformed Church*. New York: Sheed and Ward, 1965.

Martin, Germaine. *Histoire économique et financière*. Vol. X of *Histoire de la nation française*. Edited by Gabriel Hanotaux. Paris: Plon, 1927.

Marty, Martin E. *The Search for a Usable Future*. New York: Harper & Row, 1969.

Meland, Bernard E. *The Secularization of Modern Cultures*. New York: Oxford University Press, 1966.

Moltmann, Jürgen. *Theology of Hope.* Translated by James W. Leitch. New York: Harper & Row, 1967.

Monter, E. William. *Studies in Genevan Government, 1536–1605.* Geneva: Droz, 1964.

———. *Calvin's Geneva.* New York: John Wiley & Sons, 1967.

Mueller, William A. *Church and State in Luther and Calvin.* Nashville: Broadman Press, 1954.

Mumford, Lewis. *The City in History: Its Origins, Its Transformations, and Its Prospects.* New York: Harcourt, Brace & World, 1961.

Naef, Henri. *Les origines de la réforme à Genève.* Geneva: Droz, 1936.

Nelson, Benjamin N. *The Idea of Usury.* Princeton: Princeton University Press, 1949.

New Cambridge Modern History. Vol. II, *The Reformation, 1520–1529.* Edited by G. R. Elton. New York: Cambridge University Press, 1958.

Niebuhr, H. Richard. *Christ and Culture.* New York: Harper & Brothers, 1951.

Noonan, John T., Jr. *The Scholastic Analysis of Usury.* Cambridge, Mass.: Harvard University Press, 1957.

Pirenne, Jacques. *Les grands courants de l'histoire universelle.* Vol. II. Neuchâtel: Editions de la Baçonnière, 1950.

Polanyi, Karl. *The Great Transformation.* Boston: Beacon Press, 1957.

Protestantism and Capitalism: The Weber Thesis and Its Critics. Edited by Robert W. Green. Heath Series: Problems in European Civilization. Boston: D. C. Heath & Co., 1959.

Registres de la Compagnie des Pasteurs de Genève au temps de Calvin. Edited by Robert M. Kingdon and Jean François Bergier. 2 vols. Geneva: Droz, 1962, 1964. An English translation, in one volume, is *The Register of the Company of Pastors of Geneva in the Time of Calvin.* Translated and edited by Philip E. Hughes. Grand Rapids: Wm. B. Eerdmans Publishing Co., 1966.

Reyburn, Hugh Y. *John Calvin.* London: Hodder and Stoughton, 1914.

Roget, Amédée. *Histoire du peuple de Genève depuis la réforme jusqu'a l'escalade.* 7 vols. Geneva: J. Jullien, 1870–1883. The single most important work for the student of Genevan history.

Roll, Eric. *A History of Economic Thought.* 3rd ed. Englewood Cliffs, N.J.: Prentice-Hall, 1942.

Roset, Michel. *Chroniques de Genève.* Edited, with an introduction, by Henri Fazy. Geneva: Georg, 1894. This work, by Geneva's most notable councilman, was finished by 1562, but remained unpublished for more than three centuries.

Samuelsson, Kurt. *Religion and Economic Action.* Translated from the Swedish by E. Geoffrey French. New York: Basic Books, 1961.

Sanders, Thomas G. *Protestant Concepts of Church and State*. New York: Holt, Rinehart & Winston, 1964.

Schwiebert, E. G. *Luther and His Times*. St. Louis: Concordia Publishing House, 1950.

Scoville, Warren C. *The Persecution of the Huguenots and French Economic Development, 1680–1720*. Berkeley: University of California Press, 1960.

Sée, Henri, and Rébillon, Armand. *Le XVIᵉ Siècle*. Paris: Presses Universitaires de France, 1950.

Les Sources du droit du Canton de Genève. Edited by Émile Rivoire and Victor van Berchem. Vols. II and III. Aarau: H. R. Sauerländer, 1930 and 1933.

Tawney, R. H. *Religion and the Rise of Capitalism*. New York: Mentor Books, 1961. (First published in 1926.)

Thompson, James W. *Economic and Social History of the Later Middle Ages, 1300–1530*. New York: Frederick Ungar Publishing Co., 1960. (First published in 1931.)

Troeltsch, Ernst. *The Social Teachings of the Christian Churches*. Translated by Olive Wyon. 2 vols. New York: The Macmillan Co., 1950. (First published in 1931.)

Usher, Abbott Payson. *History of Mechanical Inventions*. Boston: Beacon Press, 1959.

Vahanian, Gabriel. *No Other God*. New York: George Braziller, 1966.

van Buren, Paul. *Christ in Our Place: The Substitutionary Character of Calvin's Doctrine of Reconciliation*. Grand Rapids: Wm. B. Eerdmans Publishing Co., 1957.

van Leeuwen, Arend Th. *Christianity in World History: The Meeting of the Faiths of East and West*. Translated from the Dutch by H. H. Hoskins. New York: Charles Scribner's Sons, 1964.

Walker, Williston. *John Calvin: The Organiser of Reformed Protestantism, 1509–1564*. New York: G. P. Putnam's Sons, 1906.

Walzer, Michael. *The Revolution of the Saints: A Study in the Origins of Radical Politics*. Cambridge, Mass.: Harvard University Press, 1965.

Weber, Max. *The Protestant Ethic and the Spirit of Capitalism*. Translated, with an introduction, by Talcott Parsons. New York: Charles Scribner's Sons, 1930. (First published in 1904–05.)

Whitehead, Alfred North. *Science and the Modern World*. New York: Mentor Books, 1948. (First published in 1925.)

Wilmore, Gayraud. *The Secular Relevance of the Church*. Philadelphia: The Westminster Press, 1962.

Zeller, Gaston. *Les institutions de la France au XVIᵉ siècle*. Paris: Presses Universitaires de France, 1948.

CALVIN'S COMMENTARIES

For most of Calvin's commentaries, the English-speaking world is still dependent on the Calvin Translation Society's work in the 1840's and 1850's, which were reprinted by Eerdmans in the 1940's and 1950's. However, new translations have been published of some volumes, also by Eerdmans. Of these, I have consulted volumes 4 and 5 on the Fourth Gospel, volume 8 on Romans and the Thessalonian Letters, volume 9 on I Corinthians, and volume 12 on Hebrews. The following entries follow the biblical sequence.

Calvin, John. *Commentary on the Book of Genesis*. Translated by John King, 1847. 2 vols. Grand Rapids: Wm. B. Eerdmans Publishing Co., 1948.

—————. *Commentaries on the Four Last Books of Moses Arranged in the Form of a Harmony*. Translated by Charles W. Bingham, 1852. 4 vols. Eerdmans, 1950.

—————. *Commentary on the Book of Psalms*. Translated by James Anderson, 1845. 4 vols. Eerdmans, 1949.

—————. *Commentary on the Book of the Prophet Isaiah*. Translated by William Pringle, 1851. 4 vols. Eerdmans, 1955.

—————. *Commentaries on the Book of the Prophet Jeremiah and the Lamentations*. Translated by John Owen, 1850. 2 vols. Eerdmans, 1950.

—————. *Commentaries on the Prophet Ezekiel*. Translated by Thomas Myers, n.d. 2 vols. Eerdmans, 1948.

—————. *Commentaries on the Twelve Minor Prophets*. Translated by John Owen, 1845. 5 vols. Eerdmans, 1950.

—————. *Commentary on a Harmony of the Evangelists, Matthew, Mark and Luke*. Translated by William Pringle, 1845. 3 vols. Eerdmans, 1956.

—————. *Commentary on St. John*. Translated by T. H. L. Parker. Vols. 4 and 5. Eerdmans, 1961.

—————. *Commentary upon the Acts of the Apostles*. A sixteenth-century translation edited by Henry Beveridge, n.d. 2 vols. Eerdmans, 1949.

—————. *Commentaries on the Epistles to the Romans and to the Thessalonians*. Vol. 8. Translated by Ross Mackenzie. Eerdmans, 1960.

—————. *Commentary on the Epistles of Paul the Apostle to the Corinthians*. 2 vols. Translated by John Pringle, 1848. Eerdmans, 1948.

—————. *Commentaries on the Epistles of Paul to the Galatians and Ephesians*. Translated by William Pringle, n.d. Eerdmans, 1955.

—————. *Commentaries on the Epistles to Timothy, Titus and Philemon*. Translated by William Pringle, n.d. Eerdmans, 1948.

————. *Commentary on the Epistle to the Hebrews.* Vol. 12. Translated by William B. Johnson. Eerdmans, 1963.
————. *Commentaries on the Catholic Epistles.* Translated by John Owen, 1855. Eerdmans, 1948.

ARTICLES IN PERIODICALS AND FESTSCHRIFTEN

Binz, Louis. "La population du diocèse de Genève à fin du moyen age." In *Mélanges d'histoire économique et sociale en hommage au Professor Antony Babel.* Vol. 2, pp. 145–196. Geneva, 1963.

Foster, Herbert D. "Geneva before Calvin." In *Collected Papers of Herbert D. Foster,* pp. 1–29. Privately printed, 1929. (First printed in *American Historical Review,* VIII, 2, 1903.)

————. "Calvin's Programme for a Puritan State." In *Collected Papers of Herbert D. Foster,* pp. 30–76. Privately printed, 1929. (First printed in *Harvard Theological Review,* October 1908.)

Geisendorf, Paul F. "Métiers et conditions sociales du premier refuge à Genève, 1549–1587." In *Mélanges . . . Antony Babel.* Vol. 2, pp. 239–249. Geneva, 1963.

Gerrish, B. A. "The Reformation and the Rise of Modern Science." In *The Impact of the Church upon Its Culture.* Edited by Jerald C. Brauer. Vol. II in Essays in Divinity. Chicago: University of Chicago Press, 1968.

Heyer, Theodore. "Essai de détermination de la valeur de l'argent à Genève, vers le milieu du XVIᵉ siècle." *Mémoires et documents . . . la Société d'Histoire et d'Archéologie de Genève.* Vol. 17, pp. 121–126. Geneva, 1872.

Hudson, Winthrop S. "Puritanism and the Spirit of Capitalism." *Church History,* Vol. XVIII (March 1949), pp. 3–16.

Kingdon, Robert M. "The Economic Behavior of Ministers in Geneva in the Middle of the Sixteenth Century." *Archiv für Reformationsgeschichte,* Vol. 50 (1959), pp. 33–39.

McDonnell, Kilian, O.S.B. "Calvin without Myths." *Commonweal,* Vol. LXXXI, no. 6 (October 30, 1964), pp. 163–166.

MacGregor, Geddes. "The Kenosis." *Anglican Theological Review,* XLV, no. 1 (January 1963), pp. 73–82.

Martin, Paul E. "Calvin et le prêt à intérèt à Genève." In *Mélanges . . . Antony Babel.* Vol. 2, pp. 251–263. Geneva, 1963.

Merton, Robert K. "Science, Technology and Society in 17th Century England." *Osiris,* vol. 4, part 2 (1938).

Monter, E. William. "Le change public à Genève, 1568–1581." In *Mélanges . . . Antony Babel.* Vol. 2, pp. 265–290. Geneva, 1963.

Paul, Robert S. "Weber and Calvinism: The Effects of a 'Calling.' " *Canadian Journal of Theology,* Vol. XI, no. 1 (January 1965), pp. 25–41.

Pew, J. Howard. "Our Reformation Heritage." *Christian Economics,* Vol. XVI (October 20, 1964), p. 1.

Roget, M. Amédée. "Expédition d'une compagnie de cavalerie genevoise en 1562." In *Mémoires et documents . . . de Genève.* Vol. 17, pp. 39–57. Geneva, 1872.

Sayous, André D. "La Banque à Genève pendant les XVI°, XVII° et XVIII° siècles." *Revue Économique Internationale* (September 1934), pp. 437–474.

———. "Les placements de fortune à Genève depuis le XV° siècle jusqu'a la fin du XVIII°." *Revue Économique Internationale* (May 1935), pp. 257–288.

UNPUBLISHED MATERIALS

Davis, Natalie Ann Zemon. "Protestantism and the Printing Workers of Lyons: A Study in the Problem of Religion and Social Class During the Reformation." Ph.D. dissertation, Department of History, University of Michigan, 1959. (University Microfilms, Inc., Ann Arbor, Michigan.)

Powell, Milton B. "The Abolitionist Controversy in the Methodist Episcopal Church, 1840–1864." Ph.D. dissertation, Department of History, State University of Iowa, 1963.